Newspaper Abstacts *of* ALLEGANY *and* WASHINGTON COUNTIES Maryland

1811-1815

F. Edward Wright

HERITAGE BOOKS
2008

HERITAGE BOOKS
AN IMPRINT OF HERITAGE BOOKS, INC.

Books, CDs, and more—Worldwide

For our listing of thousands of titles see our website
at
www.HeritageBooks.com

Published 2008 by
HERITAGE BOOKS, INC.
Publishing Division
100 Railroad Ave. #104
Westminster, Maryland 21157

Copyright © 1989 F. Edward Wright

All rights reserved. No part of this book may be reproduced or transmitted in any form or by any means, electronic or mechanical, including photocopying, recording or by any information storage and retrieval system without written permission from the author, except for the inclusion of brief quotations in a review.

International Standard Book Numbers
Paperbound: 978-1-58549-025-7
Clothbound: 978-0-7884-7246-6

INTRODUCTION

This book continues the series of Western Maryland newspapers abstracts. Volumes 1, 2 and 3 contain personal items for the periods, 1786-1798, 1799-1805 and 1806-1810, respectively. The newspapers available for these periods were almost exclusively those of Hagerstown and Frederick. We continue with the Hagerstown papers (Maryland Herald and Hagers-town Gazette) for the period 1811-1815 combined with a few issues of the newly established Allegany Freeman and Cumberland Gazette. The expanding coverage by newspapers of the adjoining Frederick County and the birth of Carroll County newspapers during this same period dictated that a separate volume would be published for the latter region.

These abstracts were taken from actual issues and microfilm copies held by the Maryland Historical Society and the Library of Congress.

The Maryland Herald and Hagerstown Weekly Advertiser began with the issue of June 8, 1797, under the name, The Maryland Herald and Elizabeth-Town Advertiser. It was published by Thomas Grieves. The Hagers-Town Gazette began publishing on May 16, 1809 under William Brown, until circa June 15, 1813. The (Hagerstown) Westliche Correspondenz was established in June 1795 by Johann Gruber, and continued with some apparent interruptions until 1820. The Allegany Freeman began its publication with the issue dated November 20, 1813, under the ownership of S. Magill. William Brown began printing the Cumberland Gazette early in 1814.

Abbreviations used:

a. - acres
adj - adjoining
admr - administrator (or administra-
  trix) of the estate of
co - county
dau - daughter
decd - deceased
exrn - executor (or executrix)

ft - feet
inst - instant (this month)
recd - received
regt - regiment
res - resided or residence
ult - ultimo (last month)
yr(s) - year(s)

Comments and suggestions are welcomed.

F. Edward Wright

THE MARYLAND HERALD, AND HAGERSTOWN WEEKLY ADVERTISER

1. Jan 2 1811
To be sold at the late res of Thomas WILLIAMS, decd, within 1 miles of town of Williamsport, residue of personal estate of decd, 13 negroes, cattle and other - Wm. B. WILLIAMS, admr.
Nicholas RIDENOUR adm of Conrod LONG.
Ch: CARROLL, Bellevue, to rent farm adj Hagerstown on which he resides, 700 a.
James M'COY, exr of Archibald M'COY.
Bolting Cloths - John & Hugh KENNEDY.
Michael F. MAYER, Hagerstown, seek apprentice to saddling business.
Sale of house and lot on which I now res, a few doors of the Court house square; also farm of 200 a. through which the western turnpike will probably run, 300 a., another farm of 200 a., 4 miles from town adj lands of late Gen. SPRIGG, Wendel GILBERT and others - R. PINDELL, Hagerstown.
Cheap Goods - John & George HARRY.
Luke TIERNAM & Co, Balt - have 600 boxes of best tin, English crowly and blistered steel.
Bolting Cloths - Alexander NEILL.
Storage for flour - Ezra SLIFER, Boonsboro', Washington Co.
Died Sun last, after a lingering illness, at the house of Mr. B. GALLOWAY, in this town, Elisha HARRISON, son of Dr. E. HARRISON of Balt, in his 21st year.
For rent- store and cellar fronting the square, next door to the one now occupied by Messrs. KAUSLER and GRAFF - Henry LEWIS.
Store House now occupied by Alexander NEILL, next door to George BAUMBAUGH's Tavern; apply to Philip WINGART, Hagerstown.
Sale of tract lying on Potomack river, 280 a.; the public road from Hagerstown and Williamsport to Hancock-town passes through this plantation; it lies 2 miles from the latter; Mr. HAUN, who lives on the land will shew it; apply to Jacob BARNET, Jr. for terms, Henry M'LAUGHLIN, Washington Co.
Jacob MILLER continues to carry on coverlet and carpet weaving and blue dying at his old stand near Sharpsburg.
House for sale now occupied by subscriber in Potomack st, opposite Peter HEFLEICH's - Jonathan HAGER.
Corner store house and post office room for rent, in the public square, Hagerstown, now occupied by Wm. KREPS, Esq. - Peter & Matthias MILLER.
J. SCHNEBLY certifies Capt. Gerard STONEBREAKER has taken up a stray mare

2. Jan 6 1811
J. SCHNEBLY, Hagerstown, seeks overseer for farming and management of 5-6 hands.
Jacob SMITH and Michael SMITH, exrs of Joseph SMITH.
Tavern stand now occupied by subscriber in Potomack st for sale - John COOK.
House for sale where subscriber, Henry CAKE, now lives nearly opposite Mr. BELTZHOOVER's Tavern.
Michael M'KANNA, Parkhead-Forge, has taken up two stray cows.
Philip WINGART to rent store house now occupied by Alexander NEILL, next door to George BRUMBAUGH's Tavern.
Tavern stand for rent, where the subscriber now lives, for many years occupied by him as a tavern - Thomas SHUMAN, Hagerstown.
My creditors to meet at Mr. SACKETT's, Columbian Inn, at Williamsport, Sat 19 inst to make final settlement - Conrad WALLACH.

THE MARYLAND HERALD, AND HAGERSTOWN WEEKLY ADVERTISER

James BELCH, living on Chew's Farm, has taken up a stray barrow.

3. Jan 23 1811
Trustees of Hagerstown Academy: Richard PINDELL, John T. MASON, Samuel RINGGOLD, Samuel HUGHES, jun, Charles CARROLL, Upton LAWRENCE, Frisby TILGHMAN, Otho H. WILLIAMS, Moses TABBS, William HEYSER, John KENNEDY, John HARRY, Jacob ZETTER, Christian HAGER, John I. STULL, Jacob SCHNEBLY, Thomas B. HALL, John RAGAN, sen., Matthias SHAFFNER, Alexander NEILL and Frederick DORSEY - meet and elect president and organize the institution.
Funk's (Jerusalem) Town Lottery tickets may be obtained from: Leonard SHAFER, Williamsport; Philip GROVE, Sharpsburgh; Henry LOCHER, Boonsborough; William FY, near Waynesburg; Frederick FISHACH, near the Cave; John HOLL, Inn-keeper, Cross-roads; and Major John BEARD's store.
Sale of house and lot now occupied by Thomas GARRETT, in West Franklin St, Hagerstown, adj premises in the possession of John DEITZ, book-binder - to be shewn by David HARRY - Daniel HUGHES, Junr., Trustee for the creditors of Thomas GARRETT.
Sale agreeable to last will of Michael BEARD, decd, of 2-story log house in Boonsborough - Henry B. T. BENNER, exr.
Committed to jail of Washington Co, as a runaway, negro girl who calls herself MARIA, about 20 yrs old, 5 ft, 6 inch high; had on a calico frock, check apron, and old bonnet. She says she is free and came from Charlestown, Va, and that her mother lives on Thomas HAMMON's place, near said town - Matthias SHAFFNER, Sheriff.
Dissolution of partnership of John RAGAN, Senr. and John KAELHOFER.
John COOK to sell tavern stand where he now resides in Potomack st, Hagerstown, sign of Gen. Washington.

4. Jan 30 1811
Jacob BINKLEY, Junr continues to carry on blue dying business at his old stand in Washington st, nearly opposite dwelling of Henry ARNOLD, weaver.
Frederick MILLER has just recd Paul's Patent Infallible Columbian Oil - effectual cure for the Rheumatism, consumption &c..
Peter MILLER continues to carry on coverlet and carpet weaving and blue dying at his old stand in Funks-town.
Clean Hemp seed for sale - John & Joseph M'ILHENNY.
Stone masons wanted; enquire of Patrick DUFFY, inn-keeper, Martinsburg - Jabez ANDERSON, Berkeley Co, Va.
Spanish Segars - Frederick MILLER.
John SPRINGER offers reward for silver watch lost on road to Licking Creek and Mercersburg; deliver to him in Montgomery township, Franklin Co, or to Samuel H. WHITESIDE in Mercersburg.

5. Feb 6 1811
John BOWER of Washington Co insolvent debtor, to be discharged from imprisonment.
Henry SEIBERT and John CUSHWA, admrs of Jacob SEIBERT.
Flaxseed wanted - G. & M. STONEBREAKER, Funks-town.
Thomas QUANTRILL to offer at public sale house in which he now lives, opposite dwelling of Otho H. WILLIAMS, Esq.; on premises is black-smith's shop with two fires, large coal house.

THE MARYLAND HERALD, AND HAGERSTOWN WEEKLY ADVERTISER

Frederick EICHELBERGER, near Creagers-town, will pay four cents a gallon to a distiller, that can come well recommended.
Samuel RIDENOUR to sell at the Coffee House in Hagerstown, a lot in Stull's addition to Hagerstown, 5 3/4 a..
Peter JUSTIS, Hagerstown, gives teaching rates (for spelling, reading, writing, grammar and geography- $3.50 per quater, etc.).

6. Feb 13 1811
Portion of subscription to Hagerstown Academy now required - Wm. HEYSER, Treasurer.
Mathew COLLINS, Boonsborough, cautions persons not to credit James M'CREA in the firm of James M'CREA and Mathew COLLINS, or to accept of any receipts, notes or accounts to be applied to the account with Mr. Elie WILLIAMS in said firm, as he is determined not to pay any after this date.
Robert COWEN, near Ringgold's Manor, offers reward for negro lad named SHADRACH, 16-17 yrs old, hired to subscriber by Wm. S. COMPTON, Esq. - Robert COWEN.
John YOUNG, Senr, to move to house formerly occupied by William Belch, Washington st, where he will continue to conduct a classical school.
Family Medicines of Michael LEE & Co, sold by Frederick MILLER, Druggist, Hagerstown.
Sale of life estate of 100 a. in Washington co, adj Daniel & Jacob RENCH, 1 1/2 miles of Hagerstown - Silas POMPHREY; apply to Elie BEATTY, Hagerstown

7. Sep 18 1811
Ch: CARROLL, Hagerstown, to sell farm known as Bellevue, 1100 a.
John V. KELLY continues to carry on fulling and dying business at the fulling mill of Martin BAECHTEL, near Hagerstown.
Committed to gaol of Wash co, as a runaway, negro man who calls himself John and says he belongs to James TURNER, of Hanover co, Va; about 40 yrs of age, 5 ft 6 inches.
Sale of tract 70-80 a. within 3 miles of Col. Hughes's Forge; there is an excellent mill seat within fifty yards of the house with a boring mill thereon - Henry HOCKMAN.
10th, 24th, and 8th regiments of Md. Militia to parade. The American Blues and the Washington Hussars will parade with each regiment under the command of Major Frisby TILGHMAN - By order of the Brigadier General, Tho. B. POTTENGER, Brigade Inspector.
Officers and privates of the 8th Regt of Md. Militia to meet at Jacob KERSHNER's Tavern on Conococheague - David SCHNEBLY, Lieut. Col. 8th Regt.
The American Blues will parade - O. H. WILLIAMS, Captain.
Sale at the house of the subscriber, about 3 miles from the Green Spring Furnace, and near Henry & George BRAGONIER's, horses, cows, cattle and hogs - Jacob DUNN.
George KREPS, cabinet maker, has commenced the business at the shop formerly occupied by his father Martin KREPS, Franklin st, Hagerstown.
Wanted - Assistant in a store - BEARD & KESSINGER, near Col. Hughes's Forge.
Daniel BRAGONIER cautions persons from fowling and hunting, throwing down the fences upon the Big Spring Farm, near Hagerstown.
Thomas HENNING, living about 2 miles from Robert HUGHES's and 4 miles from the Cave Tavern, offers reward for mare missing from William HAMMETT's plantation, near Col. Hughes's FURNACE.

THE MARYLAND HERALD, AND HAGERSTOWN WEEKLY ADVERTISER

Jacob MILLER, Hagerstown, offers reward for missing cow.
Thomas GRIEVES offers reward for missing horse.
Thomas CRAMPTON certifies that Andrew BOORD has taken up a stray mare.
John ADAMS has opened a tavern in Boonsborough.
Wm. O. SPRIGG admr of Otho SPRIGG.
Michael RUDISILLI, living near the great road leading from Hagerstown to Williamsport (about mid-way), offers reward for missing mare.
Pay your taxes & fees - Matthias SHAFFNER, Sheriff & Collector, Hagerstown.
John GIBBONEY, Jun., continues to carry on fulling & dying business at John HERSHEY's Fulling Mill, about 6 miles from Hagerstown and 1/2 mile from Michael HOFFER's mill; cloth will be taken in at Mr. SHAFER's store in Williamsport, John HOLL's tavern at the Cross Roads and KAUSLER & GRAFF's store in Hagerstown.
Dissolution of partnership of Lewis BIRELEY, John BIRELEY and William BIRELY, paper-makers.
Thomas HODGES, Prince George's co, 2 miles of Queen Anne, offers reward for negro woman KITTY, very black, 5 ft 8-10 inches, stout; her mother is cook to Mrs. Mary POTTENGER of Hagerstown; and also connected with the negroes of Messrs. Thomas and John BUCHANAN of Washington co.
Benjamin GUYTON, living on the plantation beloinging to the heirs of Jacob SEIBERT, decd, adj farm of John BOWLES, Esq., 1 miles from FIERY's mill, offers reward for negro man named SAM, who calls himself Samuel CHEW, about 22 yrs old, 5 ft 8-9 inches.

8. Sep 25 1811
Married Thurs evening last by Rev BOWER, Samuel D. PRICE, Merchant of Sharpsburg, to Miss Catharine B. CHAPLINE, dau of late Jeremiah CHAPLINE.
Sale at the dwelling house of the subscriber, on the farm belonging to Henry LEWIS, 2 miles from Hagerstown, horses, milch cows, cattle, sheep and hogs, and other - William DAVIS, Jun..
Solomon PHILLIPS and Uriel PHILLIPS, Balt Co, 16 miles below Liberty-town, offers reward for 2 likely young negro fellows (brothers) who ran away from them at Mr. HUNTER's tavern, near the Parkhead-Forge, Washington Co, named ZACK, aged about 25 yrs and JEREMIAH, about 24 yrs old.
Christian ARTZ has for sale a quantity of locust timber for sale.
Purchasers at my sale in April note that their obligations become due on 1 Oct - Michael KAPP.
Petition to authorize Levy Court of Washington Co to appoint Commissioners to lay out a Mill Road, to run from Henry SNIDER's Mill to intersect turnpike road near Boonsborough.
George SMITH, House painter, gilder & glazier, near opposite dwelling of Rev. RAHAUSER, Franklin st, Hagerstown.
John STONEBREAKER, 3 miles from Hagerstown, offers reward for negro man, named JOE, about 5 ft 9-10 inches, 35-40 inches, stout.
Peter GROSNICKEL, living on Catoctin creek, about 3 miles from POFFENBERGER Smith-shop and 8 miles from Middletown, offers reward for horse that strayed from David MARTIN's pasture, about 5 miles from Hagerstown.
For sale - tract of limestone land in the Great Cover, 3 miles of M'Connellsburg, Bedford co, Pa, 275 a., belonging to heirs of William ALEXANDER, decd - Charles STEUART, living within 2 miles of the premises.

THE MARYLAND HERALD, AND HAGERSTOWN WEEKLY ADVERTISER

Owners of distilleries are invited to see new distillery erected for Col. C. G. BOERSTLER, adj Gen. RINGGOLD's Mill, 5 miles from Hagerstown; rights may be purchased at Mr. SEITZ's tavern, Hagerstown.
J. E. THROCKMORTON to sell tract in Berkely co, Va, 2 miles of Bath, 532 a.
Henry LOWRYE, Funks-Town, seeks to hire journeymen joiners.

9. Oct 2 1811
Joseph SPRIGGs, living near Gen. RINGGOLDS mill, has taken up stray bulls.
Sale at dwelling of subscriber, John BEARD, 1 1/2 miles Col. HUGHES's Forge, negroes, horses, cows, wool, and more.
WILLIS & CRAWFORD, boot & shoemakers, have removed their shop to house lately occupied by Mr. A. M. WAUGH.
Black bottles for sale - Christian FECHTIG, Hagerstown.
Journeymen tailors wanted - Benjamin YOE, Hagerstown.
Journeyman wheelwright and chair-maker wanted - Jacob STATTEN, Charlestown, Jefferson co, Va.

10. Oct 9 1811
Chancery sale of tract of land in Washington co, 340 a., adj lands of Capt. Jacob ZELLER, Daniel SCHNEBLY - Jacob BARNETT, Henry M'LAUGHLIN, Trustees.
John KRAMER has rented the shop formerly occupied by Thomas QUANTRILL in Antietam st, Hagerstown, nearly opposite dwelling of Capt. Otho H. WILLIAMS, will carry on smithery, such as ironing of wagons, horse-shoeing, making and repairing locks, plating saddle trees, stove mounting &c.
Sale of corner house opposite dwelling of Col. Adam OTT, late the property of Abraham BOWER, decd - Conrod COFFROTH.
Alexander TIMS has lost in Hagerstown a silver watch.
John SEITZ, at the sign of the Buck, seeks journeymen coopers.
Committed to gaol of Washington co, a negro man by name of SAM, says he first belonged to Anne GRAY, and then to William ELLICKSON, both of city of Balt; appears to be 35 yrs old.
John YOUNG, senr., to let house, garden and stable, now occupied by himself, nearly opposite dwelling of Rev. BOWER.
Otho H. W. STULL has taken up stray bull.

11. Oct 16 1811
Williamsport Races - M. H. SACKETT, Jacob BROSIUS, Tho. EDWARDS, Williams-port, managers.
Jacob ROWLAND, about 4 miles from Hagerstown, offers reward for indented girl, named Betsey TANLEY, about 14 yrs old.
Christopher MURPHY, living in Rohrer's Addition to Hagerstown, offers reward for indented boy named Samuel NOLAND, about 7 yrs old, blind in left eye, dark hair, some freckles on his face. It is supposed that he is concealed by his mother, who lives at the Catholic Seminary near Emmittsburg, with whom he was lately left.
Wm. ARMOR, Hagerstown, seek journeymen tailors.
William KREPS and James H. BOWLES candidates for sheriff.
Two plantations for sale, one 128 a.; other, 498 a. (adj Mr. BRAGONIER's), will be shewn by George DUNN, living on premises - Christian HAGER.
Bolting cloths - R. RAGAN, Hagerstown.
Notice - Persons who gave notes at my sale are requested to call on Otho H. W. STULL - John I. STULL.

THE MARYLAND HERALD, AND HAGERSTOWN WEEKLY ADVERTISER

12. Oct 23 1811
Jacob VANTZ, Liberty town, offers reward for apprentice lad to the hatting business, John HARTZOG, about 18, 5 ft 5-6 inches, light hair, down look, speaks German and English tolerably well; took blue cloth coat, striped cotton waistcoat, yellow flowered calico waistoat, pair of dark green velvet pantaloons, pair tow lined pantaloons, black fur hat and coarse shoes.
John NEWSON, Jun, 1 1/2 mile from Hagerstown, has taken up a stray shoat.
Pocket book lost between William HEYSER's farm and Hagerstown.
Henry SWEITZER, Hagerstown, candidate for sheriff.
John GOOD to sell plantation, 400 a., on road from Swearingen's ferry to Frederick-town - "My brother William, resides on it."
James STERRETT seeks payment for mares that were put to his horse Sportsman.
Catharine SWOPE and Daniel GRIFFITH, admrs of Peter SWOPE, to sell personal estate of decd at late dwelling of decd near the Big Spring, about 13 miles from Hagerstown - and at the farm whereon Mr. Placinger resides, 1 miles of Hancock-town, residue of personal estate of Peter SWOPE.

13. Oct 30 1811
Boonsborough Races - George NICHOLS, John ADAMS.
William B. WILLIAMS, living near Williams-Port has taken up a stray colt.
John COW, living on Peter SAILOR's plantation, 1 1/2 miles from Hagerstown, offers reward for missing mare.
Charles WORLAND to sell tract, 279 a. 2 miles from Hancock-town.
John MATHEWS has opened a house of entertainment in Hancock-town, at stand formerly occupied by John PROTZMAN, sign of the Seven Stars.
Jacob I. OHR seeks journeyman tailor.

14. Nov 6 1811   pages 2 and 3 missing

15. Nov 20 1811
Died a few days ago, after a long and severe illness, Mrs. Mariam HOYE, aged 77 yrs, consort of Paul HOYE, of this co.
Died Thurs last, after a short illness, Mrs. Anne BAKER, wife of Richard BAKER, and dau of George WEBB, of this co.
Meadow land for sale, 4 acres adj Hagerstown, opposite Rope Walk of Messrs. WILLIAMS & RAGAN - Samuel ROHRER.
Quantity of good old rye whisky for sale - Isaac S. WHITE or Daniel SCHNEBLY.
For sale - tract in Washington co, 173 a., adj lands of John T. MASON, Esq. and Denton JACQUES; apply to subscriber (Jacob K. BOYER), living in Reading, Pa, or to Thomas M'CARDELL in Hagerstown.
John CRISSINGER, Hagerstown, has commenced running a handsome and convenient hack.
David LITTLE seeks to hire journeymen tailors.
Peter ARTZ has moved to the mill lately owned by Capt. Daniel STULL, near Hagerstown, and has put the same in complete order.
Jacob BINKLEY, of George, Hagerstown, seeks apprentice to blue dying business.

16. Nov 27 1811
Reward offered for negro man named HAZARD who ran away from the farm of Carlyle F. WHITTING, lying on the river Potomack, Berkeley, Va, about 25

THE MARYLAND HERALD AND HAGERSTOWN WEEKLY ADVERTISER

yrs old, 5 ft 9-10 inches; bring home to me, or to his master in D. C. - John STONE.
Committed to gaol of Washington Co, negro man who calls himself George BAILEY; says he is free and that he came from Lexington, Ky; appears to be about 30 yrs old, 5 ft 7-8 inches.

17. Dec 18 1811
Sale of tract of limestone land, 45 a. and house in Antietam st, Hagerstown; apply to subscriber, living on the premises - Leonard KUHN.
F. TILGHMAN has taken up a stray horse.
John ADAMS exr, to sell at dwelling of John LANGLEY, decd, Williams-Port, personal estate of decd, negro man, mare, and furniture.
Will be sold - at Capt. O. H. WILLIAMS's farm, 1/2 mile from William SPRIGG's, horses, cows, hogs, sheep, wagon, ploughs, hay, furniture and other - William C. HAMMETT.
Sale of improved lot on corner of Walnut and Franklin sts, Hagerstown, whereon are 3 dwelling houses, one of which is occupied by John DIETZ, book-binder - William HAMMETT.
John ADAMS exr of John LANGLEY.
Brick house for rent or sale, which has been occupied as a tavern for 14 yrs, on corner of Court-house square in Hagerstown, now kept by Christian FECHTIG - Wm. HEYSER.
Henry BARNETT and Jacob BARNETT admrs of Jacob BARNETT.

18. Dec 25 1811
Sale agreeable to last will of Henry STARTZMAN, of brick house in Washington St, Hagerstown, now occupied by Benjamin YOE, next door to dwelling of John HARRY - Martin STARTZMAN and David STARTZMAN, exrs.
Sale in town of Williams-Port of family carriage and harness, horses, cart and gears - George SANDERS, Williams-Port.
To rent two story stone house in Potomac St, Hagerstown, for many yrs occupied by subscriber as a tavern; also house occupied by Abraham FORCE, contiguous to first premises - Thomas SHUMAN.
Teacher wanted, Josiah PRICE, living about 7 miles from Hagerstown.

19. Jan 15 1812
Frederick ZIGLAR and William GABBY, admrs of George ZIGLAR, to sell at late dwelling of decd, on Antietam, near Mrs. RUSSELL's Mill personal property of decd, horses, cows, complete set of Joiner's and cabinet-maker's tools, wind-mill, furniture and other.
Committed to gaol of Washington co, as a runaway, negro woman who calls herself BETTY; says she is free and lately lived with John JEFFERSON, of Jefferson co, Va; appears to be about 45 yrs old, 4 ft 10-11 inches; has nearly lost all her fore teeth.
Sale of tract on Antietam Creek, about 2 miles from Hagerstown; apply to John ROHRER, living on the land or to Daniel HUGHES, jun., Esq., Hagers-town - John ROHRER, Peter MONG.
Cash for wheat and corn, delivered at the mill lately owned by Capt. D. STULL, near Hagerstown, and now in the possession of Peter ARTZ - P. ARTZ & EMMERT, who will keep a constant supply of flour at their store.
Jacob KNODE, near Funks-town, has taken up some stray sheep.
Henry LEWIS seeks to hire someone to the business of a saw mill.

THE MARYLAND HERALD AND HAGERSTOWN WEEKLY ADVERTISER

Elie BEATTY, exr of Daniel STULL.
Henry STRAUSE, Hagerstown, offers reward for negro man named WILLIAM, about 5 ft 7-8 inches, 22 yrs old.
Thomas M'CARDELL has found some money near the Court-house square.
William BRAZIER, Hagerstown, seeks 4-5 boys as apprentices to the Bridle-bit and stirrup making business.

20. Jan 22 1812
William GREINER, gunsmith, has commenced business at shop lately occupied by George KREPS, gunsmith, Franklin st, Hagerstown.
John CAKE, Hagerstown, has on hand a quantity of hops.
Receipts for dying silk, cotton & wool - by Peter MILLER, blue-dyer, Funks-town.
Pottery to rent occupied by Samuel SNAVELY, decd, in Shepherds-town, Va, round kiln, clay mill, glazing mill, two wheels; apply to John SNAVELY, potter, near Hagerstown, or the widow on the premises.

21. Jan 29 1812
James H. BOWLES withdraws as candidate for sheriff.
Wanted - Stone masons to construct stone locks on the Antietam creek this summer; attend at house of Christian FECHTIG - Josiah THOMSON, superintendant, for the Potomack Co.
Brick house for sale in Potomac st, opposite Lutheran Church, Hagerstown - Henry STRAUSE.
DUBUISSON, dentist, arrived here from Phila, will reside at house of Samuel BAYLY, Hagerstown Hotel until 25 Feb. He cleans, separates, files, plugs and extracts teeth, set straight those inclined to any direction, makes and places artificial ones, transplants natural teeth, cures all diseases of the gums.
John M'CLEERY will open school next door to Capt. Wm. LEWIS, Franklin st, Hagerstown.
Osborn SPRIGG wishes to sell tract on which he now lives, on North branch of Potomack, Hampshire co, Va, 800 a. and other tracts, including tract 204 a., adj Mr. OASTER who will shew it.
Blacksmith wanted - Peter FITE, living near John T. MASON's Mill

22. Feb 5 1812
Perry WAYMAN has removed to the house formerly occupied by Dr. CREAGER, next door to Mr. LEVY's Tavern in Middle-town, where he intends to carry on the saddling business. Those indebted will please to come forward and settle their balances with Jacob MOTTER, in New-town, Trap.
Henry HOUCK, living within 3/4 mile of Mr. BARTON's Tavern on Little Conococheague, offers reward for missing sheep.
Boonsborough lottery, to finish the Boonsborough Church, build a school house, &c. - Ezra SLIFER, George SHAFER, John B. T. BENNER, Conrad NICODEMUS, Robert CHENEY, John WAGGONER, managers.
Jacob STOVER, Franklin co, Pa, about 1 miles from Col. Josiah PRICE's, has taken up stray mares.
Dwelling house for rent, now occupied by Judge BUCHANAN, and 2 shops in the possession of Mr. L. FECHTIG and Wm. ARMOR - John HARRY, Hagers-town

THE MARYLAND HERALD AND HAGERSTOWN WEEKLY ADVERTISER

23. Feb 12 1812
Certifying and accounting for the money raised by the Boonsborough Church
  Lottery: John B. T. BENNER, Daniel CHRISTIAN, George NICHOLS, Ephraim
  DAVIS, John SMITH, George SHAFER, Conrod NICODEMUS, George MORDEL,
  Mordecai BOONE, Wendel SHECHTER.
Sale of a mulatto man named George BAYLY, heretofore advertised as a runaway
  - Matthias SHAFFNER, Sheriff.
Hops for sale, at his mill, about 5 miles from Hagers-town - Michael HOFFER.
To be sold - three story log house in Potomac st, Hagers-town, lately
  occupied by Peter GLOSSBRENNER as a tavern - Henry SHANE, on the premises.
Christian LANTZ admr, requests payment on sale of personal estate of
  Christian LANTZ, decd.
Samuel ROSS, living in Williams-port, offers reward for apprentice to the
  Boot and Shoemaking business named Perren BLAKENEY, about 5 ft 5-6 inches,
  17 yrs of age.
Christian SMITH and Jacob SUMMERS, admrs, request payment on sale of per-
  sonal estate of Ludwick PITRY, decd

24. Feb 19 1812
Died Thurs last, after a short illness, in the 77th yr of his age, Jacob
  PITRY, of this co.
Died Mon morning last, after a few days illness, at his farm near Hughes's
  Forge, John OSWALD, husband and father.
Henry SHAFER, Funks-town, has on hand a quantity of ground plaster of paris.
Recruiting able bodied men from 18 to 35 yrs, for the army of the U.S., for
  term of 5 yrs - John MILLER, Lieut (pay $5.00 per month).
Samuel HERR, living in Hagers-town, offers a reward of one dollar and a
  basket of chips for apprentice to the joiner's business named Jacob
  BLENTLINGER, 15-16 yrs of age, 5 ft 7-8 inches; had no blue cloth coat,
  brown cloth waistcoat, thickset pantaloons and wool hat.
Christian FECHTIG, Hagers-town, offers reward for information on evil person
  or persons who broke the lamp over the door of his tavern.
Cotton yarn - John & Joseph M'ILHENNY, Hagers-town.
Sale of furniture at his tavern in Hagers-town - George BELTZHOOVER.
Sale at plantation belonging to Henry LEWIS, 2 miles from Hagers-town, about
  170 bushels in the ground, 2 milch cows - James DAVIS.
Sheriff's sale of Tench RINGGOLD's right to his lands in Washington co, now
  in the tenure of O.H.W. STULL and Thomas WATTS, seized at the suit of John
  and George HARRY.
Journeyman cooper wanted - Thomas MULHALL, Funks-town.

25. Feb 26 1812
Married Sun evening last by Rev TOWNE, Robert DOWNEY, to Miss Barbara
  BEELOR, dau of Samuel BEELOR, of this town.
Sale at the farm on which I resided, near Sharpsburg, my stock of milch cows
  and other cattle, furniture, and other - John GOOD.
Sale at dwelling of subscriber, John BEARD, 6 miles from Hagers-town, 1 1/2
  miles from Col. Hughes's Forge, negroes, cattle, carriage, wool, furniture
  (described) and other.
Sale at dwelling house of subscriber, Leonard KUHN, Hagers-town, well seasoned cherry, walnut, pine, and poplar plank, pine joists and rafters for
  building, work benches, one turning lay, joiner's and cabinet maker's

THE MARYLAND HERALD AND HAGERSTOWN WEEKLY ADVERTISER

tools, grindstones, bee hives, one barrel of old rye liquor, 6-plate and 2 10-plate stoves and pipe, 8-day music clock, desk and bureau, &c..
Dissolution of partnership of Charles GELWICKS & John GELWICKS, Hagers-town.

Sale agreeable to last will of Henry STARTZMAN, late of Washington co, decd, at the Coffee-house in Hagers-town, of tract in Monongahela Co, Va - Martin STARTZMAN and David STARTZMAN, exrs.

26. Mar 4 1812
Pic Nic Club - to meet. The debate: Is the encouragement of the fine arts in a republic, conducive to the continuance of a republican form of government?" Affirmative: Moses TABB, T. B. POTTENGER, William HAMMOND; Negative: Tho. B. HALL, Joseph I. MERRICK, Danl. HUGHES, jun. - Wm. HAMMOND, Sen., Sec'y.
Request for volunteers to form a volunteer of Horse in Col. David SCHNEBLY's Regimental District - to meet at Baughman's Tavern, near Lantz's mill - A. NUMBER.
Otho Holland WILLIAMS promoted to command 1st Regimental Cavalry District as major and relieved of command of the American Blues. He retains in the squadron the American Blues along with Washington Hussars. Moses TABBS elected Captain of the American Blues; Jacob BARR, 1st Lieut., David NEWCOMER, Cornet.
Eve OSWALD and Benjamin OSWALD admrs of John OSWALD, to sell personal estate of decd at late dwelling, 1 mile of Abraham MAYER's Mill and 3 miles of Col. HUGHES Forge.
John PITRY and Christian SMITH,exrs of Jacob PITRY, to sell personal estate of decd, 1/2 mile of John SHERFER's mill, 4 miles of Hagers-town; also selling house and lot occupied by George BINKLEY in Washington st a few doors above Mr. BELTZHOOVER's tavern.
Sale at dwelling of subscriber in Washington st, Hagers-town, next door to Peter BELL, 2 milch cows, furniture - Christopher EMBICH. Philip EMBICH continues to carry on Blue Dying business as usuall at above stand.
Sale of Gen. RINGGOLD's Mill, upwards of 100 hogs and breeding sows, a pair of work oxen, ox cart, cows and horses, guns, corn, some whisky - Charles G. BOERSTLER.
Sale by order of Orphan's Court at his farm about 3 miles from Hagers-town, property of Jacob RIDENOUR, exr of Jacob RIDENOUR, horses, cows, windmill, farming utensils; also grain in the ground at farm where said Ridenour now lives, 1 mile of Williams-port - Philip KERSHNER, 3 miles of Hagers-town.
Sale of dwelling of subscriber in Franklin st, Hagers-town, opposite Meth Meeting House, a meadow lot under good fence adj town, milch cow, mare well calculated for the saddle or draught, furniture, a few shoemaker's seats - John EBERT.
Sale at dwelling of subscriber, on plantation where Peter ADAMS formerly lived, 2 miles of Col. David SCHNEBLY's.
Payment due for street taxes and fines in the United Fire Company - Henry DILLMAN, collector.
House to let, 2nd door above Mr. M. KERSHNER's - H. DILLMAN.
Seminary for young ladies - Mrs. CAPRON, Chambersburg.
Book binding - Samuel B. DAVIS.
William C. HAMMETT to leave this county soon, requests settlement of debts.
Dissolution of partnership of William BEECHER & Matthias NEAD, Hagerstown.

THE MARYLAND HERALD AND HAGERSTOWN WEEKLY ADVERTISER

Deserted from recruiting rendezvous in Hagers-town, William WELSH, a shoe-maker by profession; says he is 22 yrs old; born in Phila, 5 ft 11 inches, fair complexion, brown eyes, dark hair - John MILLER, Lieut., Hagers-town

27. Mar 11 1812
Married Sun evening last by Rev SCHAEFFER, William ARMOR to Miss Margaret FECHTIG, dau of Christian FECHTIG of this town.
Married last evening by Rev SCHAEFFER, John CRAWFORD to Miss Anne WHITHNEY, dau of Arthur WITHNEY of this town.
Died Sat evening last at his res, 4 miles from Green-Castle, Daniel MILLER, sen., old and respectable citizen of Franklin Co, Pa.
Dry Goods - George BINKLEY.
William DIXON, living on plantation of Major Charles CARROLL, 1 mile of Hagers-town, has furniture for sale.
Sale at farm where I now live, 3 miles of Hagers-town, all my stock and farming utensils, 100 hoges, &c. - Samuel HAMMETT.
William BEECHER has removed from his former stand to store house on corner of Court-house square, formerly occupied by William KREPS.
Dancing School - Mr. GENRES, Jun., at Samuel BAYLY's Tavern (lately BELTZHOOVER's).
Horse, Paul Jones, to cover mares at the farm of Jacob BARNETT on the Mercersburg Road, at Mr. C. LANTZ's mill on the road to Nicholson's Gap, about 6 miles from Hagers-town - John BARNETT.
Noted saddle horse, Little Johnny, formerly owned by Dr. PINDELL, will cover mares at $5.00 each mare and half dollar to the groom - John T. MASON.
Meeting of Tax Commissioners - Jacob SCHNEBLY, Clk.
John NEWSON, Jun., 1 1/2 miles of Hagers-town, seeks to employ young man to farming business.
Dissolution of partnership of William WILLIS and John CRAWFORD.
To let house lately occupied by Mr. A. M. WAUGH, 2 doors from Messrs. John & Hugh KENNEDY's store - Jonathan HAGER.

28. Apr 8 1812
Letters at Post Office, Hagers-town: Christian AVEY; John AMMERSON; James AYERS; John ALLABAUGH or Leonard WEAST; Widow ARTZ (Booth's mill); AMIS, (belonging to Webb's estate.); Doctor Edward BREATHETT; George BARINGER; William BLAKEMORE; Michael BARGELD; Peter BRUSH; Peter BURKDALE; Andrew BRANSTETTER; Clement BANKS; George BRANTNER; John BAKER; John BURGER; Mrs. Margaret BOWMAN; Mrs. Polly BUTLER; Mrs. Martha BRADSHAW; Mrs. Mary BARKMAN; Mrs. Elizabeth BARNETT; Miss Maria C. BOOTH; George COLIFLOUR, Jun; James CONNELL; John CORL; Samuel CAUFFMAN; Mrs. Mary CLARK; John DUNNX Abraham DEGROFF; Thomas L. DILLEHAY; John EADS; George EAKER, sen; William FULTON; George FOX; Casper FOLK; John D. FISHER; Maria FACKLER; Daniel GEHR; Wendel GILBERT; Thomas GRIEVES; Sophia GEERHART; Barnabas HUGHES; Adam and John HORINE; William HAMMETT (of M'Kelvie); William W. HILL; Rev. Henry HIESTAND; Jacob HERBAUGH (son of Ludwick); Mrs. HINSON; Mrs. Mary HERSHEY; George Hays IRWIN; Isaac KEEPERS; Peter KOYLER; George KEIBER; George KESSINGER; David KEMP; Jeremiah LIGGET; Elijah LEASURE; Miss Sarah LILLY; Daniel MAY; Samuel M'CONNEL; Charles M'KENNEY; Francis P. M'KEEN; Theodore MILLS; Jonas MYERS; Alexander M'CLANAHAN; John M'LAUGHLIN; Moses MURPHEY; John MAUGHMAN; Mrs. Sidy M'HENERY; Mrs. Susanna MILLER; Miss Harriot M'GOLSBERY; Ralph ORMSTON (Booth's mill); Jacob PINE; Perry A. PALMER; Mrs. Rachael PERRIN; Daniel

THE MARYLAND HERALD AND HAGERSTOWN WEEKLY ADVERTISER

RENCH; Frederick ROHRER; Matthias REIDENOUR; John SEVIER; Henry M. STEINER; Christian SHELLER; Jacob SNIDER; John SIMPSON; William SPROUL; George SWINGLE; Philip SHEFFY; John SWOPE; Henry SHOOP; Jacob SPIELMAN; Thomas SMITH (schoolmaster); Mrs. Margaret SHEETS; Mrs. Margaret SHAFFNER; Miss Sarah B. STULL; Widow SMITH; John THOMAS; Joshua FULK; Jacob TRAWINGER; William WILSON; Thomas WILLIAMS; William WEBB; John WOLGAMOT; Abraham YEITER - Wm. KREPS, P.M.
John HENNYBERGER, cabinet-maker, has removed his shop to the house nearly opposite Dr. SCHNEBLY's in Potomac st.
Wanted to hire - young man acquainted with farming business; apply to John NEWSON, Jun., 1 1/2 miles from Hagers-town.
Merchant mill for rent, a complete distillery and 200 acres of land adj, 5 miles from Hagers-town; apply to Charles G. BORSTLER on the premises or Thomas KENNEDY, Esq. near Williamsport.
Subscribers to the Antietam Loan are notified that the first instalment is due - J. THOMSON, Sup't P.C..
John SMITH, Antrim twp, Franklin co, offers reward for missing filly.
John WOLFERSPERGER forewarns persons from taking assignment on bond given to Job M'NAMEE, of the state of Ohio.
Members of the Agricultural Society are requested to meet at Samuel BAYLY's Hotel. The present members are: F. TILGHMAN; William FITZHUGH; Martin KERSHNER; Jacob ZELLER; Samuel RINGGOLD; Daniel HUGHES; John BUCHANAN; John T. MASON.
William ARMOR, tailor, continues his business in the shop lately occupied by Lewis R. FECHTIG, next door to his former stand.
John SEITZ has removed from his late stand sign of the Buck, to the tavern stand formerly occupied by Thomas SHUMAN, sign of the Golden Swan, a few doors above the dwelling of Col. Adam OTT, in Potomac st.

29. Apr 15 1812
J. STALLSMITH, Boots & Shoe manufacturer, continues his business, nearly opposite Mr. F. MILLER's Apothecary shop, in Potomac st.
David SPEALMAN, Boonsborough, offers reward for Jacob GUNN, formerly by the name of Jacob MILLER, about 20 yrs of age, 5 ft 7 inches, well made, bound to the subscriber to learn the trade of a stone mason and brick layer. It is supposed that he is gone to Virginia, near Martinsburg, to his step-father, Caleb FULLER.
George BINKLEY has declined store-keeping and sold out his stock of goods; requests payment of debts.
Christian LANTZ has opened a House of Entertainment at the stand formerly occupied by John SEITZ, in Potomac st, Hagers-town.
Christian LANTZ, Hagers-town, offers reward for apprentice to the tanning business named Andrew PUTTER, about 18 yrs of age.
William ROBEY, admr, to sell at late dwelling of Susanna ROBEY, decd, on the road from Sharpsburg to Williamsport, 2 1/2 miles from Zeigler's store, personal estate of decd.
John YANDES, 6 miles north of Liberty Town, offers reward for William HARTZOCK, apprentice to the wagon making business, about 15 yrs of age, stout and well made, low in stature, broad face and very cross eyed

THE MARYLAND HERALD AND HAGERSTOWN WEEKLY ADVERTISER

30. Apr 29 1812
Agreeable to last will of Jacob RENCH, to be offered at sale, part of real estate of decd: (1) 11 acres, adj lands of Daniel RENCH, the heirs of John RENCH, jun. decd, and Jacob YOUNG; (2) 10 acres, adj lands of Jacob YOUNG and heirs of John RENCH, jun; (3) 38 3 1/6 acres; also part of the land conveyed by Peter RENCH to Jacob RENCH, and a conveyance from Charles CARROLL, Esq. to Jacob RENCH and a part conveyed by John BUCHANAN, Esq. as trustee for John RENCH's estate to Jacob RENCH - Daniel SCHNEBLY and Isaac S. WHITE, Exrs.
Martin FUNK continues to carry on wool carding business at his farm, near the widow Funk's mill and 1/2 mile from Martin BAECHTEL's Fulling Mill and 1 1/2 mile from Hagers-town.
Joseph WOLF exr of Daniel SPEIS.
Notice to those having business in Washington County Levy Court - O.H. WILLIAMS, Clk.
Jacob DUNN and Andrew KERSHNER have in operation a carding machine at the mill lately erected by Martin KERSHNER on the road from Hagers-town to Hancock-town, 1/4 mile from Holt's Tavern at the Cross Roads.
Apprentices to the Tailor's trade wanted - Benjamin YOE, Hagers-town.
Philip MAINS certifies that Andrew BLAIR has taken up a stray mare.
Matthias SPITLER, Adams co, Mount Pleasant twp, near Gettysburg, Pa, offers reward for missing mares.
Rezin WELLS, living with 2 miles of Williamsport, has taken up a stray bull which came to the plantation where the subscriber lately lived, on Ringgold's Manor, 3 1/3 miles from Williamsport.
Daniel BRAGONIER cautions against fowling or hunting, throwing down the fences, mustering or feasting at any of the Springs, or trespassing in any manner upon the Big Spring Farm, near Hagers-town.
For sale - a large stone paper mill, 3 stories high, adj two story Vat house on two sides; also a small grist mill near the above with pair of French burs and a saw-mill. These mills are situate on Antietam creek; apply to subscribers, living on said premises and near Hagers-town - George MILLER, Henry MILLER, and Moses M'NAMEE.

31. May 8 1812
Married at Hanover, York co, Pa, a few days since, by Rev MEISHEIMER, George EMMERY, merchant of Hagers-town, to Miss Catharine WARTZ, dau of Christian WARTZ, of that place.
Sale of tract in Berkeley Co, Va, on the waters of Sleepy Creek, 1 1/2 mile from Johnston's mill, 413 acres - Jacob REICHARD, in Bath.
John WELLS, Druggist & Apothecary, has commenced business in the house lately occupied by John P. HERR, next door to Bayly's tavern.
Officers belonging to the 1st and 2d Battalion, 10th Regt, Md. Militia are ordered to meet on 14th at 10 o'clock, A.M. in uniform, at Carey's Cross Roads - John BLACKFORD and Daniel MALOTT, Majors.
Jacob ROWLAND, living about 4 miles from Hagers-town, offers reward for apprentice girl by name of Betsey TANLEY, about 15 yrs of age.

32. May 13 1812
Died suddenly, Monday evening last, Robert NEILL, son of Alexander NEILL, merchant of this town, in the 9th year of his age.

THE MARYLAND HERALD AND HAGERSTOWN WEEKLY ADVERTISER

Conrod SMITH, continues to carry on wool carding business at his old stand, at Isaac HOTTMAN's mill (formerly John ALLISON's), 1/2 mile of Greencastle, near the road leading to Mercersburg.
Rockville Academy Lottery - Richard ANDERSON, Upton BEALL, Honore MARTIN, Solomon HOLLAND, Commissioners.
Arthur WITHNEY, Hagers-town, has taken up a stray mare.
Leonard SWINGLE, living on Conococheague, has taken up a stray mare.
John HUNTER (L.S.) certifies that George RIZER has taken up a stray mare.
Jacob & Michael CONRADT are now erecting in Funks-town next to Henry SHAFER's mill, a factory for all kinds of woolen cloths, cassimers, kerseys, flannels, blankets &c..
Conrad FOREMAN, Greencastle, offers reward for mare stolen out of the stable of Abraham STONER, in Greencastle, Franklin co, Pa.
Sale at dwelling of the subscriber in Funks-town, furniture, milch cow, gig &c. - Henry SCHRADER, Senr

33. May 20 1812
Rifleman attention! Rifle Corps of Volunteers forming, to consist of 4 companies - John RAGAN, Junr..
KEEN, KAIGHN, & Co. have established a hat manufactory in Washington st.
Bolting cloths - R. RAGAN.
Those persons who have subscribed money for the purpose of erecting a bridge over the Conococheague, at Williams-Port, are hereby notified that a call for money has become necessary because of the expense of raising stone pillars under the arch for the security of the bridge - Jacob T. TOWSON, Treasurer at Williams-Port.
Chancery sale made by George C. SMOOT, trustee, of the real estate of George SHARKEY, decd.
Jacob SHOLL continues to carry on the rope making business at his old stand in Hagers-town, opposite Gottleib ZIMMERMAN's. He makes mill and wellropes, bed cords, halters, plough liners, all kinds of twin, &c.
Warrented bolting cloths - Alexander NEIL & Co., Hagers-town.
2d Battalion, 24th Regt, to meet - John REYNOLDS, Major.
Samuel HAMMET lost on parade, a brass pistol, mounted with silver.
The Washington Hussars are ordered to muster in full uniform at Mr. MUIR's Tavern in Williams-port - E. G. WILLIAMS, Captain, Hagers-town.

34. Jun 10 1812
Benjamin GALLOWAY, Washington Co, will serve as an elector of the next President and Vice-Pres of the U.S. if chosen by the voters.
George BEIGLER, baker, has removed to house lately occupied by Arthur JOHNSTON, nearly opposite Lutheran church, Hagers-town, where he carries on the bread and sugar baking business, nearly opposite Mr. SAILOR's tavern, sign of the White Swan and next door to Mr. BEECHER's store.
Sale at the late dwelling of Peter REYNOLD, decd, on Beaver Creek, 1 1/2 miles of Cave Tavern, of personal estate of decd.
Died Wed morning last at his res near Williams-Port, after a short illness, Nicholas BAKER, in his 52d year; native of Germany, but for many yrs an inhabitant of this co, husband, father.
Edward G. WILLIAMS, Springfield, near Williams-Port has taken up 2 stray mares.

THE MARYLAND HERALD AND HAGERSTOWN WEEKLY ADVERTISER

Deserted from the barracks at this place, on 2d inst, a recruit named George BROWN, about 23 yrs of age, 5 ft 8 1/2 inches, fair complexion, blue eyes, black hair, stout and well made, by profession a labourer; born in Dauphin co, Pa - Thomas POST, Lieut., U.S. Army.
John WOLGAMOT, living five miles of Hagers-town, has taken up stray mare.
James NOWELL, Williams-port, offers reward for missing mare.
Chancery sale of Jacob BARNETT and Henry M'LAUGHLIN, trustees for sale of real estate of Elizabeth BARNETT.
Joseph HUNTER, has taken up stray steers which came to his plantation at Parkhead-forge.
Henry SCHRADER, at Gerard STONEBREAKER's, has a four wheel carriage for sale, with plated harness.
Sale of negro man - Emanuel FRANCIS

35. Jun 17 1812
Meeting of Washington Rangers at Mr. STINE's Tavern; John RENCH of Peter called to the chair and John B. POTTENGER appt'd sec'y. Thomas B. HALL elected as Captain, Henry C. SCHNEBLY of Jacob, 1st Lieutenant, Isaac CELLER, 2d Lieutenant, and John BARNETT, Cornet.
Hagers-town Hotel, formerly the Indian King Tavern (Beltzhoover's), prepared for the reception of travellers and boarders - Samuel BAYLY. A convenient hack, a pair of gentle horses and a careful driver, may be had at the shortest notice.

36. Aug 5 1812
Sale of personal property of Thomas SHEARER, decd, at late dwelling of decd, Falling Waters, Berkeley co, Va.
Edward APRICE, Chaptico, St. Mary's Co, offers reward for negro man HARRY, about 5 ft 8-9 inches, hired to Michael MALOT, near Hagers-town, from whom he ran away; deliver to James MUIR, Williams-Port, or to subscriber, Edward Aprice.
James PRATHER certifies that George LOWE, living near the Big-Spring Tavern, has taken up a stray horse.
John SHAFER, living on Antietam Creek, offers reward for negro nam named DICK, about 26 yrs of age, 5 ft 10-11 inches, speaks English and German.
Tho: M'CARDELL has two story brick house for sale in Antietam st, Hagers-town, including kitchen, smoke house, carriage house, stable and garden.
Henry SWEITZER, Hagers-town, candidate for sheriff.
John CROMWELL, Frederick-town, offers reward for apprentice boys, bound to carpenter's business, Corbin JACOBS, about 20 yrs of age, 5 ft 8 inches; other named John BARRICK, about 20 yrs of age, about 5 ft 6 inches.
Daniel SCHNEBLY and Isaac S. WHITE, exrs, request payment on notes due from sale of personal estate of Jacob RENCH, decd.
Catharine SWOPE and Daniel GRIFFITH, admrs, request payment on notes given at sale of personal estate of Peter SWOPE, decd.
Carpenter wanted to finish the steeple on German Lutheran Church in this place; apply to David HARRY, Theobald EICHELBERGER, or Christopher EMBICH.
William KREPS candidate for sheriff.
Married at Chambersburg, Sunday evening last by Rev MILLER, Mr. G. H. IRWIN, merchant, to Miss Mary LOTTERBERGER, both of this town.
Married same evening by same, Wm. SHAW to Miss Mary RIDENOUR, both of this co.

THE MARYLAND HERALD AND HAGERSTOWN WEEKLY ADVERTISER

Married last evening by Rev RAHAUSER, George HESS, to Miss Hannah WOLGAMOT, both of this co.
American Blues ordered to parade in full uniform - Joseph M'ILHENNY, 1st Sergt..
Deserted from the Volunteer Company in Hagers-town, attached to the 24th Regt of Md. Militia a few days since, James BEATTY, about 25 yrs of age, 5 ft 9-10 inches, fair complexion, grey eyes, by profession a cabinet maker; also Richard HALL, about same age, 5 ft 10-11 inches, dark complexion, black eyes, same profession - Thomas QUANTRILL, Captain, Hagers-town.
John WEST exr of Jeremiah HAYES, to sell at dwelling of decd, on Potomac river, 4 miles of Mr. ZEIGLER's store, and 2 from Mr. GALLOWAY's Mill, all personal estate of decd: negro boy, horses, cows, furniture, &c.
Sarah BAKER and Nicholas FRITZ, admrs, to sell at late dwelling of Nicholas BAKER, decd, 1 mile from Williams-Port, personal estate of decd, negro boy and girl, horses, farming utensils, &c..
George KREPS continues to carry on cabinet making busines in Fraklin st at his present stand.
George HEDRICK adm of Benjamin TYSON, to sell personal estate of decd.
Ann BERRY, adm of John BERRY to sell at late dwelling of decd, residue of personal estate of decd.
John CRAWFORD, boot & shoe manufacturer, has commenced business at stone house on corner of public square, directly opposite Messrs. John & George HARRY's store.
Henry SCHNEBLY, living near Fiery's Mill has taken up a stray horse, certified by Adam OTT.
House for sale in Potomac st, Hagers-town, near the Presby Church. John KING
Benjamin BELL to sell the farm whereon he resides, on Opeckon Creek, 5 miles of Martinsburg, Va.
John STALLSMITH, Hagers-town, offers reward for apprentice to boot & shoe making business, John STANTON, about 14 yrs old, 4 ft 9-10 inches, sandy hair, very much freckled in his face.
Persons are forewarned against making assignment on a note give to Dr. Emanuel FRANCIS with endorsement of Alexander NEILL. Wendel GILBERT

37. Aug 12 1812
George ECKERD, living neaar Union Town, offers reward for missing gelding.
Volunteers attached to my company are ordered to repair to my quarters for the purpose of being uniformed. They are to bring their arms with them, as they will be supplied with new arms for the purpose of marching immediately, according to orders. Thomas QUANTRILL, Capt, Hagers-town.
Daniel HEFFLEBOWER, insolvent debtor, discharged from imprisonment.
George MARTIN, Hagers-town, offers reward for missing cows and calf.
Grocery store - Matthias NEAD has received fresh supply of groceries and liquors.
Adam M'CHESNEY, 5 miles from Middlebrook, upper end of Augusta co, Va, offers reward for yellow man slave, CHARLES.
Robert DOAK, Henry HAWPE, Robert STEELE, living near Greenville, upper end of Augusta co, Va, offers reward for mulatto man named BEN belonging to Robert DOAK, light made fellow named TOM of Henry HAWPE and dark coloured man named CARTER of Robert STEELE.

THE MARYLAND HERALD AND HAGERSTOWN WEEKLY ADVERTISER

Ordered that the Officers and Privates of the Battalion commanded by Major John M'CLAIN in the 8th Regt, Md. Militia, meet at Capt Joseph HUNTER's near Parkhead Forge, 14th inst, and Officers and Privates of the Battalion commanded by Major Christian HAGER meet at Mr. STINE's Tavern (Cross Roads) on 15th inst, each at 9 o'clock in the morning for purpose of furnishing their respective quotas. The commanding Officers of Companies in the 8th Regt will enrol every white male person in their district, between 18 and 45 yrs of age, who does not produce a certificate according to law, dated since the last June session, as the old certificates are all void. The Commanding Officers of Companies will make out plain copies of the enrolments and make return thereof to me on the mornings of the above mentioned days. David SCHNEBLY, Lieut. Col., 8th Regt, M.M.
Philip EMBICH to remove from this county in a short time, requests persson indebted to make payment.
David HARRY, Jun'r seeks two journeymen wagon makers.
Casper MOUDY, living 3 miles from Williams-Port, on road to Little Conococheague, has taken up a stray gelding. Certified by James M'CLAIN, Justice of the Peace.
Frederick ROHRER, near Hagers-town, has taken up a stray horse.
American Blues are ordred to parade in full uniform in front of the Captain's quarters at 10 o'clock A.M. with 6 rounds of blunt cartridges. Joseph M'ILHENNY, 1st Serg't.

38. Aug 19 1812
Died Mon last in this town, after a short illness, Maxwell WELCH, in his 53d yr, leaving wife and 8 children. His remains were interred in the German Lutheran Burying ground.
William ROBEY exr of Owen ROBEY; also admr of Susanna ROBEY.
Susanna BELCH and William SIMKINS, admr of James BELCH, to sell at late dwelling of decd, on Chew's Farm, 2 miles of William ZEIGLER's Store, and 1 1/2 mile from Mr. GALLOWAY's Mill, personal estate of decd.
2d Brigade orders to parade. S. RINGGOLD, Brig General; Tho. B. POTTENGER, Brigade Inspector. Regimental orders of 24th Regt, John RAGAN, Jun'r, Lieut. Col., to parade in Potomac st, Hagers-town; and 10th Regt, Daniel MALOTT, Lieut. Col., ordered to parade at Carey's Cross Road.
To be sold at the store house of William MOORE, late of the borough of Carlisle, decd, his entire stock of goods. James GIVIN, William IRVINE, admrs.
George MILLER has received new cards for his machines at his fulling mill near Hagers-town.
Reward offered for red morrocco pocket book containing ten dollar notes wrapt in a paper from Thomas BRENT to Leonard SHAFER. Deliver to Mr. KNABLE near Hancock-town or John GELWICKS, Innkeeper in Williamsport.
Henry SNYDER has commenced the bridle bit and stirrup making business, 2 doors from the dwelling of William BRAZIER, Franklin st, Hagers-town.
William DELAHUNT near Sprigg's Mill has taken up a stray horse.
George MARTINI, Hagers-town, has taken up stray cows and calf.

THE MARYLAND HERALD AND HAGERSTOWN WEEKLY ADVERTISER

39. Aug 26 1812
On Mon last the Volunteer Corps of the 24th Regiment, Maryland Militia, marched from this place, under the command of Capt. Thomas QUANTRILL, for the city of Annapolis, all in good spirits, and willing to defend the rights of their country. They were escorted a few miles by Capt. TABBS's volunteer troop of horse, together with large concourse of their fellow citizens.
It is with pleasure we announce, that on Monday the 17th of August, Captain David CUSHWA's company of infantry, was paraded in front of his Quarters, for the purpose of furnishing their quota of Militia. The captain informed the men, that if volunteers could not be had, a draught would be resorted to, and to the satifaction of every one present the quota allotted to the company turned out to a man; and, we verily belive if as many more had been wanted, they could have been had - So great a desire among young men to volunteer in defence of the rights and liberties of their country, we never witnessed - and it is with pleasure we record the names of those young patriots, who have so nobly volunteered their services - Philemon CROMWELL, Robert CHAMBERS, George STINEMETZ, David STOLTZ, Stephen CROMWELL, James MYERS, Philip TROXELL and Abraham WATSON.
Married Tues 18th inst by Rev KENNEDY, John BARNETT, to Miss Sally PRICE, dau of Col. Josiah PRICE of this co.
James LITTON, Parkhead Forge, has taken up stray steers.
Plantation for sale on Beaver Creek, near John WITMER's mill and 6 miles from Hagers-town, 116 a. Enquire of William FORD on the premises.
Ordered that 8th Regt, Md. Militia, parade at Jacob KERSHNER's Tavern. David SCHNEBLY, Lieut. Col.
Wendel GILBERT, 3 miles from Hagers-town, offers reward for negro boy named ELIJAH, about 15 yrs old, 4 ft 3-4 inches, purchased of William EVANS of St. Mary's co.
Coverlet & carpet weaving & blue dying - Daniel STOVER has commenced the business in the shop adj dwelling of Jacob FUNK, 3 miles from Hagers-town.
Charles M'PIKE offers reward for mare missing from Roger JOHNSON's Furnace, near the mouth of Monocacy, Frederick co.
Journey man blacksmith wanted by Randolph WOODEN, Mercersburg, Pa.

40. Sep 2 1812
The Agricultural Society will meet at Mr. BAYLY's Tavern. U. LAWRENCE, Sec'ry.
William SHERIDAN, Hughes's Furnace, offers reward for missing mare.
John GIBBONEY, Sen., and James LOCHRAY, have commenced the fulling & dying business at the fulling mill of Martin BAECHTELL, near Hagers-town.
John GIBBONEY, jun. continues the fulling & dying business at John HERSHEY's fulling mill, 6 miles from Hagers-town and 1/2 mile from Michael HOFFER's mill.
Those persons who have coloured yarn laying at the subscriber's shop in Hagers-town these 3 yrs past, are requested to call for the same as it will otherwise be injured by vermin. The subscriber continues the dying busines at his old stand, opposite Samuel RIDENOUR's Tan-yard. Jacob BINKLEY, sen.
Simon YANDES, Jun'r. has lost a black pocket book.
Michael BOWARD, Stull's Addition to Hagers-town, offers reward for missing cow.

THE MARYLAND HERALD AND HAGERSTOWN WEEKLY ADVERTISER

41. Sep 9 1812
Died Wed 2d inst at the house of Dr. Jacob SCHNEBLY, William LEE, formerly an inhabitant of this town.
- On Fri morning last at the res of Daniel RENCH, Mrs. Elizabeth RENCH, in her 75th yr.
Letter from G. W. BOERSTLER, to his father, Dr. C. BOERSTLER in Funks-town, dated Williamsburg, O, Aug 20th, 1812, stating that "my dearly beloved brother Jacob" was killed on 8 Aug, leading his company against the enemy, his scull was fractured by a ball. He lived until they carried him to Detroit... our army was surrendered to the British... "Today, brother-in-law HUBER started with a corps to protect our frontiers."
Mrs. LITTON has just arrived at Mr. BAYLY's Hotel, where she has opened an assortment of millinery & fancy articles.
Sale at the dwelling of the subscriber, 1 mile from Stephen BARTON's Tavern, on Little Conococheague, 2 miles from Big Spring, negro woman and her two children and 2 negro boys, milch cows, and other. John OLIVER.
Philip KERSHNER, 3 1/2 miles from Hagers-town, offers reward for missing heifer.
John HERSHEY, on Conococheague Creek, 6 miles from Hagers-town, offers reward for missing hogs.
Purchasers of property at the sale by the subscriber of the property of Jacob RIDENOUR, are informed that their notes will be due on 13th.
Samuel MARTIN has taken his son Thomas into partnership, under the firm of Samuel Martin & Son, in the blacksmsith business. Samuel Martin.

42. Sep 16 1812
John Lee BEALL, insolvent debtor, discharged from gaol.
Charles M'GEE has again commenced the fulling & dying business at George MILLER's Factory near Hagers-town.
Man wanted who understands the fulling & dying business. James GRAHAM, Bedford co, Pa.
George SMITH, 3 miles from Frederick town, offers reward for missing mare.

43. Sep 23 1812
Supported by "Friends of Peace" - For Congress: Roger B. TANEY; for the Assembly: Robert HUGHES, John BLACKFORD, Thomas BRENT, Otho H. W. STULL.
Sale at the farm on which I now live, 2 1/2 miles from Hagers-town, horses, cows, 1-2 negro womn, &c. Christian HAGER.
Sale on farm on which I now live, adj Gerhart BUCKWALTER's plantation near John & George HARRY's Mill, furniture, wagon, horses, cows, sheep, hogs, &c. Barnabas FASTNAUGHT.

44. Sep 30 1812
Died Mon morning last in this town, Miss Ann M'ILHENNY aged 20 yrs.
Republican ticket - Congress: Gen. Samuel RINGGOLD; electors of the president: Frisby TILGHMAN, Joshua COCKEY; for Assembly: John BOWLES, Henry LEWIS, Wm. B. WILLIAMS, Wm. O. SPRIGG.
Williamsport Races - James MUIR, M. H. SACKETT, managers.
Barton CARICO has opened a House of Entertainment in house of Jacob HOFFMAN, town of Cumberland.
Sale at dwelling of the subscriber, Hagers-town, hogs, wheat in the straw, furniture. Leonard KUHN.

THE MARYLAND HERALD AND HAGERSTOWN WEEKLY ADVERTISER

John SEITZ continues the cooper's busines in Potomac st, where tight and
flour barrels can be had.

45. Oct 7 1812
Sale at dwelling of Wm. DAVIS, decd, on Chew's Farm, 1 1/2 miles from
   Zeigler's store. Mary DAVIS and Stephen DAVIS, exrs.
Daniel BRAGONIER cautions against fowling or hunting, &c. at any of the
   Springs, or trespassing upon the Big Spring Farm, near Hagers-town.

46. Oct 14 1812
Died Tues morning 26th ult at his farm near Hancock-town, after a long and
   severe illness, Denton JOHNSON, in his 27th yr.
Died Sat morning last at his farm in this co, after a tedious illness, Henry
   GAITHER, husband and father.
Uriah KITCHIN will commence a school for writing at the stone house, corner
   of Court house Square.
George KERSHNER, living near Mr. HOLL's Tavern, at the Cross Roads, offers
   reward for horse stolen from Mr. SAILOR's Tavern.
William YATES has timothy seed for sale.
List of letters left at the Post Office [omitted here]
Sale at his farm adj Hagers-town, horses, cattle, carriage, &c. Frederick
   ROHRER.
Price list of master cordwainers of Hagers-town established [and published
   here] - John CRAWFORD.
Sale in pursuance of last will of Samuel TURNER, decd of farm in Montgomery
   co, late res of decd, 700 a. Thomas TURNER, Samuel TURNER, exrs.
George BEAN, near Hagers-town, has taken up a stray mare.

47. Mar 10 1813
House for sale in which Moses TABBS, Esq. now lives adj Mr. HEYSER's and
   within a few doors of the public square. R. PINDELL, Hagers-town.
Peter SAILER, admr of Henry SHENEFELT.
   Will sell at late dwelling of decd, near Rohrer's mill, 2 1/2 miles from
   Hagers-town, personal estate of decd, horses, cows, sheep and hogs, wagon,
   ploughs, harrows, farming utensils, grain in the ground, furniture.
For sale or rent - Brick house in Franklin st, Hagers-town, near the public
   spring, now occupied by subscriber, Susanna ORNDORFF.
Five rooms for rent in the house where the subscriber, Frances MONAHAN, now
   lives, in Franklin st.
Warranted bolting cloths - Alexander NEILL, & Co.
Married Sun evening last by Rev SCHAEFFER, Robert HAYS to Miss Sally
   RICHARDSON, all of this town.
- Last evening by Rev E. TOWNE, Charles COX, to Miss Nancy WENDALL, all of
   Washington Co.
Died Mon 1st inst, after a short illness, Samuel MARTIN, son of Samuel
   MARTIN, of this town in the 24th yr.
Nicholas CLOPPER, Greenfield, Frederick Co, to commence the mercantile
   business again, will sell the farm on which he now lives, on west side of
   Monocacy, 12 miles south of Frederick-town, 400 acres clear.
Hagers-town Academy - Persons in arrears for subscriptions to the Academy
   are informed that the last instalment is due. O. H. WILLIAMS, Pres.
Smart active negro woman for sale, about 22 yrs of age. John SLEIGH.

THE MARYLAND HERALD AND HAGERSTOWN WEEKLY ADVERTISER

The horse, Young President, will stand this season at Conrod HILDEBRAND's stable, 2 miles from Peter NEWCOMER's Mill on road from Funks-town to Boonsborough, and at George COLIFLOWER's stable, 1 mile from Cave Tavern. John COLIFLOWER.
Henry SHAFER, Funks-town, has on hand a quantity of ground plaster paris to sell.
Will be sold at the house of the subscriber in Williams-Port, milch cow, furniture, tubs, iron pots, hog's lard, bacon. Albert HUMRICKHOUSE.
Sale at the farm where the late Jacob PITRY formerly lived, 1 1/2 mile from John SHARER's mill, 4 1/2 miles from Hagers-town, furniture, 34 a. of wheat and 11 a. of rye, farming utensils, geese, potatoes, and other. Christian SMITH.
For sale - at the late res of Leonard BEVENS, decd, on Licking Creek, 3 miles from Parkhead Forge, Washington co, horses, cows, young cattle, hogs and sheep, wagon, cart, ploughs, harrows, and other; also tract called Leonard's Rest, 500 a., Washington Co, to be shewn by Leonard BEVENS, living on the premises; tract of 400 a. in Air Twp, Bedford co, Pa, to be shewn by Basil BEVENS, living on the premises; tract on Fifteen Mile Creek in Allegany Co, called Sugar Bottom, 300 a., to be shewn by Henry BEVENS, adj the premises; tract in Warren twp, Franklin co, Pa, 160 a., to be shewn by Elie BROWN, living on the premises. Leonard BEVENS, John ADAMS, exrs.
Jacob MOATS, living 2 miles from Mr. STOVER's Tavern, and 9 miles from Hagers-town, offers reward for stolen horse.
Sale of personal property by Joseph SPRIGG, at his res 3 miles from Williams Port, 26 negroes, 200 head of cattle, 120 sheep, 200 hogs, 40 horses, wagons, furniture, 225 a. of grain in the ground; also a tract of land on Potomack River, 840 a. with distillery, merchant mill and saw mill.
For rent - office now occupied by John CRAWFORD, rooms above the office of George C. SMOOT, frame house occupied by Mr. STEELE, next door to Dr. DORSEY, and other property [listed]. Henry LEWIS.
The co-partnership of Daniel WEISEL and Albert HUMRICKHOUSE, Williams-Port, dissolved.
Tract of land for sale, 232 3/4 a. 1 1/2 miles from Jacob ANGLE's mill on West Conococheague creek, Franklin co, Pa. Josiah PRICE, 7 miles from Hagers-town, on road to Mercersburg.
Sale at the late dwelling of Daniel SPEISS, decd, 2 miles from Hugh's Furnaces, residue of personal estate of decd. Joseph WOLF, exr.
Journeyman fuller wanted at his fulling mill near Hagers-town. George MILLER.
A new tavern in Hagers-town. L. PRICE has taken the stand lately in the occupancy of Mr. BAYLY.
Christian GOOD admr of Barbara BARR.
Jacob SHOLL continues to carry on the rope making business at his old stand, opposite the dwelling of Gottleib ZIMMERMAN, pump maker, near the Lutheran Church in Hagers-town.
Tract of land for sale 7 miles from Hagers-town, 340 a., to be shewn by John C. CROMWELL, adj the premises. Nathan CROMWELL, near Hagers-town.
Daniel MILLER, 1 1/2 miles below the Broad fording on Conococheague creek, 7 miles from Hagers-town, has found a pocket book with some money near Middletown.
Peter CRAMER, Hagers-town, has taken up a stray cow.

THE MARYLAND HERALD AND HAGERSTOWN WEEKLY ADVERTISER

48. Mar 17 1813
Married at York, Pa, Tues 2d inst by Rev GHEISTWEIT, Henry MILLER, son of George MILLER of this place, to Miss Elizabeth LENHART, dau of Wm. LENHART, of York co, Pa.
- On Thurs last in the afternoon, at his res, near the seat of Gen. Samuel RINGGOLD by Rev RAHAUSER, Michael MALOTT, to Miss Catharine TRITCH.
- On same day in the afternoon, by Rev RAHAUSER, at the house of his aged parents, Elias MALONE, to Miss Catharine STEFFY.
- On Sun last in Hagers-town, by Rev RAHAUSER, Daniel MILLERE to Miss Elizabeth SNYDER, all of this co.
Election to be held at the Banking-house - Elie BEATTY, Cash'r.
David BRUMBAUGH, living near Col. David SCHNEBLY's has taken up a horse, certified by A. OTT.
Sale of lot adj lots of Peter HEFLEIGH and George BENDER, in Rohrer's Addition to Hagers-town. John CRUMBAUGH, jun'r, Samuel CRUMBAUGH.
Sale at the dwelling house of subscriber, near Harry's town, horse, cart, 8-day clock, furniture. Margaret BOWART.
Sale at res of Christian GERHART, 3 miles from Hagers-town, negro woman and child, horses, and other.
Sale at the subscriber's tavern in Hagers-town, mare, furniture. Christian FECHTIG.
Jacob SAYLOR has removed from his late stand, sign of the Swan, to the Tavern stand lately occupied by Christian LANTZ, sign of the Indian King.
Troop of Washington Hussars are ordered to muster in full uniform at Muir's Tavern in Williamsport. E. G. WILLIAMS, Capt.
Fresh Hemp seed just received at the store of P. ARTZ & EMMERT.
Fresh clover seed just received at the store of John & Jos. M'ILHENNY.
The subscribers to the Antietam Loan to the Potomack Co. are requested to pay unto the Hagers-town Bank the 3rd instalment of the loans. Joseph BREWER, Treasurer.

49. Mar 24 1813
Hat Manufactory - Nathaniel POSEY just received an addition to his old stock at his shop lately occupied by Abraham FORCE, in Potomac st, 2 doors below P. ARTZ & EMMERT's store.
Nicholas BREWER, late Register of the Court of Chancery, offers his services at solicitor of that court.
Merchant mill and 120 a. for sale, 4 miles from Hagers-town, 2 miles from Mr. OGLE's Tavern, at the Cross roads. John SCHERCH.
Sale of furniture. John HUMRICKHOUSE, Hagers-town.
Matthew MURRAY, Middle-town, Frederick Co, will commence plough making this spring.
Sale at late res of Henry SHRIVER, decd, 1/2 mile from Christopher BARKHART's mill, 7 miles from Hagers-town, furniture, grain, farming utensils. George HARBAUGH, John STRITE, admrs.
J. STALLSMITH, boot & shoe manufacturer, opposite Mr. F. MILLER's Apothecary shop in Potomac st, Hagers-town.
School master wanted. John M'CLAIN, Henry ANKONY, 8 miles from Hagers-town, on west side of Conococheague creek.
Henry LEWIS will receive proposals for quarrying and laying 500-600 perches of stone, in Hagers-town.

THE MARYLAND HERALD AND HAGERSTOWN WEEKLY ADVERTISER

50. Mar 31 1813
I forewarn persons from trusting or boarding my wife Elizabeth CARR on my account. Nicholas CARR.
The horse, Herculian Cub, will stand this season at KIRKPATRICK's tavern at the Big-Spring, and at subscriber's stable in Williams-Port. Samuel ROSS.
George KREPS continues to carry on Cabinet Making at his old stand in Franklin st.
Squadron Orders. The officers commanding the Troops of Cavalry forming the Squadron under my command are requried to inspect the arms of their repspective Troops... O. H. WILLIAMS, Major.
Head miller wanted. John & Geo. HARRY, Hagers-town.

51. Apr 7 1813
[Letters at Post Office ommitted here.]
Perry WAYMAN, saddle & harness maker, has commenced business in the corner house lately occupied by Zachariah SHUGART, next door to the dwelling of Col. Adam OTT, directly opposite Henry MIDDLEKAUFF, in Potomack st.
John HENNYBERGER, cabinet maker, has removed to the shop formerly occupied by Leonard KUHN, next door to the dwelling of Otho H. WILLIAMS, Esq., in Antietam sts.
By order of the board of Directors of the Hagers-town Bank, the house now occupied by Christian HAWKEN, will be sold. The house must be removed from the lot immediately after the sale. Wm. HEYSER, Pres't.
Sale at the house of the subscriber in Hagers-town, family carriage, new still containing 80 gallons, bar utensils, liquors, furniture; also 150 a. of Mountain land in Frederick Co and 550 a. near Morgan-town, Va. Christian LANTZ.
Michael KAPP, to run a handsome and convenient Hack.
William BUTLER forewarns persons from trusting his wife, Letty BUTLER, on his account.

52. Apr 14 1813
On Fri and Sat last a detachment of 312 regulars, from the state of Virginia, under the command of Lieut. Col. James PRESTON, reached this place, and early on Mon morning pursued their march for Black Rock.
The Commanding Officers of Cavalry composing the Squadron commanded by major O. H. WILLIAMS are ordered to parade on Sat. Col. TILGHMAN will inspect the Squadron. Tho. B. HALL, Adjutant 1st Regt, Cavalry.
Levi PRICE, Hagers-town, offers reward for negro lad named JIM.
Christian STEMPLE offers reward for information on persons who broke into his garden.
John BRADSHAW, wheelwright & chair maker, has removed his shop to house below Mr. HESS's cooper, Franklin st.
S. PETTIT has taken well known inn, lately occupied by Jacob SAYLOR.
Theobald EICHELBERGER, house joiner and cabinet maker, has removed to the house lately occupied by George SMITH, merchant, 5th door above John & Hugh KENNEDY's store, opposite Dr. J. SCHNEBLY's office. Mrs. EICHELBERGER continues to carry on the milliner and mantua making business.
Samuel HAGER, saddle & harness maker, has removed his shop to house lately occupied by William BROWN, next door to his former stand, directly opposite the German Printing Office.

THE MARYLAND HERALD AND HAGERSTOWN WEEKLY ADVERTISER

The horse, Independence, will stand for mares this season at the subscriber's tavern. Samuel PETTIT.
Members of the Military School will parade on Wed, with arms in complete order. Wm. ROBERTSON.
John STOVER, living at the Cross Roads, has taken up a stray cow.

53. Apr 28 1813
Wm. WILLIS, boot & shoe maker, has removed his shop to house lately occupied by Samuel HAGER, 1 door from his former stand, directly opposite Dr. SCHNEBLY's.
George BRUMBAUGH has for sale a quantity of Hops.
Frederick KINSELL, barber & hair dresser, has arrived from George-town, and has opened a shop in the corner room adj William BEECHER's store, and lately occupied by George BEIGHLER, confectioner.
Bar-keeper wanted. L. PRICE.
Proposals will be received for building a bridge across Big Conococheague at the Broad Fording. David MARTIN, trustee.
Warranted bolting cloths for sale. Richard RAGAN.
Married last evening by Rev RAHAUSER, Samuel WEIS to Miss Catharine MILLER, dau of Geo. MILLER, near this town.
Peter & Matthias MILLER have lately removed from Hagers-town to Williamsport, and lodged their notes & books of accounts in the hands of William KREPS, Postmaster for collection. All those indebted to the firm of MILLERs & JULIUS, MILLERs & BEATTY, and Peter & Matthias MILLER, are requested to discharge their dues to said Kreps.
Philip BINKLEY, admr of Henry BECKLEY, sen., to sell at late dwelling of decd, 1/2 mile from Hagers-town, on road to Williams-port, all property of decd, consisting of 2 cows, 1 3/4 a. of wheat in the ground, bed and bedstead, cupboards, tables, chairs, and articles too tedious to mention.
John B. SHOWMAN, jun. has taken up a stray horse, certified by Thomas CRAMPTON.
John TEISHER, 3 miles from Hagers-town, offers reward for negro man named JAMES, about 25 yrs of age, 5 Frederick-town 6-7 inches, stout; his mother lives in or near Washington city.
Wm. O. SPRIGG, near Hagers-town, offers reward for bright mulatto man named JAMES, sometimes calls himself James SNOWDEN, 22 yrs old, 5 Frederick-town 7-8 inches.
Sale at late dwelling of Barbara SMITH, decd, 3 miles from Hagers-town, residue of the late Nicholas SMITH, decd, negro girl about 15 yrs old, cows, hogs, furniture. George CELLAR, Benjamin SWINGLE, exrs.
George MILLER and William JACKSON have entered patnership in the fulling and dying business at the fulling mill and factory adj Hagers-town.

54. May 5 1813
Sale of some furniture of Major Charles CARROLL. John SLEIGH, Auctionier.
Conrod SMITH continues to carry on the wool carding business at his old stand at Isaac HOTTMAN's mill (formerly John ALLISON's) 1/2 mile of Greencastle, near the road leading to Mercersburg. His price for picking, breaking and rolling wool is 9 cents per pound.
Washington County Levy Court to adjourn 24th inst. O. H. WILLIAMS, clerk.
Josias POTTER has taken up a stray gelding, certified by William YATES.

THE MARYLAND HERALD AND HAGERSTOWN WEEKLY ADVERTISER

William SMALL, 1 1/2 miles from Mercersburg, 1 mile from Dickey's mill, Peter's twp, Franklin co, Pa, offers reward for missing horse.
Henry M'LAUGHLIN, living near Col. David SCHNEBLY's has taken up a stray mare, certified by J. SCHNEBLY.

55. May 12 1813
Pocket book lost on road between Williams-Port and John BARTLETT's. Michael KREPS.
Sale at late dwelling of Christian ROHRER, decd, 1 mile from Hagers-town, personal estate of decd. Samuel ROHRER, admr.
John TROVINGER admr of William SCHYCAW, to sell at res of decd, 1 mile from Hagers-town, his personal estate.
Frederick MILLER, Druggist & Apothecary, has just received a fresh supply of drugs and medicines and paints.
Sarah PETER, Geo. PETER, and L. H. JOHNS, exrs of David PETER, to sell at the Union Tavern in George-town, lands in Montgomery co, Carderock, 1704 1/2 a.; The Hay Park, 40 a.; Dowl's Discovery, 127 a.; part of James's Park, 149 a.; The Ferry Landing, 22 a.; part of tract of 220 a., called The Resurvey on Honesty - to be shewn by Barton DULY who lives near the lands.
Trustees of the Hagers-town Academy to meet at Mr. PRICE's Tavern. Tho: B. HALL, sec'ry.
Elisha WILLIAMS, living on Abraham BOYER's plantation, near George MARKER's mill, 1 1/2 miles from the main road leading from Hagers-town to Middle-town, offers reward for missing mare.
Persons are forewarned against taking assignments on notes of hand given to John M'COY of Frederick co. Jacob ZUCK.
Two journeymen house carpenters wanted. Henry LOWRYE, Funks-town.

56. May 19 1813
Married yesterday by Rev SCHAEFFER, John MILLER, to Miss Susanna KREPS, both of this co.
Any gentleman having a gold epaulette lent him by Judge BUCHANAN, please leave it at the Office of the Maryland Herald.
L. PRICE offers reward for missing cows.
Persons are cautioned against passing through our enclosures and fishing in the Creek. George MILLER, Henry MILLER.
Two negro men for sale, at Mr. STRAUSE's Tavern, Hagers-town. James DAVIS.
Eve FRANZ and Henry E. FRANZ, admrs of Dr. Emanuel FRANZ.
Robert T. FRIEND has taken up a stray gelding, certified by Wm. VAN LEAR.
Peter HAMMOND, living near Wm. ZEIGLER's store, has taken up a stray gelding, certified by Isaac HOWSER, Jun. (L.S.)
John RAGAN, Jun'r. has plank for sale, Hagers-town.
Meeting of Commissioners of the Tax for Washington Co. J. SCHNEBLY, Clk.

57. Jun 2 1813
Martin FUNK continues the wool carding business at his farm, near the widow FUNK's Mill, 1/2 mile from Martin BACHTEL's Fulling Mill.
Died at Pomons in Baltimore Co, Mon 17th ult, after a short illness, Rev. George RALPH, in his 61st yr.
Daniel BRUMBAUGH, near Sprigg's quarter, offers reward for missing colt.
Charles YOCUM, Franklin co, Pa, has repaired his carding machine near John WORLEY's Sickle Shop, 4 miles south of Greencastle.

THE MARYLAND HERALD AND HAGERSTOWN WEEKLY ADVERTISER

Matthias SPONSG living on the widow GROUND's farm, near Sharpsburgh, has taken up a stray horse, certified by John BLACKFORD.
Sarah BAKER and Nicholas FRITZ, admrs of Nicholas BAKER, request persons pay on notes due from sale of personal estate of decd.
Charles DOWNS, living near Sharpsburgh, has taken up a stray colt, certified by George SMITH.
Daniel HUYETT, 1 1/2 miles of the Cave Tavern, offers reward for negro man named GEORGE about 20 yrs of age, 5 ft 7 inches.

58. Jun 9 1813
Married at George-town a few days since, by Rev ADDISON, George HARRY, merchant, of Hagers-town, to Miss Sarah CHESLEY dau of the late Alexander CHESLEY, Esq. of that place.
Simon KIESACKER, living 1 mile from Col. David SCHNEBLY's, had taken up a stray cow.

59. Jun 16 1813
A Meeting of the Home Spun Volunteers and others who wish to become members of a uniform company, to consist of 100 men, at PETTIT's Tavern. Thos. QUANTRILL.
The Co-partnership of GAREY & ZIGLAR was dissolved inconsequence of the death of Mr. Garey. William ZIGLAR.
Co-partnership of BAKER & ZIGLAR formed at the Crossroads, 4 miles from Sharpsburg.

60. Jun 23 1813
Sale by virtue of will of George GARY, 330 a., 10 miles from Hagers-town. Jonas HOGMIRE, George SMITH, exrs.
Purchasers of the personal property of Robert M'KEE, decd, are notified their notes are due. John M'KEE, admr.
John BOYD and Michael KAPP continue to run a line of mail stages from Frederick-town via Middle-town, Boonsborough, Hagers-town and Greencastle to Chambersburg, 3 times a week.
Samuel M'CORMICK, near Millwood on Spout Run, offers reward for negro man named TOM, shoemaker by trade, 35 yrs old, 5 Frederick-town 10 inches.
Leonard BEVENS has taken up a stray mare, certified by Philip MAINS.
Martin BILMYER, 2 miles from Shepherds-town, Va, offers reward for negro man who ran away from the farm of William TAYLOR, near Shepherds-town, Va, of yellow complexion, red eyes, 6 Frederick-town 1-2 inches.
John GELWICKS forewarns persons from taking assignment on note give to Chrisitan LANTZ, given for negro woman who is unsound.
George SMITH wants boy as an apprentice to house painting and glazing business.
John BROWNING offers reward for mare which strayed from James M'COY's plantation, 1 mile from Funks-town.
Geo. C. SMOOT will attend to the professional business of U. LAWRENCE, Esq., in his absence. Mr. Lawrence will himself attend, at his office, regularly on Tues and Thurs.

61. Jun 30 1813
John & Joseph M'ILHENNY, have removed their store to the coffee house Corner, lately occupied by C. FECHTIG as Tavern.

THE MARYLAND HERALD AND HAGERSTOWN WEEKLY ADVERTISER

Wool carding, common and merino, done at the woollen cloth factory, in Funkstown. J. & M. CONRADT.
Died Fri night last at his res near this town, Jacob YOUNG, in his 55th yr.
- On Sun last at his farm, near Funks-town, Gerard STONEBREAKER, in his 70th yr.
Mary DAVIS and Stephen DAVIS exrs of William DAVIS.
Agreeable to last will of James STERRETT, William-Port, will be sold lot and half lot adj William-Port, to be shewn by Jacob T. TOWSON, or Milton H. SACKETT, in Williams-Port. Jacob T. TOWSON, Wm. M'CLELLAND, exrs.

62. Jul 7 1813
John HARRY & Co. have purchased the Tan Yard and Stock of Mr. A. CLAGETT. They will also give the highest price for hides and skins at the Yard, or at the store of George I. HARRY.
Michael FIRESTONE, near the subscriber's mill, has taken up a stray gelding. Christopher BURCKHARTT.
Tract of land for sale, 250 a., 8 miles of Winchester, Va. Thomas CAMPBELL, Hagers-town.
[Omitting Letters at P.O.]

63. Jul 14 1813
Purchaser at the sale of George MARSTELLER's property are informed that their notes will become due on 17th inst. James ADAMS.
Improved spinning wheel for sale at tavern of John SEITZ in Hagers-town.

64. Jul 21 1813
O. H. W. STULL, offers reward for negro slave who ran away from Salubria, near Hagers-town, who calls himself Bill GUY, raised by Benjamin HARRISON of West River where he has a mother.
Detrick BOYER, 5 miles from Liberty, offers reward for missing mare.
Persons are forewarned against carrying away sand from the sand bank near the new Paper Mill. George MILLER and Henry MILLER.
Columbia Inn - Christian FECHTIG has removed to the house lately possessed by Capt. George SHALL, Washington St, next door above Post Office.
Jacob BOSTATER, 3 miles from Hagers-town, has taken up a stray mare.
William H. BATES, Lieut., 38th Regt, U. S. Infantry, Hagers-town, offers reward for John CLARK, recruit, aged 43 yrs, 5 Frederick-town 11 inches, dark complexion, black hair, first joint of his little finger is off his left hand, by trade a shoemaker.
Gera SOUTH, Hagers-town, offers reward for missing cow.

65. Jul 28 1813
Died Thurs last, in this town, Mrs. Mary COOKES, widow of late Adam COOKES, formerly Inn-keeper of this place, in her 64th yr.
Married Tues 20th inst, by Rev SCHAEFFER, Martin RIDENOUR, to Mrs. Anna CLAPSATTLE, both of this co.
- On Sun evening last by Rev RAHAUSER, Stephen NORRIS, of Georgetown, to Miss Charlotte MADEIRA of this place.
Mrs. Anna WHITMORE, living near Daniel SCHNEBLY's, 5 miles from Hagers-town, has taken up a stray colt.
Journeyman weaver wanted - William M'ELROY, Shepherds-town, Va.

THE MARYLAND HERALD AND HAGERSTOWN WEEKLY ADVERTISER

66. Aug 4 1813
Sale of tract in Loudon co, on broad run, 2 1/2 miles above the bridge; enquire of John MATHIAS, Leesburg. Richard H. LOVE.
To sell two story sotne house and lot in Washington St, Hagers-town, opposite Mr. LEIGHT's Tavern, late property of John RAHP, decd, with blacksmith's shop. Elizabeth RAHP and Matthias SHAFFNER, exrs.
Sale by order of Orphan's Court, at late dwelling of Jacob YOUNG, decd, 2 miles from Hagers-town, personal estate of said decd. Jacob YOUNG, Jacob HERSHEY, admrs.
Merino sheep for sale - John JOHNSTON, at his farm 3 miles of Kershner's Fording on Conococheague.
Whereas my wife Susanna hath left my bed and board, without any just cause, this is to forewarn persons from harboring her or trusting her on my account. John COW.
Persons are cautioned against fowling or hunting, throwing down the fences, from going to any of the springs or orchards in the enclosures, without my leave, or trespassing in any manner upon the Big spring Farm, near Hagers-town. Daniel BRAGONIER.

67. Aug 11 1813
Barbara HACKMAN and Jacob LAMBERT exrs of Henry HACKMAN.
Robert DOUGLASS, Hagers-town, continues to carry on the weaving business, at his old stand nearly opposite the Lutheran Church.
Hugh M'CAULEY, living near Joseph SPRIGG's Mill, on Potomac river, has taken up a stray mare, certified by Isaac HAUSER, junr.
Two journeymen copper-smiths wanted. Tho. SHUMAN, Hagers-town.
Elie BEATTY, Hagers-town, offers reward for negro man, who calls himself John JOHNSTON, 45-50 yrs old, left handed.

68. Aug 18 1813
Peter SMITH continues to act as auctionier or vendue crier; apply to him at his dwelling, a few doors above Mr. KING's Blacksmith's shop, Franklin st.
Will be sold at the subscriber's res, 2 miles from Boonsborough, 2 miles from BOOTH's Mills, one negro girl, 14 yrs of age, cows, horses, furniture and other. Christopher FLORY.
Two story log house for sale in Potomack st, Hagers-town, now occupied by subscriber as a tavern; also horse and gig, milch cow, furniture. Henry SHANE.
James WILLIAMS to sell farm, 240 a., in Bullskin settlement, Jefferson and Frederick counties, Va.
Daniel M'COY, near Fleming's Ferry, offers reward for Chambers PAYTON, apprentice to the cooper trade.

69. Aug 25 1813
Married at Frederick-town Tues evening, 17th inst by Rev David F. SCHAEFFER, David BARR, of this place, to Miss Christiana MANTZ, dau of Francis MANTZ, merchant of Frederick-town, Md.
George KERSHNER, 4 miles from Hagers-town, 1 mile from Mr. OGLE's Tavern, at the Cross Roads, offers reward for missing colt.
Josiah PRICE, having frequently suffered by impudent persons fishing with lights, and being apprehensive of further injury, forewarns persons from fishing in any of the waters, particularly in that part of the Conoco-

THE MARYLAND HERALD AND HAGERSTOWN WEEKLY ADVERTISER

cheague included in his patents, that is from the fish dam next below the mouth of Daniel MILLER's lane to the state line.
Pay your taxes and fees. Henry SWEITZER, Sheriff & Collector, Washington Co.
Tho. B. CRAWFORD and John MATHEWS, Allegany co, admrs of William H. BURNS, late of Allegany Co.
John NEWSON,Junr, 1 1/2 miles from Hagers-town, has taken up stray sheep.
To be sold at the subscriber's res 2 miles from Jacob KERSHNER's tavern and 2 miles from John FIERY's Mill, 50 head of horned cattle, 70 sheep and other. Abraham DITTO.
Brigade Orders, 2d Brigade, 3d Division opf Md. Militia. 8th Regt, 10th Regt, 24th Regt, The American Blues and the Washington Hussars to parade. 8th Regt to parade at OGLE's Tavern, Cross Road, with arms and accoutrements - David SCHNEBLY, Lieut. Col.; 10th Regt to parade at Carey's Cross Roads - Daniel MALOTT, Lieut Col.; 24th Regt to parade in Potomac st, Hagerstown - John RAGAN, Junr., Lieut. Col.
Sale at late res of Henry STINE, decd, 5 miles from Hagers-town, at the Cross Roads leading to Mercersburg, furniture, horse, 3 milch cows, cart and other. Elizabeth STINE and William KREPS, admrs.

70. Sep 1 1813
Anthony B. MARTIN & Co. have commenced the Drug & Apothecary Business at the store formerly occupied by John WELLS, Jun., in Washington st.
600 working hands wanted by Charles M'KENNEY, contractor of the U.S.Turnpike Road above Cumberland. Call on Mr. CARRICO, Innkeeper, Cumberland.
One story brick house for sale adj the jail. Peter GLOSSBRENNER.
A camp meeting will be held by the people called Methodists, on land of John NEWSON, 1 1/2 miles from the Big-spring, between that and Potomac.
Sale in pursuance of the last will of Anthony BELL, of plantation 8 miles from Hagers-town and 4 miles from Waynesburg, adj the Rock Forge, the lands of Frederick BELL and others, 208 a. Andrew BELL, Jacob BELL, Conrod MENTZER, exrs.
Jacob KERSHNER will sell at the res of Philip KERSHNER, 3 miles from Hagerstown, personal estate of Philip Kershner, horses, cows, sheep and hogs, wagon, ploughs, harrows, farming utensils, furniture.
John GIBBONEY, junr, continues to carry on the fulling & dying business at John HERSHEY's Fulling Mill, 6 miles from Hagers-town, and 1/2 mile from Michael HOFFER's Mill.

71. Sep 8 1813
Married last evening by Rev SCHAEFFER, William MOFFITT, merchant, to Miss Elizabeth SHUMAN, dau of Thomas SHUMAN, of this town.
Died Fri morning last, at the house of William BRAZIER in this town, on his way from the state of Virginia to his family in Chambersburg.
- Samuel B. DAVIS in his 45th yr, leaving widow and 4 small children.
- On Sat last at his res near Williamsport, William BEATTY, aged 31 yrs.
Mr. CEZERON has opened a dancing school at Mr. PRICE's Tavern.
Hagers-town Races to be run. H. STRAUSE, S. PETTIT, L. PRICE, Managers.
Just received - flax linen, tow linen, twill'd bagging, twill'd bags, shoe thread. Alex. NEILL & Co.
The Hussars are ordered to parade completely equipped at Mr. OGLE's tavern. Tho. KENNEDY, Sec'ry.
Thos. QUANTRILL, Hatter, has taken up a stray cow.

THE MARYLAND HERALD AND HAGERSTOWN WEEKLY ADVERTISER

72. Sep 15 1813
Republican ticket for members of Assembly: John T. MASON, Frisby TILGHMAN, Martin KERSHNER and William GABBY.
Steuart GAITHER and Edward GAITHER admrs of Henry GAITHER.
Joseph HUGHES and Patrick BRIDLEY, Emittsburg, Frederick Co, have applied to the High Court of Chancery for redress of grievances, respecting a fraudulent sale made by John EVANS to them of a plantation on Fifteen Mile Creek, in Allegany co, Md.
Sale of dwelling house in Washington st, Hagers-town, next door to Rev Geo. BOWER, and now occupied by George SMITH, Grocer. Robert DOWNEY.
Two lots in Potomac st, Hagers-town for sale, whereon two story weather boarded house with a two story back building adj a large shop, 35 by 25 Frederick-town, 1 1/2 stories high, barn and stable, the lower part built with stone, stone spring house and smoke house, and a never failing pump of water at the door. John WEIS.
Assistant in a mill wanted. Peter ARTZ.
Flaxseed wanted at their store, in Hagers-town. KAUSLER & GRAFF.
Peter RENCH, 4 miles from Hagers-town, has taken up a stray mare.

73. Sep 22 1813
On Saturday last a detachment of 160 Regular Troops from Virginia arrived at this place, and on Sunday morning pursued their march for Niagara.
Steuart GAITHER offers reward for watch lost somewhere in Hagers-town.
Daniel SCHNEBLY candidate for sheriff.
James M'CLAIN, Jun'r gives notice that notes give at the sale of property of Jacob NISBETT, are due on 27th inst.
Sale of brick house on Potomac St, Hagers-town, opposite the Coach maker's shop of Peter HUMRICKHOUSE, sen., a few doors above SEITZ's Tavern. Peter HUMRICKHOUSE, junr.

74. Sep 29 1813
Mrs. GEISENDORF has just opened in Mr. JOHNSTON's Front Room, next door to this Printing Office, an assortment of dress bonnets and caps.
Edward GAITHER has taken up stray sheep at his farm.
Fleet SMITH, Leesburg, Loudon Co, Va, offers reward for man servant called Billy JACKSON, around 23 yrs old.
E. EASTON, on the premises, Pleasant Valley, offers for sale a house 5 miles below Sharpsburg, 1/2 mile below the Pleasant Valley Meeting house.
Robert GRIMES, Martinsburg, offers reward for horse which broke out of Joshua LINTON's yard in Hagers-town.

75. Oct 6 1813
3500 a. for sale in Loudon and Fairfax, Va. Edgar McCarty, Esq. will shew the lands. Enquire of John T. Mason, Esq., near Hagers-town regarding the titles. John W. BRONAUGH, George-town, District of Columbia.
Wishes to employ workmen to make 20,000 shingles. U. LAWRENCE.
John SCHNEBLY, Junr, offers reward for yellow dog.
Sale at house of Christian STEMPLE, Franklin st, Hagers-town, milch cow, shoats, furniture. Caspar KELLAR.
Big Springs Estate to be sold, 1260 a.- George Washington BALL, Fayette BALL, Charles Burges BALL, heirs and devisees of B. BALL, decd, Leesburg, Loudon co, Va.

THE MARYLAND HERALD AND HAGERSTOWN WEEKLY ADVERTISER

Sale at the late res of Henry HACKMAN, decd, near Abraham MEYER's Mill, and 1 mile from Major John BEARD's store, personal estate of decd. Barbara HACKMAN and Jacob LAMBERT, exrs.
Sale of lot in town of Mercersburg, whereon subscriber now lives, on which are erected two story brick house, large brewery, stable, smoke house and other out-houses. Isaac TAYLOR.
Peter KRICK, 2 miles from Hagers-town, 3/4 mile from John and George HARRY's mill, offers reward for stolen cows and heiffer.
[Letters at Post Office omitted]

76. Oct 13 1813
Died Thurs last, after a lingering illness, Mrs. Cassandra SCHNEBLY consort of Dr. Jacob SCHNEBLY of this town, in her 42d yr, leaving husband and 7 children. Her remains were interred in Episcopal burying ground.
Died Sat last near Williamsport, after a short illness, Mrs. Elizabeth BEATTY, widow of the late William BEATTY, and dau of Peter MILLER, formerly of this town.
Sale of second hand gig and harness at Mr. SAYLOR's Tavern, sign of the Indian Chief.
John SNYDER, 6 miles from Hagers-town, on the Hancock town road, has taken up a stray cow.
Sale of tract of 88 a. in Allegany co. John DEAKINS.

77. Oct 20 1813
Married Tues evening, 12th inst by Rev IRVING, Daniel SPRIGG, to Miss Elizabeth CHESLEY, dau of late Alexander CHESLEY, Esq., of George-town.
HEFLEICH & NEAD, continue to carry on the Grocery business at the old stand, next door to George I. HARRY's store.
John COSS, 1 1/2 miles of Williams-port, offers reward for negro man named JACK, 35-40 yrs of age.
Daniel SCHNEBLY will sell on the farm whereon he now lives, all the stock attached to the farm, farming utensils and grain.
Michael FIRESTONE, 6 1/2 miles from Hagers-town, and 1/4 mile from BAUGH-MAN's Tavern, near the road to Nicholson's Gap, has taken up a stray calf.
Peter and Matthias MILLER offer reward for horse which strayed from their mill near Williams-Port.

78. Oct 27 1813
Died yesterday morning in this town, after a short illness, Jonathan KRAMER, in his 23d yr.
Jacob KESSINGER candidate for sheriff.
Sale of two story log dwelling house in Franklin st, nearly opposite the jail. John FREANER, living on the premises.
Persons are forewarned against taking assignment on two bonds given to Joseph SPRINGER and David REISHER, exrs of Matthias SPRINGER, late of Washington co, decd, one which remains in the hands of Ann SPRINGER, widow of the decd. Benjamin EMMERT.
James KAY has opened a Select School in Franklin st.
Christian ARTZ, 3 miles from Hagers-town, has taken up a stray cow.

79. Nov 3 1813
Died in this town, Mon evening last in his 33rd yr, Dr. William DOWNEY.

THE MARYLAND HERALD AND HAGERSTOWN WEEKLY ADVERTISER

Warranted rifle powder. Daniel & George BOERSTLER, Funks-town.
Henry S. TURNER, to sell 347 a. on the Bull-skin stream, Jefferson Co, Va.
Sale of plantation on Conococheague, near the Union Mills, at the Broad
  ford, part of real estate of Jacob BARNETT, late of Washington co, decd.
  Jacob ZELLER, John SCHNEBLY, David SCHNEBLY, Walter BOYD, Nathan CROMWELL,
  Commissioners. Apply to Henry or Jacob BARNETT, who live near the land.
James ROBARDET to open a dancing school.
Dissolution of partnership of Peter ARTZ and George EMMERT. George Emmert
  to carry on business of Dry Goods and Groceries.
Distiller wanted - William B. WILLIAMS, near Williams-Port.
WILLIS and FRANKENBERY, boot and shoe makers, have commenced business in
  Potomack st, Williams-Port, below the Church, and nearly opposite Mr.
  KREPS Hatter's shop.
Alexander MONTGOMERY, tailor & woollen draper, has opened a shop in town of
  Sharpsburg, next door to Mr. MILLER's store, near the public square.
Dissolution of partnership of George STONEBREAKER and Michael STONEBREAKER,
  Funks-town. M. Stonebreaker will carry on business where he has received
  assortment of seasonable goods and hardware and groceries.
Tract of land for sale, 230 a., 1 1/2 miles from Williamport, on which is
  erected a merchant and saw mill, formerly known by SWINGLEY's mill,
  distillery lately erected, 4 dwelling houses, barn and out-houses. Peter
  MILLER and Matthias MILLER, on the premises.

80. Nov 10 1813
Married Thurs evening last, by Rev SCHAEFFER, William M'CARDELL, to Miss
  Margaret POWLAS, both of this town.
Sale of 600 a. of land in Washington co, adj Ringgold's Manor, to be shewn
  by Jacob SPEILMAN, living on the premises. Elie BEATTY.
Sale by virtue of the last will of Owen ROBEY, tract of 180 a., 5 miles from
  Williams-port. William ROBEY, exr.
George BOWER, Hagers-town, to sell brick house in which he res, directly
  opposite Mr. LAWRENCE's.
The mill adj Hagers-town, late the property of Daniel STULL, decd, for rent.
  Elie BEATTY.
Asa ROBINETT and Jeremiah ROBINETT, offer reward for horse which strayed
  from plantation of Jeremiah CHENEY, 6 miles from Hagers-town.
John & Geo. HARRY, Hagers-town, offer reward for negro boy named GEORGE,
  19-20 yrs old, purchased of Daniel HUYETT, who bought him of Wm. SIMKINS.

81. Nov 17 1813
Dissolution of partnership of Henry KEALHOFER and John KEALHOFER,
  Hagers-town. H. Kealhofer to carry on the saddle and harness making
  business. John Kealhofer has opened a saddler shop opposite the German
  Printing Office.
An overseer is wanted to manage the Poor-house of Washington co. John
  SLEIGH, Tho. GRIEVES, Wm. KREPS, Trustees.
John O. KING & Co. carry on the wagon making business at the shop of Jacob
  KING.
Henry SWEITZER, Sheriff of Washington co, has committed as a runaway a negro
  man who calls himself WILLIAM and says he belongs to Samuel WILSON of
  Berkeley co, Va. He is 16-18 yrs old, 5 ft 10-11 inches.

THE MARYLAND HERALD AND HAGERSTOWN WEEKLY ADVERTISER

Susanna GORDON and Robert DOWNEY, admrs of Dr. William DOWNEY, to sell at late dwelling of decd, nearly opposite Mr. PRICE's Tavern, the personal estate of decd.
Journeyman cooper wanted at John CUSHWA's mill, 2 miles from John T. MASON's. Jacob TROXELL.
George FRENCH will sell at the res of Thomas FRENCH, decd, adj Boonsborough, horses, hogs, cattle, sheep, farming utensils, &c. Apply to Leonard HURDLE, Boonsborough.
Bolting cloths at his store by the Market house in Shepherds-town, Va. James S. LANE.
Robert HAYDON, living on the plantation of Jacob SEGUR, 1 mile from Hughes's Furnace, has taken up a stray cow.
Chancery sale of real estate of Jacob ROOT, decd, 240 a. on Beaver Creek. George C. SMOOT, Trustee.
Saddle lost on second day of the Hagers-town Races - Edward BOND, 5 miles from Hagers-town.

82. Nov 24 1813
David BOUDON, Painter, from Geneva Switzerland, has opened a subscription for teaching drawing, painting flowers, landscapes, &c.
Ezra SLIFER, Boonsborough to sell tract adj Boonsborough, 109 a.
Sale of dwelling house of late Col. George WOLTZ, decd, next door to Mr. COOK's tavern in Hagers-town.
Peter SEIBERT, living on Beaver Creek, 6 miles from Hagers-town, has taken up some stray sheep.
Sale of plantation, 145 a., 2 miles from Peter MIDDLEKAUFF's mill, on Little Conococheague, adj lands of John NEWSON and others. John BRYAN on the premises will shew the land, or James AMOS near Wiliams-Port. Apply to Daniel HUGHES, Jun'r, Hagers-town
Persons who purchased property at my sale are informed that their notes will become due on 9 Dec. Leonard SHAFER.

83. Dec 1 1813
Married Thurs evening last by Rev SCHAEFFER, David SHAUMAN, of this co, to Miss Frances SHEETS, of this town.
- On same evening by same, William HARRY, son of David HARRY, to Miss Mary WOLFARTH, all of this town.
Died Fri evening 19th ult at his res in Washington co, about 9 miles from Hagers-town, Henry FIERY, aged about 48 yrs.
Persons who purchased property at the sale of personal estate of William ROUCH, are informed that their notes will become due on 4th inst. Philip ROUCH, John JONES, exrs.
Henry GERLACH, near OGLE's Tavern, Cross roads, has taken up a stray cow.
Cave Tavern for sale, with 12 a. Wm. ALLINDER, on the premises.

84. Dec 8 1813
Married Sun evening last by Rev SCHAEFFER, John MILLER, to Miss Catharine POWLAS, all of this town.
Sale at the late dwelling of Eve RIDENOUR, decd, in Funkstown, personal property of decd, beds, bedding, bedsteads, tables, chairs, stove and pipe and other. Gerard STONEBREAKER, exr.

THE MARYLAND HERALD AND HAGERSTOWN WEEKLY ADVERTISER

Tavern for sale on corner of the public square in Hagers-town, opposite John & Hugh KENNEDY's store. Also lot in Antietam st, adj property of Major O. H. WILLIAMS. Terms will be made known by Henry STRAUSE.
House for sale now occupied by William T. T. MASON, Esq., a few door of the Court-house square.
1300 a. of land for sale in Anne Arundel co. Nicholas MERIWEATHER, who lives on the farm.
Sale of his farm near Christian LANTZ's mill. John KELLER who lives on the premises will shew the place. Also the brick tavern now occupied by Levi PRICE and formerly kept by John RAGAN, one of the oldest tavern establishments in Hagers-town. Henry LEWIS.

85. Dec 15 1813
House and lot for sale on main st, Williams-Port. This property has been occupied as a tavern for 8-10 yrs. John KISSINGER.
H. DILLMAN is authorized to collect the subscriptions to the Hagers-town Academy.
Sale of brick house now occupied by the subscriber in Potomac st, Hagers-town, a few doors above Alexander NEILL's store. John WEITZEL.

86. Dec 22 1813
Married yesterday by Rev RAHAUSER, Jacob KNODE, to Miss Mary BENCE, dau of Henry BENCE, of this co.
Amos YATES, near Hancock-town, Md, has taken up stray cattle.
A ball will be held at PRICE's Tavern, Hagers-town.
J. STEPHENSON will sell the Stone House Tavern, on Mill creek, Berkeley co, Va, at present occupied by Francis SILVER, 200 a., two distilleries, one in complete operation upon the steam principle. The water is raised in the still house by a hydron.
Coverlet, Carpet and Table Linen Weaving and Blue Dying - Jacob MILLER, has removed his shop to Sharpsburg.
Paul HOYE to sell farm where he resides, near Williamsport, 204 1/2 a.
Tract of land for sale, 100 a., on Potomac river, 4 miles above Williams-Port, 1 mile from Peter MIDDLEKAUFF's mill. John NEWSON, Sen'r., living within 1 mile of the premises.
James STEVENSON will sell the farm on which he now lives, 27 3/4 a., 1/2 mile from Cave Tavern.
John SHAUMAN, 4 miles from Williams-Port, 2 miles from Foreman's Ferry, offers reward for missing hogs.

87. Jan 5 1814
Died Fri morning last, after a short illness, Frederick ALTER, overseer of the Alms and Work-house in Washington co, in his 73d yr.
- On same day, Mrs. Catharine DIEHL, wife of Henry DIEHL, of this town, in her 27th yr.
Married Thurs last by Rev RAHAUSER, John RENCH to Miss Catharine SHAFER, dau of John SHAFER, all of this co.
- Yesterday by Rev RAHAUSER, Daniel SCHNEBLY son of John SCHNEBLY, to Miss Ann Maria RENCH, dau of Daniel RENCH, all of this co.
Jacob YOUNG and Jacob HERSHEY, admrs of Jacob YOUNG.
Jacob POWLAS, Hagers-town, offers reward for apprentice boy to the house joiner's business, named William HALBERT, 18-19 yrs old, 5 ft 5 inches.

THE MARYLAND HERALD AND HAGERSTOWN WEEKLY ADVERTISER

Letters remaining at Post Officer [omitted here]
Chancery sale of farm called Nelson's Folly, property of George SCOTT and
  Robert T. CARY's heirs, adj town of Boonsborough, 580 a. Apply to Leonard
  HURDLE on the premises. George FRENCH and Michael HAUSER, Trustees.
Tan Yard for sale containing 21 vats, in Greensborough, Greene co, Pa, adj
  the new Geneva Glass Works. John EBERT, Frederick-town.
David HARRY, Jun'r has commenced the wagon making business in Salisbury st,
  Williamsport, opposite the dwelling of Jacob BYERS.
Stamped paper for sale. William KREPS at the Post Office.

88. Jan 26 1814
Two story stone house in Potomac st for rent, a few doors above the dwelling
  of Col. A. OTT, occupied by John SEITZ as a Tavern. Thomas SHUMAN.
Lost between Strauss's Tavern and Conrad OSTER's farm, 2 1/2 miles from
  Hagers-town, a double skirted man's saddle, with common stirrup irons.
  Samuel OSTER
Merchant mill and saw mill for sale in Berkeley co, Va, on Opeckon creek.
  James FORMAN, living on the premises.Samuel BUTLER to sell farm on which
  he now lived, formerly owned by Samuel DEHART in Rockingham co, Va, 180 a.
Appointments for Washington Co - Justices of the Levy Court: William
  FITZHUGH, John HARRY, Lancelot JACQUES, John WAGONER, John HERSHEY, George
  SMITH and William VAN LEAR. Justices of the Peace: Adam OTT, William
  YATES, James M'CLAIN, George SMITH, Jacob SCHNEBLY, John BOWLES, James
  PRATHER, Robert HUGHES, John BLACKFORD, Edward BOTELER, George NICHOLS,
  James D. MOORE, John WITMER, John BARR, Christopher BURCKHART, John
  HERSHEY, William VAN LEAR, William FITZHUGH, jun., Isaac HAUSER, jun.,
  Alexander GRIMM, Edmund H. TURNER, Jonas HOGMIRE, Joseph INGRAM, Matthew
  VAN LEAR, Frederick GROSH, David NEWCOMER, Lancelot JACQUES, Cornelius
  FERREE, Jeremiah MASON, Ephraim DAVIS and John ADAMS.
John MARTINEY, wheel-wright & chair maker, has commenced business in
  Franklin st.
Daniel SCHNEBLY, admr of Christian WITMER, to sell at late res of decd, 1/2
  mile of Mrs. STINE's Tavern, personal estate of decd.
Farm for sale in Jefferson Co, Va, 480 a.; apply to Isaac SWEARINGEN, living
  at Gen. RINGGOLD's near Hagers-town. Wm. P. FLOOD, Jefferson co, Va.
Farm and mills for sale, Shenandoah co, Va, 1109 a. Apply to James ROACH
  near Hillsborough, Loudon co, Va, or Mahlon ROACH, living on the premises.
William BODENHAMER, Balt Co, offers reward for person who circulated a false
  report about him.
Jacob KESSINGER and Daniel SCHNEBLY candidtes for sheriff.
George MILLER seeks apprentices to the fulling and dying business at his
  factory near Hagers-town.
Martha K. ALLEN and Elisha EASTON admr of James ALLEN.

89. Feb 2 1814
On Thurs night a barn of Henry LEWIS, 2 1/2 miles from Hagers-town, was
  consumed by fire.
Sale at subscriber's res, 1 1/2 mile from BURCKHART's mill, horses, cows,
  cattle, furniture, &c. Benjamin WINTER.
George EMMERT has received supply of books of all kinds.
Stone house for rent now occupied by Dr. A. HANENKAMPF and room adj occupied
  by William ARMOR as a taylor's shop. John HARRY.

THE MARYLAND HERALD AND HAGERSTOWN WEEKLY ADVERTISER

Jacob YAKLE, Hagers-town, offers reward for apprentice to the tinner's business named Lawrence HOWARD, about 19 yrs old, 5 ft 8-9 inches, light hair, fair complexion.

90. Feb 9 1814
Married in Balt on Mon evening 31st ult by Most Rev Archbishop CARROLL, David WILLIAMSON, jun. to Miss M. A. TIERNAN, dau of Luke TIERNAN, all of that city.
On Mon last a fire broke out in the house of George BEIGHLER, of this town, but was extinguished without doing any material injury.
Elizabeth WELLS, 2 miles from Williams-Port, has taken up a stray bull.

91. Feb 16 1814
Chancery sale of farm of Samuel BOWLES, decd, 124 a., 12 miles from Hagerstown, adj lands of J. T. MASON, John CUSHWA and Henry SEIBERT. U. LAWRENCE, Trustee.
John HENNEBERGER, Hagers-town, offers reward for apprentice to cabinet making business named Samuel M'CULLOCH, about 20 yrs of age, 5 ft 8-9 inches, fair hair & grey eyes.
Christian STOVER and Chrisitan ROWLAND admrs of Christian ROWLAND, to sell at late dwelling of decd, 1 mile from Fountain Rock, 4 miles from Hagerstown, personal estate of decd.
Christian MILLER, Sunbury, Northumberland co, Pa, gives notice that his wife, Elizabeth MILLER, formerly Elizabeth FUNK, left him some yrs past, and in the latter end of August last, went from Lancaster, far advanced in pregnancy, for the neighbourhood of Hagers-town, to lay in with some of her friends. She is a likely, middle sized woman, has a wart on one of her cheeks, and seems virtuous in hearing her talk. As said Elizabeth has again returned to the neighbourhood of Lancaster without having a child with her, the subscriber offers reward to peron who will give him information where, and with whom said Elizabeth was brought to bed.
L. PRICE, about to remove from this co, requests payment of debts.
John SCHLEIGH has obtained licence as an auctionier or vendue crier.
Edward O. WILLIAMS, near Martinsburgh, Berkeley co, Va, offers reward for negro man named JAMES, about 40 yrs of age.
Peter SMITH, Hagers-town, offers his services as auctionier of vendue crier.
For rent - dwelling house, blacksmith shop, stable and garden. Daniel REICHARD.
William WILLIS having declined business, has transferred his book accounts unto KAUSLER and GROFF.
Negroes for sale at STRAUSE's tavern. Richard DAVIS.
Persons indebted to late firm of Henry & John KEALHOVER are requested to settle their accounts.
Sale at subscribers mill on Conococheague creek, 1 1/2 miles of Williamsport, wagon, 4-5 horses with gears, plantation wagon, carts, cows, &c, 230 a. with merchant mill, saw mill, new distillery. Peter & Matthias MILLER.
Farm worker wanted. O. H. W. STULL, Salubria.
Eve BINKLEY and Wm. KREPS, admrs of George Binkley, to sell at late dwelling of decd, Hagers-town, nearly opposite the Post Office, stock of dry goods and groceries, furniture.
Ludwick YOUNG, 2 miles from Hagers-town, has taken up 2 stray cows.

THE MARYLAND HERALD AND HAGERSTOWN WEEKLY ADVERTISER

92. Feb 23 1814
Married Sun evening 13th inst, at the Seminary near Emittsburg, by Rev DUHAMEL, Philip MILTON, to Mrs. Frances MONAHAN, both of Wash co.
- On same evening by same, Otho ADAMS, son of John ADAMS, to Miss Mary CHARLTON, both of Wash co.
- In Chambersburg on Tues 14th inst by Rev MOELLER, Matthias NEAD, to Miss Catharine DECKERT, dau of Mr. DECKART, member of the Legislature of Pa.
Died yesterday morning, at Hagers-town Academy, after a lingering illness, Mrs. Patsey IRVING, consort of Rev IRVING, in her 43d yr.
Chancery sale of property of Jacob ROUCH, decd, 168 a., adj lands of late Col. James WALLING, 1 mile from Henry NEWCOMER's mill.
Sale at subscriber's res, 3 miles from Hagers-town, on road to Broad fording, of 10 1/2 a. with stone dwelling house, 2 stories high, blacksmith shop, stable; also furniture. Gustavus BRUA.
House for rent in Antietam st, Hagers-town, lately occupied by John CRISSINGER, a few doors above Col. John RAGAN's. John STALLSMITH.
Arthur JOHNSTON, clock & watch maker, silver smith and jeweler, has removed his shop a few doors from public square, 2 doors from Printing Office.
Tavern for rent in Potomac st, below the Lutheran Church now occupied by the subscriber; also dwelling house in front, now occupied by Wm. BRENDEL (room painter). Henry SHANE.
Negro man committed to gaol as runaway, who calls himself LONDON, 23-24 yrs old, light complexion; says he lately belonged to R. M'GINNIS of Montgomery co, Md, who sold him to Joseph SMITH of Frederick co, Md, and subject to spasms, a dispute took place about him, in consequence of which he was turned at large.
Walter B. SELBY, Shepherds-town, Va, offers reward for negro man named BILL.
Sale or rent - farm, 190 a., 3 miles from Hagers-town, on road to Greencastle, property of late Nicholas SMITH. George KELLAR, Senr., living adj the premises.
John DEITZ, Hagers-town, seeks boy as apprentice to book-binding business, who can read and write.
Jacob KESSINGER admr of Nicholas BEARD, requests claims against decd.
Wagon making - David HARRY who has continued this business these 40 yrs past, has taken his won William into partnership.

93. Mar 2 1814
Died at her res 5 miles from Hagers-town, Tues 15th ult, Mrs. Mary WOLGAMOT, in her 75th yr.
Sale of 526 a., of James CHESTON, now under rent to Wm. STARLING, part of Ringgold's Manor, adj Judge BUCHANAN's Farm, 1 mile from the Potomac and 3 miles from Williams-Port. Elie BEATTY, Hagers-town.
New store - Christian LANTZ & Co., now opening next door to Jacob SAYLOR's.
Farm for sale, 180 a., Berkeley co, Va. Samuel VAL, near Richardson's ferry, 15 miles above Williamsport, on the Potomac river.
Isabella OTTO and Matthias OTTO, exrs of Henry OTTO, to sell at late res of decd, 2 miles from Green-Spring Furnace, personal estate, negro woman and her 6 children, eldest of whom is 14 yrs old, horses, cows, furniture &c.
Dissolution of partnership of firm of Keene, Kaighn & co. Thomas KEENE, Wm. KAIGHN, John RAGAN, Senr.
Ludwick YOUNG to sell at his res, 2 miles from Hagers-town, horses, cows, hogs, &c.

THE MARYLAND HERALD AND HAGERSTOWN WEEKLY ADVERTISER

94. Mar 9 1814
Died at Georgetown, Sat last, after a lingering illness, Mrs. Anne Barbara
   WILLIAMS, consort of Elie WILLIAMS, Esq., formerly of this co.
- Yesterday after a short illness, in the bloom of life, Miss Sally
   SCHNEBLY, dau of Dr. Jacob SCHNEBLY of this town.
Joseph FIREY and Jacob FIREY, exrs of Henry FIREY, to sell at late dwelling
   of decd, 3 miles from Jacob KERSHNER's tavern, on Conococheague, personal
   estate of decd.
Sale of 7 bales of New Orleans cotton at Mr. LEWIS's store house. Jacob
   HAWKEN.
Sale at subscriber's res on farm where Wm. S. COMPTON, Esq. formerly lived,
   2 1/2 miles from Williams-Port, on road to Sharpsburg, horses, cows, wind-
   mill, furniture, &c. Emanuel NEWCOMER.
George EMMERT has removed to store room lately occupied by Messrs. Ale'r
   NEILL & Co. where he has fresh supply of books.
George BEAN at his res on farm where Major CARROLL formerly lived, 2 miles
   from Hagers-town, to sell negroes, horses, wagons, &c.
John BROWN, at Ringgold's mill, offers reward for missing mare.
Lucinda BOWER, Elie BEATTY, Alexander NEILL, exrs of Rev George BOWER.
Leonard KUHN exr of Frederick ALTER, to sell personal estate of decd: 8-day
   clock, chest of drawers, beds and bedsteads, tables, chairs, one ten-plate
   and one six-plate stove, milch cow and other.
Anthony SNYDER has taken up a stray calf.
John WORLEY, sickle maker, has on hand at his shop near Green-Castle sickles
   of the best quality, which can be purchased at Alexander NEILL and Co's
   Store, Hagers-town.
Apprentices wanted to the fulling & dying business at John HERSHEY's cloth
   factory, 7 miles from Hagers-town, 1/2 mile from Michael HOFFER's mill.
John DOWNIN, Jun'r, now at Funks-town Factory.
Negroes for sale - Enos SCHELL.
To be sold at subscriber's dwelling near Presby Church, a few doors above
   Mr. SEITZ's Tavern, family negroes (seven in number, being the undivided
   part belonging to Peter HUMRICKHOUSE and Son), cow, furniture. Peter
   HUMRICKHOUSE, Jun. Partnership of Peter Humrickhouse & Son is dissolved.

95. Mar 16 1814
Married last evening by Rev SCHAEFFER, George SHANE, to Miss Catharine ADAM,
   all of this town.
Agreeable to last will of Philip GROUND, decd, the subscriber (atty in fact
   for George GROUND, surviving exr of said decd) will sell plantation, on
   the Potomac river, 2 miles of Sharpsburg, 230 a., 2 dwelling houses, 2
   barns and other out houses. George SMITH
Jacob BAECHTEL, 8 mils from Hagers-town, 1 mile of Cave Tavern, offers
   reward for indented mulatto boy named Dick SHORTER, 14-15 yrs old, very
   small for his age.
Samuel LYNCH, 2 miles from Galloway's mill, has taken up 3 stray hogs.
Leonard SHAFER will attend at James MUIR's tavern in Williams-Port 2 Apr
   next; persons indebted to him are requested to make payment at that time.
The horse Boston will stand at the farm occupied by the sucscriber, 3 miles
   from Hagers-town. O. H. W. STULL
Two story brick house for rent, near the square, now occupied by John
   HERSHEY, Esq. Apply to Matthias SHAFFNER or Henry LEWIS.

38

THE MARYLAND HERALD AND HAGERSTOWN WEEKLY ADVERTISER

Thomas JONES, Senr. will sell small home on which he now lives at the head of Pleasant Valley, near Casper SNAVELY's mill and Mr. SNYDER's mill. Sale of 1200 a. 6 miles from Hancock Richard G. BELT, on the premises.
A piece of woollen cloth was left at the subscriber's tavern during the Hagers-town Races in Oct last. Christian FECHTIG

96. Mar 23 1814
Married last evening by Rev IRVING, Dr. William HAMMOND, to Miss Mary TILGHMAN, dau of Dr. Frisby TILGHMAN of this co.
Died Tues 15th inst, Mrs. Esther WILLIAMS, widow of Richard WILLIAMS, late of this co.
Sale of 1070 a. on Shenandoah River, half way between BERRY's and SNICKER's ferry, with merchant mill. John HOLKER, res on said plantation.
Perry WAYMAN, saddler & harness maker, has removed to shop lately occupied by Nathaniel POSEY, hatter, next door to Mr. M'PHERRIN's Printing Office, Potomac st. Mrs. Wayman has on hand at the house adj the shop an assortment of straw and silk bonnets.
Plantation of 200 a. for sale, 1 mile from Big Spring. Jacob P. KERSHNER, on the premises.
Chancery sale of real estate of Christian ROHRER, decd, who in his will bequeathed to his wife Frances all his real and personal estate, during her life and after her death the real estate to be sold and money divided amongst his seven children. His wife hath died. Said Christian Rohrer left the following heirs: Daniel ROHRER, and Barbara wife of Daniel BRAGONIER, the petitioners, and Christian ROHRER, Samuel ROHRER, Jacob ROHRER, Maria (married to Abraham TROSEL) and Ann MILLER. Christian, Samuel and Maria reside out of the state of Md.
Abraham BAKER, 2 miles from Burckhartt's mill, has taken up a stray mare. Certified by Christopher BURCKHARTT.
Subscription book of the Hagers-town and Westminster Turnpike co. will be opened at Price's tavern. John SCOTT, Treasurer.
The firm of YOUNG & VAN LEAR dissolved. Dr. VAN LEAR has removed his medicines to his lodging rooms in the house of George BENDER, Wheel-wright, next door to the German Printing Office.
John FREANER, Hagers-town, requests persons indebted to him to make payment.
The horse, Jolly Farmer, to stand at John STOVER's Tavern, and Christian MILLER's stable, on place formerly owned by Dr. Wm. DOWNEY. Elijah LEASURE.
The horse, Young Pilgrim, owned by James M. STERRIT, to stand at stable of John ADAMS, Inn-keeper and stable of Gideon H. IRWIN, Inn-keeper.

97. Mar 30 1814
Died Sat morning last, after a short illness, John NEWSON, jun. of this co, leaving widow and 8 children. His remains were interred in the Meth burying ground in this town. Discourse delivered by Rev Louis FECHTIG.
White Swan Inn, Hagers-town. G. H. IRWIN, successor to Samuel PETTIT, has opened well known and long established Tavern.
J. STALLSMITH, boot & shoe-maker, has removed to house of the late Capt. George BINKLEY, opposite the Post Office.
Sale of tract near Charlestown, Jefferson co, Va, 390 a. Samuel SWAYNE, Winchester, Va.
Fresh hops - Jno. & Jos. M'ILHENNY.

THE MARYLAND HERALD AND HAGERSTOWN WEEKLY ADVERTISER

Subscribers have commenced running a line of mail stages from Chambersburg, via Green-Castle, Hagers-town, Boonsborough, Middle-town, Frederick-town and from Frederick-town to Balt and Georgetown in one day. Michael KAPP, Joseph BOYD, Joshua HALLER, William LAUMAN, William CRAWFORD, John WINEMILLER.
Election of five commissioners to regulate the police of Hagers-town. Adam OTT, John HERSHEY.
Daniel WELTY and David WESTENBERGER, exrs of Peter SNIDER, to sell at late res of decd, 1 mile of Samuel FUNK's Mill, personal estate of decd.
John COOK, Inn-keeper, Hagers-town, requests payment of debts.
Isabella OTTO, to sell tract, 150 a. on Potomac river, 2 1/2 miles from Big Spring.
The horse, Independence, to stand at Henry STRAUSE's stable. Caleb HARLAN.

98. Apr 13 1814
Letters remaining at Post Office [Omitted here]
Daniel MALOTT admr of Peter MALOTT, to sell at late res of decd, adj Ringgold's Manor, personal estate of decd.
Jane NEWSON and Joseph P. NEWSON admr of John NEWSON.
Elected commissioners for Hagers-town: Henry LEWIS, Richard RAGAN, George BRUMBAUGH, Charles SHAFFNER, John M'ILHENNY.
John SEITZ, cooper, has removed his shop to house in whch Mr. M'CLEERY formerly kept school, in Franklin st.
FRANKINBURY & ROSS have commenced boot & shoe making business next door to Messrs. TURNER and HESLETINE, opposite Muir's Tavern, Williams-Port.
Dr. HAMMOND has opened a shop of medicine 2 doors east of the shop formerly occupied by the late firm of DORSEY, NANENKAMPF and HAMMOND.
For sale - House of Entertainment, sign of Columbus. Christian FECHTIG.
George SHANK, Jun., has commenced the saddler & harness making business in Funks-town, at the house of Jacob BRUNNER, directly opposite the dwelling of Jacob KNODE and 2 doors from Mr. STONEBREAKER's store.
The subscriber having given 2 notes to Lawson LUCKETT of Md, forewarns persons from taking assignment. William ABERNATHY, Berkeley co, Va.
Hat Manufactory - Nathaniel POSEY has removed to the house lately occupied by Messrs. P. ARTZ & EMMERT as a store.
John WINTER, near the Cave Tavern, on the Charlton's Gap Road, has taken up a stray mare. Certified by Robert HUGHES.
Adam GLOSSBRINNER, house joiner & cabinet maker, has removed to shop in which Mr. KAY lately kept school in Franklin st, near the Public Spring.
Commissioners of the Tax for this co have adjourned. Jacob MYERS, Clk.
Sale of house in William-Port formerly the property of James GREGORY, decd. William GREGORY, admr.
Sale of farm in Montgomery co, on 672 1/2 a., will be shewn by Mr. WADE, the tenant. Daniel SCHNEBLY, Hagers-town.
Jacob KESSINGER, admr of Henry COOK, to sell at late dwelling of decd, 1 1/2 mile from Cave Tavern, personal estate of decd.

99. May 18 1814
Wm. W. BAXTER has taken up a stray mare. Certified by William YATES, J.P.
2d Battalion, 24th Regt, ordered to meet for exercise, at the Courthouse Square in Hagers-town, provided with 6 rounds of blunt cartridges and arms and accoutrements in complete order. John REYNOLDS, Major.

THE MARYLAND HERALD AND HAGERSTOWN WEEKLY ADVERTISER

Job HUNT has commenced the coppersmith business in Potomac st, at the house lately occupied by Mr. WEITZEL, hatter.

George KERSHNER, 1 mile from Mr. Ogle's tavern, at the Cross roads, offers reward for missing colt.

Whereas my wife Catharine has left my bed and board without any just cause or provocation, I forewarn persons from crediting her on my account. John WOMELDORFF.

The Troop of American Blues are to meet at Mr. Strause's Tavern in full uniform, to elect the Captain. Jacob BARR, 1st Lieut.

Sale of house and lot whereon he lives in Washington st, Hagers-town, next door to Post Office. On the premises there is a Brewery in complete order, with two malt kilns, calculated to dry 60 bushels of malt per week; also 2 a. adj lands of Peter HUMRICKHOUSE, 1 mile from town. Henry CAKE.

Catharine GIERHART and William SIMKINS, admrs of Christian GIERHART, to sell at res of decd, 1/2 mile of Hughes's Furnace, personal estate of decd: negro woman and her 4 children, horses, gig, farming utensils, &c.

Died Fri last, after a lingering illness, Mrs. Barbara TUTWILLER, wife of Jonathan TUTWILLER, of this town, in her 58th yr.

Christopher SCHIOLER, painter & glazier, has lately removed from Balt to Hagers-town and has commenced business in the stone house formerly occupied by Christian LANGENECKER, Franklin st.

Will be sold at the late dwelling of John CONRAD, decd, Hagers-town, personal estate of decd, consisting of complete set of house carpenter's tools, cow, beds and bedsteads, furniture, copper kettle and other. Joseph GRAFF, admr.

J. SCHNEBLY, offers reward for negro SAM who absconded from his farm near Rench's mill. He is about 30 yrs old and fond of liquor.

Catharine MILLER exr of Robert MILLER, to sell at late res of decd, 1/2 mil from John WOLFERSBERGER, personal estate of decd.

Instalments are due on shares of stock in Conococheague Bank. Samuel A. CHEW, Cash'r.

Petry's Rifle and rock powder - Philip PETRY & Co. have completed their powder mill, 2 miles below Funks-town.

Tract for sale, 338 7/8 a. for sale, 3 miles from Big Spring; enquire of George HEBB, Esq., Cumberland. Aquilla JOHNS.

George SHRYOCK, pump maker, continues business above the Hagers-town Bank, Washington st.

John DOWNIN, Jun. and Henry CAKE have erected a carding machine at John HERSHEY's fulling mill, 1/2 mile from Michael HOFFER's mill.

Susanna GORDON and Robert DOWNEY, admrs of Dr. William DOWNEY.

Edward GAITHER to sell 50 a. of land 4 miles from Hagers-town, adj lands of Henry RINEHART, late of Daniel SPEECE.

Persons are forewarned from hauling away clay or trespassing in any manner on lot no. 188, lately purchased by me of the heirs of George LOTTEBERGER, in the hollow where the Gallows formerly stood, in Hager's Addition to Hagers-town. James DICKSON

Dr. A. HANNENKAMPF has removed his medicines to shop formerly occupied by Dr. WOLTZ, near the Stone Church.

Rope Factory - Jacob SHULL & BUTLER have entered into partnership at Jacob Shull's former stand, opposite the dwelling of Gottleib ZIMMERMAN, pump-maker, near the Lutheran Church.

THE MARYLAND HERALD AND HAGERSTOWN WEEKLY ADVERTISER

100. May 25 1814
Died Tues morning, 17th inst, after a tedious illness, Mrs. Barbara M'CLAIN, consort of James M'CLAIN, Esq., of this co, age about 66 yrs.
Married at Martinsburg, Sun evening last, by Rev REVENACHT, George HAGER of this place to Miss Eleanor WAUGH, of Berkeley co, Va.
- Last evening by Rev RAHAUSER, George FRENCH of George-Town, to Miss Maria BOOTH, dau of John BOOTH, Esq. of this co.
No persons will be permitted to fish within the premises of the subscribers: Henry MILLER, Moses M'NAMEE, Andrew SHANAFELD, Henry FUNK, John ROHRER, John FUNK, Abraham SNYDER, Christian NEWCOMER, Jacob ROHRER.
Jacob SCHNEBLY, admr, to sell at the house of John MILLER, late of Hagers-town, decd, personal estate of decd.
Partnership under firm of ROHRER & BARR is dissolved. - Frederick ROHRER and David BARR. David Barr continues the Tanning business at the old stand.
John LONG and Daniel BRUMBAUGH admr of John LONG, to sell at the late res of decd, 4 miles from Hagers-town, personal estate of decd.
James EARECKSON, Junr., offers reward for negro men, BEN, about 6 ft and 24 yrs old, and CHARLES, about 5 ft, who ran away on the road from Frederick-town to Pittsburg.
John BUMBERGER, living on Little Beaver Creek, 1/2 mile from Peter NEWCOMER's Mill, 3 miles from Boonsborough, has taken up a stray colt.

101. Jun 1 1814
Gerrard RICKETTS, Williams-Port, has taken up a stray mare.
Jacob KESSINGER admr of Nicholas P. BEARD, to sell at res of Andrew BEARD, near the dwelling of Major John BEARD, personal property of Nicholas P. Beard, decd, riding mare, cow, furniture.
Benjamin WINTER, Frederick-town, offers reward for negro man named NACE, 5 ft 7-8 inches, raised in st. Mary's co.
Citizens of Hagers-town are prohibited from taking water from my Spring after 9 o'clock at night. Nathaniel Posey.
John GEORGE, 2 miles from Col. Hughes's Forge, has taken up a stray bull.
George MILLER has commenced carding at the mill of Major Martin Kershner.
Locust posts for sale - George Coliflower, Jun'r, living at the Cave Tavern.
Pine plank for sale. John P. Herr.

102. Jun 8 1814
Died Thurs 19th ult, at his res in Shenandoah co, Va, after an illness of about 3 weeks, Col. Henry SHRYOCK, late of Hagers-town, aged 78 yrs.

103. Jun 15 1814
Died Mon last, at his res about 6 miles from Hagers-town, William ADAMS, aged 87 yrs.
- Same day in this town, Samuel WOLTZ, aged 32 yrs, leaving a wife and 2 small children.
- yesterday in this town, after a short illness, Michael F. MAYER, in his 29th yr.
Books for subscriptions of stock in Farmers' and Mechanics' Bank in Green-Castle, will be opened at the house of John BESHORE, Waynesburg; house of Michael COSKERY, Hagers-town; house of Henry STRAUSE and David HAMMOND's tavern on road from Hagers-town to Mercersburg. Commissioners: William

THE MARYLAND HERALD AND HAGERSTOWN WEEKLY ADVERTISER

ALLISON, Daniel MILLER, Joseph SNIVELY, Jun., William BLEAKNEY, Matthew LIND, John M'LANAHAN, Jun., Archibald M'CUNE, Archibald RANKEN.
John COOK, Innkeeper, Hagers-town, has flour for sale.
Joseph SMITH, Sharpsburg, Md., offers reward for apprentice to the hatting business named William MORROW, 16 yrs old, about 5 ft high, fair complexion.
Daniel M'CURTIN of Balt apptd professor of Belle Lettres and Dr. Jacob SCHNEBLY treasurer, of Hagers-town Academy. Tho. B. HALL, Sec'ry.
Sale at the late dwelling of Jacob KLOTZ, decd, in Franklin st, furniture and complete set of joiners' tools. George I. HARRY.
Mills and land for sale on north branch of Rappahannock river, Culpepper Co, Va. John ALLCOCK, Culpepper Co.
Elie RENCH has taken up stray geldings. Certified by A. M. WAUGH, J.P.
Negro man committed to jail, who calls himself Jerry CARTER; says he belongs to General RIDGLEY near Baltimore.

104. Jun 22 1814
Berkeley Springs, Va - Robert BAILEY has removed a number of nuisances, built and repaired buildings and put all the baths in complete order. He wishes to sell his dwelling called Bailey's Retirement in Frederick co, Va, and two farms in Berkeley co, one in Hampshire co.
Washington Hussars are ordered to meet at Williams-Port. E. G. WILLIAMS, Capt.
James LYNES and Thomas I. FUET have entered into partnership in the coach making business, under the firm of LYNES & FUET.
The Antietam Woollen Manufacturing Company wishes to employ book-keeper. Henry SHAFER, Pres't.
George EMMERT has jusst received and is now opening at his store, assortment of Dry Goods, Groceries and Queen's Ware.
John HENNEBERGER, cabinet maker, continues business in Antietam st, a few doors below dwelling of Rev SCHAEFFER.
To let the building of a stone meeting house at a place called the Falling Water Meeting House, Berkeley co. Deliver proposals to Jacob ZUCK, merchant at Capt. NEWKIRK's mill.
Henry STOLTZ, living near the Pa line, Washington Co, Md, 12 miles from Hagers-town, near the old road leading to Mercersburg, past Christian HAGER's mill, has taken up a stray gelding.
John FIEDT, with neighboring landholders in Wash co, to petition General Assembly to open a road from end of new road opened by state of Pa, leading from Mercersburg to the division line between Pa and Md., in Jacob LEAR's plantation, and from thence to river Potomack.
Elie RENCH has taken up stray geldings.

105. Jun 29 1814
John CUSHWA, 2 miles from John T. MASON's mill, offers reward for negro man, John SIVLEY, about 22 yrs old, probably in company with negro fellow named Jack BUTLER, property of John SNIVELY.
Daniel STAUFFER, Chambersburg, has lost out of his wagon on great road between Green-Castle and Williams-Port, 2 pieces of home made linen.
Thomas FLEMING has commenced the weaving business in Funks-town in the street adj the creek, next door to Mr. SCHILLING.
James RIED, Montalto Furnace, near Waynesburg, Pa, offers reward for missing gelding.

THE MARYLAND HERALD AND HAGERSTOWN WEEKLY ADVERTISER

106. Jul 13 1814
George FEAGUE admr of David WEST.
Joshua HICKMAN, Poole's Store, Montgomery co, offers for sale, horse called young Canadian.
Reward offered for negro man named JERRY who ran away from the subscriber at Martinsburg on his way to Tennessee. He is about 23 yrs old, purchased of Mrs. BOND of Talbot Co; has wife near Elkton. George E. DAVIDSON.
Samuel MARTIN, Hagers-town, offers reward for apprentice to blacksmith business named John WILSON, about 19 yrs old, 5 ft 7-8 inches high, fond of gambling.
The American Blues will parade in Hagers-town, in complete uniform, with swords and pistols in good order, and three rounds of blank cartridges each. Jacob BARR, Capt.
Fine of 1 dollar to be imposed by moderator on owners of hogs allowed to run at large. Henry LEWIS, moderator, George BOWER, clk.
Sale of property adj Pugh-town, Frederick co, Va, called White House. James O'BOYLE, Pugh-town.
Sale of 183 merino sheep. O. H. W. STULL, Salubira, near Hagers-town.
Sale of plantation 1 mile from Hancock-town, with merchant mill on Little Conoloway creek, with two pair of stones, one French burrs and the other Country stones, carding macine near the mill, and other houses. Henry DAVIS.
Letters at the Post Office [omitted here]

107. Jul 20 1814
Died Sun morning last, after a short illness, Benjamin WITMER, son of Henry WITMER, of this town, in his 18th yr.
Jacob TRESSLER, living on Mr. SWOPE's old place, 1 mile from Mr. BARTON's Tavern, on Little Conococheague, offers reward for muley bull, cow and 5 calves.
Sale at late dwelling of Michael F. MAYER, decd, Washington st, Hagers-town, personal estate of decd; also 40 new man woman's saddles, bridles, harness, &c. and all saddler tools of the decd Ann B. LEIBLEY and Joseph GRAFF, admrs.
Isaac HARTMAN, 1/2 mile from Green-castle, offers reward for missing horses.
James KAY has a vacancy for a few pupils of either sex at his school-room.

108. Jul 27 1814
On Sun last, upwards of 100 draughted militia, from the 24th Regiment, commanded by Lieut. Col. John RAGAN, under the requisition of the President of the U.S., marched from this place for the city of Baltimore; and, on Thurs 120 of the states' quota, from the same regiment, left this for the city of Annapolis. They are all healthy, good looking men, and went off in high spirits. The militia from the upper part of this state, are expected to pass through this place in a few days.
Samuel LYNCH, 1 mile from benjamin Galloway's mill, on Potomac river, has taken up a stray horse.
Joseph KEAN, Capt., 4th U.S. Rifle Regt., Bedford Rendezvous, offers reward for Henry HOFFMAN, private in the 4th U.S. Rifle Regt, who deserted from Bedford, Pa, 7 Jun, 36 yrs old, 5 ft 8 inches, dark complexion, hazel eyes, black hair, shoemaker by trade; has been seen in town of Hancock, Md; calls himself Sergeant STINE.

THE MARYLAND HERALD AND HAGERSTOWN WEEKLY ADVERTISER

109. Aug 3 1814
Joseph GRAFF admr of John CONRAD.
Catharine WOLTZ to sell at late dwelling of Samuel WOLTZ, decd, Potomac st, persons property of decd.
Peter LONG, son of John LONG, decd, 4 miles form Hagers-town, near William SPRIGG's has taken up a stray horse.
Ordered that the officers of the 10th Regiment, Md. Militia, meet at Stover's Tavern for drill exercise. The officers commanding companies will notify the delinquents of their respective companies, who refused to march on Wed the 2th ult to attend on said day, at said place, to shew cause why they did not march, before a Regimental Court Martial. Daniel MALOTT, Lieut. Col. 10th Regt.
House for sale in Franklin st, adj Abraham KING's Blacksmith's shop. Nicholas LANTZ.
William WEBB to sell 100 head of sheep at his res near the Cave Tavern.
John CHENEY and David CHENEY, exrs of Jeremiah CHENEY, request accounts be settled.
John WOLGAMOT exr of Mary WOLGAMOT.
Chancery court - ordered that the sale made by Upton LAWRENCE, trustee, in the cause of Daniel DAVIS and wife against Daniel BOWLES and others be ratified; that the sale by Upton Lawrence, trustee in the cause of Jacob KESSINGER vs George KESSINGER and others be ratified; that the sale made by George C. SMOOT, trustee for the sale of real estate of Jacob ROOT, be ratified.

110. Aug 10 1814
Died Sun morning last in this town, after a short illness, Master James POTTENGER, in his 16th yr.
Silver Greys - It is proposed that all of our fellow citizens above the age of 45, meet at the Court-house, on Friday evening next, at 4 o'clock, for the purpose of forming a company, and electing their officers, to defend the town when called upon.
Jacob LECKRON of Simon and Jacob LECKRON, exrs of Simon LECKRON.
George KREPS continues the cabinet making business at his old stand formerly occupied by Martin KREPS, decd, in Franklin st.
Daniel HUGHES, Junr. wants to purchase 4-5 wagon horses.
16 feather beds for sale at Pettit's tavern. Samuel HAMMETT.
Joseph BARKDOLL, 3 miles from Nicholson's Gap, offers reward for Jacob MILLER, apprentice to the blacksmith business, 18-19 yrs of age, 6 ft 1 inch high, sandy hair, blue eyes, fair complexion.

111. Aug 17 1814
Died Thurs last in this town, Everard GRUBER, father of the sen'r Editor of the German Western Correspondent, in his 79th yr, leaving wife to whom he had been married 51 yrs; had 10 children of whom 7 were living; remains interred in the burying ground of the German Reformed Congregation.
Thurs morning last, the squadron of Cavalry composed of Capt. Edward G. WILLIAMS' company of "Washington Hussars" and "Capt. Jacob BARR's company of "American Blues," under the command of Major Otho H. WILLIAMS, well mounted and equipped marched from this place for the lower counties of this state - all in high spirits, and determined to come home crowned with laurels, or die in defence of their country.

THE MARYLAND HERALD AND HAGERSTOWN WEEKLY ADVERTISER

We have accounts from our squadron of Cavalry which arrived in George-town Sat morning, all well - They are now awaiting further orders.
Yesterday, about 270 Militia from Allegany county arrived at this place, and this morning pursued their march, part, we understand, for Baltimore and part for Annapolis.
John KENNEDY will sell at the house of George BUEHLER, a lot of ground and buildings, 2 a., in the bourough of Harrisburgh, Pa.
Jacob MUMMA, 1 mile from Sharpsburg, offers reward for negro man, Sam TILMAN, about 18 yrs of age.
John ECARD, Stone Mill, near Harper's Ferry, has taken up a stray gelding. Certified by Alexander GRIM, Justice of the Peace.
Nicholas MARTIN, living on the Welch run, Franklin co, Pa, 2 miles from John CUSHWA's Mill, has taken up a stray mare. Certified by A. OTT, Justice of the Peace of Washington Co, Md.
Miller wanted - Edmund RUTTER, at Mrs. RENCH's mill, 3 miles from Hagerstown.

112. Aug 24 1814
From the Washington Squadron of Cavalry - On Saturday morning we arrived in George-Town - and remained there until Tues evening, when we took up our line of march for Washington City, and pitched our tents at Camp Stuart, in a skirt of woods near a beautiful spring - Men all well, and in good spirits - Good far and plenty of it - The Squadron has been much admired in the City and George-Town. Our future destination is yet unknown, but we are ready to march wherever it may be necessary.
Deserted from Camp Stuart, near Washington City, on 17th inst, George KERSHNER, private in Capt. Jacob BARR's Troop of Cavalry. He resided near Kershner's cross Road, Washington co, about 30 yrs of age, 6 ft high, robust, strong looking man. The commanding officer regrets, that he is compelled to advertise any member of a volunteer troop - but however painful the duty, the crisis, demands the strictest discipline and attention. O. H. WILLIAMS, Major, 1st Regiment Maryland Cavalry. N. B. Benjamin MALONE, residing near Sharpsburg, and James AYRES, residing near Hancocktown, Privates in troop of Horse commanded by Capt. Edward G. WILLIAMS, are ordered to join the Squadron without delay, or measures will immediately be taken to bring them to military trial.
A woman's saddle was left with Levi PRICE some months ago.
Sale at the late res of Simon LECKRON, decd, 1 mile from Hagers-town, personal estate of decd, horses, milch cows, farming utensils, hemp, flax, potatoes, pork, lard, furniture and other. Jacob LECKRON of Simon and Jacob LECKRON, exrs.

113. Aug 31 1814
Dade P. NOLAND, Loudon co, Va, to sell tract of land on which he now lives, on Potomack river, within 200 yards of Noland's Ferry.

114. Sep 21 1814
Died yesterday morning in this town, after a short illness, Jacob SHULL, in his 33d yr, leaving widow and 4 small children.
Committed to jail of Washington co as a runaway, negro man who calls himself PHIL; says he belongs to Ferdinand FAIRFAX, esq. of Jefferson co, Va. He appears to be 40 yrs of age and 5 ft 6 inches high.

THE MARYLAND HERALD AND HAGERSTOWN WEEKLY ADVERTISER

Joseph FORD admr of William BLAKEMORE.
Hiel PECK, living on the premises, to sell merchant mill with 4 pair of stones, saw-mill, 300 a., known as Middlebrook, on post road from George-town to Frederick-town, 21 miles from each.
Sale at late dwelling of John LIGHTER, decd, near Andrew BAUGHMAN's tavern, personal property of decd. Catharine LIGHTER and Andrew LIGHTER, admrs.
Sale at late dwelling of Henry HAHN, decd, in Church st, Hagers-town, near Mr. BOWSART's Brick Yard, personal estate of decd: one cow, 6 sheep, 2 hogs, 3 weaver's looms and tackling, beds and bedsteads, tables, chairs, 1 tenplate stove with pipe and other. Jacob LAMBERT, admr.
Anthony O. ROW, living near William ZEIGLER's store, has taken up a stray colt. Certified by Isaac HOUSER, Jun'r, Justice of the Peace.
Thomas M'CARDELL, has taken up a stray filly at his farm known as Salisbury Spring.
John DOWNIN, Jun'r, and Henry HUNSBERRY, has commenced the business of fulling & dying at John HERSHEY's fulling Mill.
Dissolution of the firm of Jacob SHULL & BUTLER. Jacob SHULL and Jacob BUTLER. Rope-making business will be carried by Jacob Shull at the old stand.
Sale of tract of limestone land 3 miles from Hagers-town, late the property of Nicholas SMITH, decd, 188 a. George CELLAR.
Christian HOUSER, near Wm. ZEIGLER's, has taken up stray geldings.
Ludwick HAUVERMALE, near Jacob MUMMA's mill, has taken up a stray horse.
Peter MILLER offer reward for French Watch, stolen out of his Tavern, 2 miles from Parkhead Forge.
Samuel WEIS, Hagers-town, offers reward for apprentice to the blacksmith business, Patrick MAGRAW, about 16 yrs of age, 4 ft 10-11 inches.
Joseph BLACKISTON, overseer for Mr. D. COOK, offers reward for negro man named CHARLES, who sometimes calls himself Charles HINTON, about 21 yrs old, who ran away from David COOK's farm (formerly Dr. F. TILGHMAN's), 7 miles from Hagers-town.
Raccoon Skins - MIDDLEKAUFF & JULIUS, Hagers-town, have received large quantity of fur.
Pock book lost - William FITZHUGH.
Henry POPST, Frederick-town, offers reward for stolen mare.
Purchasers of Benjamin WINTER's property are notified that their notes are due. Christopher BURCKHARTT.
3,300 racoon pelts for sale, caught by Indians near Fort Detroit and Lake Michigan. George STONEBRAKER, Boonsboro'

115. Sep 28 1814
Conococheague Rolling Mill & Nail Factory - BROWN & WATSON, Chambersburg.
George NEEDY, living on John CELLAR's land, 3 miles from Hagers-town, has taken up a stray cow.
For rent: Tavern opposite the New Bank, now occupied by L. PRICE; dwelling house occupied by Capt. Thomas QUANTRILL; farm 6 miles from Hagers-town, now occupied by John KELLER. Henry LEWIS.
Committed to jail, small negro man, who calls himself BOB; says he belongs to Nicholas DORSEY of Anne Arundel co, about 25 yrs old; also mulatto man who calls himself BOB, says he belongs to Samuel HAMILTON, near Bladensburg, hired to Lewis HARPER; was at work at the above mentioned Mr.

THE MARYLAND HERALD AND HAGERSTOWN WEEKLY ADVERTISER

Dorsey's for Mr. Harper, who was putting up a building for Mr. Dorsey, from whence Mr. Dorsey's fellow and himself run away.
G. M. CONRADT, one of the late owners of the cloth Factory in Funks-town, has rented Martin BAECHTEL's Fulling Mill near Hagers-town.
Sale at the late dwelling of Jacob SHULL, decd, Potomac st, personal property of decd. Theobald EICHELBERNER, admr.

116. Oct 5 1814
David FUNK and John HOFFER, admrs of Jacob SNAVELY.
Letters remaining at the Post Officer [not listed here]
Sale of horses, cows, sheep, set of carpenter's and set of cooper's tools, and other. Michael FIRESTONE
Sale at the place where the subscriber now lives, on Gen. RINGGOLD's Manor, 4 miles from Hagers-town, negro woman about 25, boy age 14 and a girl. John COMBS.
David WESTENBERGER, near Gen. Samuel RINGGOLD's, offers reward for negro man named HEZ, about 20 yrs of age, 5 ft 6-7 inches.
Catharine WOLTZ admr of Samuel WOLTZ.
David SCHNEBLY, 6 miles from Hagers-town, has taken up a stray mare.

117. Oct 12 1814
William GABBY denies that he brought Col. John BOURNS from Pennsylvania and furnished him with a ticket and endeavoured to procure him a vote, as asserted by Christopher BURCKHARTT.
Samuel HAMMETT, living at Messrs' Peter & Matthias MILLER's Mill near Williams-port offers reward for missing sheep, purchased at George BEAN's.

118. Nov 2 1814
Jacob BARR and Jacob ROHRER admrs of John ROHRER, to sell at res of decd, formerly Funk's Mill, 2 miles from Hagers-town, personal property of decd.
Robert T. FRIEND and Eleanor FRIEND, admrs of Jacob FRIEND, to sell at res of decd, personal property of decd: young negro woman and her 2 children, wheat, rye, corn, hay, horned cattle, hogs, sheep, furniture.
Sale at farm on which he res on Potomack river, 5 miles from Williams-Port, variety of property [listed]; to rent farm on which he resides, 600 a., with exception of the house, garden and spring-house which he now occupies and about 15 a., and saw and grist mills on the river bank. Joseph SPRIGG
Sale at the farm of subscriber, where Joseph BLACKISTON now lives (late the property of Dr. Frisby TILGHMAN), 6 miles of Hagers-town.
Sale at dwelling of Peter CREAGER, near the Poor-house, clock, desks, stoves, tables, beds and bedsteads, hemp.
The Troop of Horse "American Blues," to parade in Hagers-town 19 Nov. Jacob BARR, Capt.
Samuel BROGUNIER and John HARRY, admrs of David BROGUNIER, to sell at late res of decd, personal estate of decd.
"Dr. HAMMOND Informs the public, that he has returned from his Military tour, and is again ready to attend those who may require his professional services."
Persons are forewarned not to take assignment of a bond executed to John OLIVER. Jacob HERSHBERGER.
Committed to jail as a runaway, negro man, about 21 yrs old, who calls himself LEROY, and says he belongs to Ruben HUTCHESON of Loudon co, Va.

THE MARYLAND HERALD AND HAGERSTOWN WEEKLY ADVERTISER

Hides & skins wanted, now carrying on the Tanning business in Williams-Port, in the Yard formerly owned by James STERETT. Robert M'CULLOH & Son.
James ROBARDET to commence a Fencing School.
William ARMOR, Hagers-town, offers reward for apprentice boy to the Tayloring business named George HUNTSBERRY, 16-17, 5 ft 2-3 inches, slender made, dark complexion and light hair.
Chancery sale by George C SMOOT, Trustee, of lots in Elizabeth-town [Hagerstown], late property of Frederick ALTER, decd, one of which is lot on which he died, lot no. 263 of Hager's Addition to Elizabeth-town.
Chancery sale by George C. SMOOT, Trustee, of tract, property of Christian ROHRER, decd, called Establishment, 119 a., 1/4 mile from Hagers-town.
Sale on premises and late dwelling of Solomon DIDIE, decd, near Antietam creek, 2 1/2 miles from Sharpsburgh, 1 mile from Mr. BRIEN's forge, several young negroes, wagon, horses and gears, milch cows, steers, mill-wright tools, furniture, &c.; also the plantation of decd, 256 a.; and another tract of decd, 1 1/2 miles below Brien's iron works, 115 a. Jacob MUMMA and John BEARD, exrs.
Dividend of the effects of Moses TABBS, to be paid to persons with claims against him. Daniel HUGHES, Jun. and Henry SWEITZER, Trustees.
James ROBINSON, Sharpsburgh, authorised by Benjamin ODEN, Prince George's Co, to offer at sale, at the house of John KNODE, Sharpsburgh, 40 slaves.

119. Nov 9 1814
Reply by Christopher BURCKHARTT to earlier statement by William GABBY. He says that Gabby had "ordered a writ to be issued against my son Henry, who, he said had just voted without the prescribed residence. I replied that I was ignorant of the fact, and was sorry he had voted; however, remarking at the same time, that it was nothing more than he himself had been guilty of at a former election..." Following is statement of John BOURNS who says that when he voted, he had his home at John GABBY's.
Barbara WEEKER and Geo. MARTINEY exrs of Melchor WEEKER.
A. P. REA, to teach penmanship in Hagers-town.
Joseph WOLF, 2 miles of Jacob ROHRER's mill on Antietam, has taken up a stray heifer.
Samuel LONG to sell tract of 60 a., 5 miles from Hagers-town, late the property of Robert M'KEE, decd.
John JULIUS, Hagers-town, has taken up a stray horse.
James Lowry DONALDSON who was killed in the action near North Point, on 12th ult, was a native of Ireland, but has resided in this country from the time he was 11 yrs old. He was the 3rd son of Col. Wm. LOWRY, of this city, his name having been changed by an act of the Assembly of this state, in compliance with the wishes of a relation. Mr. Donaldson received a liberal education, and was bred to the profession of the laws which he was practising in this city with much reputation and success. For 3 successive yrs he was elected delegate to General Assembly. He was about 33 yrs of age, left a widow and 5 small children. He acted as Adjutant of the 27th Regiment. Balt. Fed. Gaz.
John ADAMS to sell plantation, 234 a. 1 mile from Kershner's fording on Conocoheague; also horses, hogs, farming utensils, furniture.
Samuel NUNAMOCAN has taken up a stray mare.

THE MARYLAND HERALD AND HAGERSTOWN WEEKLY ADVERTISER

Persons who gave notes for purchases at sale of personal estate of Christian ROWLAND, decd, are notifed that the notes are due. Christian STOVER and Christian ROWLAND, admrs.
Fuller wanted - Benjamin BELLER.

120. Nov 16 1814
Daniel SCHNEBLY admr of Jacob BRUMBAUGH, to sell at late res of decd, 2 miles of Col. David SCHNEBLY's, personal estate of decd.
John GELWICKS has commenced brewing business at his old stand in Williams-Port.
Purchasers at sale of subscriber's property last March, are notified that their obligations are due and lodged with William VAN LEAR of William-Port. Emanuel NEWCOMER.
Sale of 2 story house in Potomac st, Hagers-town, now occupied by subscriber, near the Lutheran Church, opposite the dwelling of Col. D. HUGHES. Henry SHANE

121. Nov 30 1814
David BRUMBAUGH and John M'KEE admrs of Peter RENCH, to sell at dwelling house of decd, personal estate of decd.
Matthias STINE, 6 miles from Hagers-town, has taken up a stray gelding.
Sale of 7 negroes and a road wagon. Henry SWEITZER.
On Wed evening last, a Volunteer Company of Infantry, 120 in number, from Brownsville, Pa, under the command of Capt. Valentine GIESEY, arrived in this place and yesterday morning proceeded on their march for Balt. Capt. Giesey and Officers and men under his commande return their sincere thanks for the particular attention paid them by the citizens of Hagers-town.
Sale of farm, 430 a. in Montgomery co, Md., 3 miles of Middlebrook (res of late Gen. LINGAN), 1/2 mile of Francis C. CLOPPER's merchant mill on Big Seneca. Apply to Griffith HENDERSON at Middlebrook or Archibald HENDERSON living on the premises.
Whereas Thomas M'CUMSEY has been employed to purchase cattle for me 8-9 months past, he is no longer in my employ. Henry BECKLEY.
Matthew THOMPSON, Franklin co, Pa, 6 miles from Mercersburg, and 1 1/2 mile from Jacob ANGLE's mill, has taken up a stray heifer.
John SNAVELY, 6 miles from Hagers-town, has taken up a stray shoat.
Samuel HAMMETT, living at Messrs. Peter & Matthias MILLER's Mill near Williams-Port, has taken up stray sheep.

122. Dec 7 1814
HUGHES & FITZHUGH, Washington Co, offer reward for negro SCIPIO, aged 22 yrs, who ranaway from their Nail Factory near Hagers-town.
For sale - 70 a., 1 1/2 mile of Mercersburg, 1/4 mile of John SHAFER's mill. Elliott T. LANE, Mercersburg
Sale at house of Jacob MILLER in Williams-Port, watch, bureau, feather bed and bedding, negro boy, being property of William BEATTY, decd. Peter MILLER, admr. Also offered for sale: 3 houses and lots in Williams-port, Potomac st, one formerly the property of Henry HAHN - P. & M. MILLER
Sale of plantation, 1 3/4 miles of Mercersburg, Montgomery twp, Franklin co, Pa, 143 a. William T. M'KINSTRY.

THE MARYLAND HERALD AND HAGERSTOWN WEEKLY ADVERTISER

Jacob BINKLEY of George, Hagers-town, to move to Ohio Apr next, to sell his blue dying apparatus, consisting of one copper boiler, 3 vats, a mill for grinding Indigo, and sundry other articles.
Benjamin HOWARD to open a Seminary for instruction of young ladies. Letter from Mary Ann SMITH, Phila, attesting that Benjamin Howard who superintended her school, was a young man of unexceptionable morals and recommended him as a good teacher.
Men attached to my Company will meet at Henry BECKLEY's Tavern in Funks-town, 17th inst. Gerard STONEBREAKER, Capt.
For sale - house adj jail. Peter GLOSSBRENNER

123. Dec 14 1814
John HARMAN, Boot & Shoemaker, from Baltimore, has commenced his business in the house formerly occupied by Major Martin KERSHNER, Washington, Hagers-town.
Jacob LAMBERT, admr of Henry HAHN, wishes to settle accounts of decd.
Sale of plantation, 200 a., 1 mile from Big Spring. Jacob P. KERSHNER.
Sheriff's sale of property of John CAKE, insolvent debtor: still of 35 gallons, 25 bushels of malt, 8 malt tubs.
John SCHNEBLY, Jun., 5 miles from Hagers-town, has taken up a stray calf.
Purchasers of personal property of Henry OTTO, decd, are informed that their notes become due on 17 Dec. Isabella OTTO and Matthias OTTO, exrs.
House and half lot in Antietam st, Hagers-town, for sale, nearly opposite dwelling of Rev SHAEFFER. Casper FULK.

124. Dec 21 1814
Died in this town Mon morning, Jacob KAELHOFER, in his 32nd yr.
Moses GIBBONS, living near Charles-Town, Jefferson Co, Va, offers reward for negro man named JAMES, about 30 yrs of age.
Sale for use and benefit of William M'PHERRIN's creditors, the Printing establishment of late Hagers-town Gazette, viz. one press and 5 fonts of types, with necessary apparatuses to conduct a Country Paper. Henry SWEITZER, Trustee.
Sale of plantation whereon he now resides, on Raystown branch of Juniata, 2 miles west of Bedford, Pa, 300 a. Michael SPRENGLE.
Red Morrocco Pocket Book lost - George CUTAR. In the book are written the names of John BEAVER, Jacob MOWEN and George CUTAR.
Samuel MILLER, 1 mile of Kershner's Ford, on Conococheague, has taken up a stray heifer.

125. Dec 28 1814
John FREANER accuses Wm. WILLIS of attempting to raise the price of boots and shoe whereas he (Freaner) considers a price increase at this time would be a burden, and inappropriate during the War.
John DOWNIN, 5 miles from Hagers-town, has taken up a stray hog.
William M'CONLEY cautions persons from trusting his wife Elizabeth M'CONLEY on his account.
Deserted from Camp, near Baltimore, from the 24th July to 22d Dec, 1814. [rearranged alphabetically]: Resin BARBER; Hezekiah BERNET; John BORTLE (Drummer); John BOWSER; Joseph BOYER; John BUCK; William CARROLL; Benjamin DOWNES; Basil DOWNEY; William EICHELBERGER; Peter GAY; William GILPIN; Thomas GRIFFIN; Henry HAREGROVE; Elisha HERBERT; Jacob HINE; David HOPE;

THE MARYLAND HERALD AND HAGERSTOWN WEEKLY ADVERTISER

Gabriel ISENBERGER; Joshua JONES; Adam KUHN; Edward MINCHER; Benjamin POTTER; John PRICE; Richard RAY; John REPP; Charles SEAMON; Abraham SHONG; Samuel SMALLWOOD; Ephraim SMITH; Jonathan SMITH; Youst SMITH; Jacob SONTMON(?); Richard SPICER; Jacob STAKE; John STAKE; Hansim(?) TUCKER; Henry WEEKS; John WILHELM - William CURTIS, Capt. 1st Regt, 11th Brig. Md. Militia, Annapolis.
Deserted from Camp, near Baltimore, between 4th of August and 5th of Dec 1814, the following men from Washington co, detached from 24th Regt. Md. Miltia, viz. John BLACKBURN, Moses BOWER, Joseph GRAYBILL, Jacob GOWER, Zebulon LOVER, David THOMAS, Jeremiah LEANARD, George RINULL, Josiah TALLY, William YUTSLER, Samuel TUFTS. The following men were transferred to my company from Capt. FARQUIER's from Frederick co, who also deserted between 4 Aug and 5 Dec, viz. James SARGENT, George SARGENT, Philip FLENNER, William DAWSON, Wm. PATTERSON, Peter GARDNER. George SHRYOCK, Capt. 1st Regt, 11th Brig. Md. Militia, Annapolis.
Hatters Attend! 7,000 racoon skins and 170 pounds of beaver - Samuel SWAYNE, Winchester.
To be rented - large and convenient 2 story stone house in Franklin st, Hagers-town, near the Public Spring (now occupied by George DOYLE and William ARMOR).
Abraham WHETSTONE offers for sale tan-yard in Westmoreland co, Pa, 1/2 mile from Young's Town.

126. Jan 4 1815
Jacob BARR candidate for sheriff.
Dissolution of partnership of Anthony B. MARTIN & Co is dissolved. George WILLIAMSON and Anthony B. MARTIN. The business previously conducted under the name of George Williamson, Jun. in the city of Balt, will be conducted in the future by George Williamson.
Letters at the Post Officer [Not listed here]
Jacob LAMBERT admr of Sophia GERHART.

127. Jan 11 1815
Michael GEISER, 1/2 mile from Abraham MAYER's Mill, 3 miles from HUGHES's Forge, offers reward for missing mare.
Daniel SCHNEBLY candidate for sheriff.
Stephen DAVIS forewarns persons from taking asssignment on note given to Michael MILLER in the state of Kentucky for a negro man which he purchased, as said negro has proved to be unsound.
Reward offered for stolen kersimere pantaloons and red morocco pocket book which contained promissary notes one on Thomas KELLAR for $500 and other on Christian F. GOLL for $125.28, stolen out of my lodging room at Mr. Samuel PETTIT's, Hagers-town, between 25 and 30 Dec. Joseph CELLERS.
Otho LAWRENCE, Atty at Law, has opened office in small brick house lately occupied by Dr. SCHNEBLY as a shop.

128. Feb 1 1815
Died Thurs evening last at his res about 6 miles from Hagers-town, Jacob MONG, in his 57th yr.
Death of Rev. Solomon SCHAEFFER, Pastor of the Lutheran Congregations of this place and its vicinity, who died Mon last, in his 25th yr. In his 20th yr he took charge of these congregations. [long obit.]

THE MARYLAND HERALD AND HAGERSTOWN WEEKLY ADVERTISER

Edward B. BAILEY has taken large and commodious house in Hagers-town, lately occupied by Levi PRICE. He informs ladies and gentlemen travelling to Bath, that there will be a stage running every other day from his house to Major Robert BAILEY's at Bath, during the season.

The commissioners of the Farmer's and Mechanic's Bank of Greencastle, call for payment of second instalment on each share. Commissioners: William ALLISON, Daniel MILLER, Archibald RANKIN, Joseph SNIVELY, Matthew LIND, John M'LANAHAN, Jun., William BLEAKNEY, Samuel M'EWEN.

Sale of plantation in Pleasant Valley, 3 miles from Harper's Ferry, 190 a., to be shewn by Thomas BOTELER, near the premises. Jonas HOGMIRE, Zachariah CLAGETT, Joseph C. KELLAR, John ECARD, Commissioners.

Farm for rent adj STOVER's Tavern. Benjamin YOE

129. Feb 8 1815

Died 3d inst, William M. M'PHERRIN, late Editor of the Hagers-town Gazette, and son of the late Rev M'PHERRIN, of Franklin co, Pa.

George SHALL, Hagers-town, offers reward for apprentice to boot & shoe making business named Archibald SERGEANT, about 18 yrs of age, 5 ft 9-10 inches; had on blue cloth coat, bottle green cloth roundabout, new fur hat.

Theobald EICHELBERNER and David F. SCHAEFFER admrs of Rev. S. SCHAEFFER of Hagers-town, to sell personal estate of decd: horse and carriage with gears and other items [listed].

Joseph WOLF, 4 miles from Hagers-town, has taken up a stray cow.

Franklin ANDERSON, Atty at Law, has opened office in the corner of square near Messrs. John & Joseph M'ILHENNY's Store.

All soldiers of the 1st Regt, Md. Militia, who have not received their pay, will call on me at Funks-town, before the 12th inst at which time I must close my accounts. G. W. BOERSTLER, Pay-Master.

130. Feb 15 1815

Partnership under firm of Alexander NEIL & Co. dissolved. Alexander NEILL, David TUTWILER, Hagers-town.

Thomas M'ELFISH, 10 miles from Cumberland, Md, near the road to Hancock-town, offers reward for negro girl named BECK but sometimes calls herself Mary BARNES, about 18 yrs of age, 5 ft 6 inches, mulatto colour, taken up as a runaway on 12 Jan near road from Waynesburg to Hagers-town.

Grist mill and saw mill (property of heirs of late Henry COOK, decd) for rent, near Cave-Town. Jacob KESSINGER, near Hughes' Forge.

Peter BOYER, living on Salisbury, 1/2 mile of road from Hagers-town to Williams-Port, has obtained licence as Auctioneer or Vendue Crier.

Sale of 2 stills, hogsheads, wheat and rye in the ground, and other, at the farm of the late David HAMMETT. Jonathan HAGER.

Conrad HOGMIRE, living on the Marsh, 8 miles from Hagers-town, offers reward for missing mare.

WILLIAMS & RAGAN to sell house and lot occupied by John A. DONALDSON, Antietam st, near opposite res of O. H. W. STULL, with blacksmith shop, two pair of bellows, anvils and tools.

Creditors of Samuel BOWLES, decd, are to exhibit their claims. U. LAWRENCE, Trustee.

THE MARYLAND HERALD AND HAGERSTOWN WEEKLY ADVERTISER

131. Feb 22 1815
Sale in Sharpsburg, of stone house, 40x35 ft. and several small tracts. Enquire to subscriber, Gabriel NOURSE or Mrs. Elizabeth CHAPLINE, near Sharpsburg.
Henry ARNOLD, Hagers-town, to move from this town, to Ohio next spring, requests those indebted to make payment.
To be rented - farm, 130 a., and tan yard with 5 vats, 1 1/2 miles from Big Spring, late property of Dr. Emanuel FRANZ, decd. Martin MYER, guardian.
Sale of house and lot adj lots with Jacob TUTWILER, Potomac st.
E. G. WILLIAMS, to sell his distillery apparatus.
Sale of plantation 1/2 mile from Boonsboro', 189 a., with saw mill. George SHAFER and Henry LOCHER, Jr., Boonsboro'.
Tract of land for sale, 150 a., on Potomac river, 2 1/2 miles from Big Spring. Isabella OTTO.
Jacob MIDDLEKAUFF, Jun'r, 2 miles from Henry NEWCOMER's Mill, offers reward for apprentice to farming business named Thomas HARRIS, about 11 yrs old, 4 ft 6 inches; had on green linsey jacket, black linsey overalls, pair of patent shoes and wool hat.
Journeymen coopers wanted. John SEITZ.
Henry KEALHOFER, admr of Jacob KEALHOFER, to sell at late dwelling of decd, his personal property: cart, set of butcher's tools, 8-day clock, bureau, kitchen cupboard, beds and bedsteads, tables, chairs, ten-plate stove with pipe and other items.
John SCHNEBLY, senr., 3 miles from Hagers-town, has taken up a stray boar shoat.
Public sale at res of subscriber, 1 mile of Ogle's Tavern, Cross Roads, negro woman about 20 yrs old with male child, horses, cows and other. John KERSHNER.
George KERSHNER, 1 miles of Ogle's Tavern, Cross roads, has taken up a stray bull.
Abraham STARLING and Horatio WATKINS, on Ringgold's Manor, 2 1/2 miles from Williams-Port, have taken up a stray sow.

132. Mar 1 1815
Wm. FITZHUGH, will sell in Hagers-town, a number of slaves, as he contemplates removal of his family to state of New York.
The paper making business carried on at Valley Paper Mill, under the firm of LEWIS & William BIRELEY, will be in future, be conducted by subscribers, Lewis BIRELEY, Thomas OGLE, Middletown Valley, Frederick Co.
Sale at res of subscriber, on Ringgold's Manor, 1 1/2 mile from Williams-Port, horses, cows, sheep, ploughs, furniture - Elizabeth WELLS
Co-partnership of SMITH & KELLER dissolved. Geo. SMITH, Thos. KELLER.
Dissolution of partnership of David HARRY and William HARRY under the firm of David HARRY and Son.
William HARRY will sell milch cow, new 8-day clock, clothes press, bureau, beds and bedsteads, all sorts of wagon maker's stuff and tools. At the same time and place David HARRY will sell Meadow Lots adj Philip KELLAR's, opposite dwelling of Joseph BOYD in Hagers-town.
Sale at dwelling house of George SHALL in Franklin st: milch cow, 8-day clock, furniture.

THE MARYLAND HERALD AND HAGERSTOWN WEEKLY ADVERTISER

Sale at house of subscriber in Hagers-town, furniture [listed], five weaver's looms, meadow lot adj Wm. KREPS and George BRENDLE, in Rohrer's Addition to Hagers-town. - Henry ARNOLD
The Antietam Woollen Manufacturing Co. have opened a store in Hagers-town, in the large stone house on the public square, where they offer for sale assortment of domestic cloths. W. DICKEY, agent for the company.
Sale at res of John BARTLETT on Ringgold's Manor, 2 miles from Williamsport, horses, cows, cattle, wagons, wind mill, and other.

133. Mar 8 1815
Died Mon, 27th ult, after a short illness, at his res on Conococheague, Jacob KERSHNER, Inn keeper, in his 58th yr.
Partnership under the firm of TURNER & HESLETINE is dissolved. Edmund H. TURNER, Charles HESLETINE.
Barbara MONG and Jacob B. MONG admrs of Jacob MONG, to sell at res of decd, near Hughes's Furnace, 5 miles from Hagers-town, personal estate of decd.
Sale at plantation where subscriber now lives, on Gen. RINGGOLD's manor, 4 miles from Hagers-town, work horses, milch cows, set of blacksmith tools, road wagon, farming utensils, ten-plate stove, furniture. John COMBS
Sale at subscriber's res on Little Antietam, 1/2 mile from Abraham MAYER's Mill, horses, cows, sheep wagon, &c. Christian GOOD.
Moses M'NAMEE, at the New Paper Mill, 1 1/2 mile from Hagers-town, offers reward for negro boy named Joseph BRISKER, apprentice to farming business, 15-16 yrs of age, 5 ft 3-4 inches; had on bear skin roundabout, black velvet pantaloons, pair of patent shoes and old fur hat.
40 negroes for sale at Court-House in Hagers-town. Ch: CARROLL, of Belle Vue.
Sale at house of subscriber, Potomac st, desk, kitchen furniture, 3 weaver's looms, and other items [listed]. James GARRETT
Sale at dwelling house of subscriber in Church st, near SPRIGG's Brick Yard, mahogany bureau, tables, cart blacksmith tools and other. John DAVIS.
Sale at house of Thomas SHUMAN, Potomac st, beds and bedsteads, tables, chairs, bureau, cupboard and chest, kettles and other - William MOFFETT
John GROFF, 8 miles from Hagers-town, has taken up two stray sheep.
Samuel BAYLY, insolvent debtor, earlier confined to county jail is now discharged.

134. Mar 15 1815
Married last evening by Rev RAHAUSER, John HARRY of this town, to Miss Mary ASHBURY, dau of Capt. John ASHBURY of this co.
Died in this town, Thurs morning last, Samuel ALTER, in his 24th yr.
- On Thurs last in Montgomery co, James PRATHER, Esq. of this co. His remains were interred near the Big Spring.
Board of Managers for Hagers-town Turnpike Road now receiving first installment on stock subscribed by persons residing on west of the South Mountain. Walter BOYD, Robert HUGHES.
Persons who gave their notes at sale of personal estate of John LONG, decd, are notified that notes are due. John LONG, Daniel BRUMBAUGH, admrs.
Frederick WORSTER and George KLINK, living in and near Hagers-town, intend going to Germany May next. They will go up the river Rhine, to Alsace, Suabia and Swisserland and other parts of Europe. Those wishing to send letters may call or send them to Hagers-town.

THE MARYLAND HERALD AND HAGERSTOWN WEEKLY ADVERTISER

Meeting of United Fire Company - Tho: GRIEVES, Clk.
Mary RIDENOUR and Adam RIDENOUR, admrs, to sell at res of Charles RIDENOUR, decd, near Frederick UNGER's mill, 1 mile from Cave-Town, personal estate of decd.
Jacob BOWER, 1 mile from Hagers-town, has taken up a stray heifer.
Thomas FLEMING continues to carry on weaving business at his old stand in Funkts-town, in the street adj the Creek, next door to Mr. SCHILLING, where he will weave linen, woollen and linsey.
The horses, Young Pilgrim and Canadian Draught horse, property of James M. STERRITT, will stand for mares this season at stables of Jacob REBECK, Inn-keeper, Sharpsburgh, stables of John STOVER, Inn-keeper at the Crossroads, and at the stable of Christian ARTZ, Inn-keeper, Boonsborough.
Edward GAITHER offers for sale 30 a. of limestone land, 4 miles from Hagers-town, adj lands of Henry RINEHART and late Daniel SPEECE.
Sale at subscriber's res 1 1/2 miles from Hagers-town, on road to Sharps-burg, work horses, mares, milch cows, sheep, hogs. Jane NEWSON
Sale agreeable to last will of Jeremiah HAYES, decd, 147 a., on Potomac river, adj land of Thomas BUCHANAN, and Samuel LYNCH; also half of an island in Potomac, 7 3/4 a. Apply to Benjamin MEADES, living on Chew's farm and near the premises. John WEST, exr.
Red Morocco Pocket Book lost - John JONES

135. Mar 29 1815
Negro woman for sale and her 2 children. Peter MONG, 9 miles from Hagers-town, 3 miles from Messrs. BEARD & KESSINGER's Store.
Jacob BUTLER & Co. will pay the highest price for hemp; deliver to their Rope Factory, opposite the dwelling of Gotleib ZIMMERMAN, Pump-Maker, near the Lutheran Church.
The horse, Chester Ball, to cover mares this season at John SCHAFFER's Mill (formerly Buckwalter's) in Montgomery twp, Franklin co; and at Mrs. STINE's Tavern. Jacob HOSLER
Farm and mills for sale in Allegany co, on the Little Crossings, 22 miles west of Cumberland, 100 a. cleared, occupied as a Tavern. Joseph TOMLINSON, Youghany Mills.
Furs and Peltries - John TRAVERSE, Auctionier.
Married last evening by Rev RAHAUSER, William HOBLITZELL, merchant, of Cumberland, to Miss Mary RIDENOUR, of this town.
The horse, Young Shepherd, will stand this season at John SCHNEBLY's farm, 3 miles from Hagers-town. Jacob SCHNEBLY, Jun'r.
William ANIBA has on hand, Liquid Blacking; enquire at Geo. EMMERT's Store.
Jacob TRESSLER, living 5 miles from Williams-Port, on Little Conochogeaague, offers reward for horse stolen from his wagon at Mr. NEIFF's Tavern, 2 miles from Middle-town, on the Balt Turnpike road.
The books for receiving subscriptions for the stock in the George-town Importing and Exporting Co., will be opened at Bailey's Tavern in Hagers-town. U. LAWRENCE, F. TILGHMAN, O.H. WILLIAMS, J.B. CLAGETT, and John HARRY, Commissioners.
Sale at late res of Jacob KERSHNER, decd, on Conococheague Creek, 7 miles from Hagers-town, personal estate of decd: negro man and wife and 4 chil-dren. Jacob KERSHNER, exr. Also renting farm of 100 a. cleared land adj lands of John T. MASON, Esq.

THE MARYLAND HERALD AND HAGERSTOWN WEEKLY ADVERTISER

Report of Receipts and Expenditures by the Moderator and other Commissioners of Hagers-town. George BOWER, Clk. and Henry LEWIS.
Rent due on lot no. 220 in Williams-Port by Henry CRAFT, senr.
As I intend to leave Martin BAECHTEL's Fulling Mill on 14 Apr, persons who have not yet taken away their cloth, should do so. G. M. CONRADT, Junr.

136. Apr 5 1815
Elected Directors to the Conococheague Bank: Jacob T. TOWSON, Thomas BUCHANAN, Wiliam B. WILLIAMS, Charles HESLETINE, John BOWLES, Matthew VAN LEAR, Michael A. FINLEY and John HOGG.
The following will be supported at the next Election as Directors of the Hagers-town Bank by a large number of stockholders: Frederick DORSEY, Upton LAWRENCE, Jacob SCHNEBLY, Thomas B. HALL, Alexander NEILL, O. H. WILLIAMS, Frisby TILGHMAN, Matthias SHAFFNER.
The following will be supported as Directors of the Hagers-town Bank, at the ensuing election, by a large number of Stockholders: Matthias SHAFFNER, Jacob SCHNEBLY, Henry LEWIS, O. H. WILLIAMS, Upton LAWRENCE, Frederick DORSEY, Jacob ZELLER.
Died Tues 28th ult at the res of Dr. Wm. B. WILLIAMS, near Williams-Port, after a tedious illness, Mrs. Eleanor DAVIS, relict of the late Col. Rezin DAVIS of this town, in her 56th yr.
James M'CULLUGH, has commenced the Weaving business in Funkstown, in the house lately occupied by Charles RICE, on lower corner of the back st, adj Mr. SHAFFER's meadow lots.
Sale of furniture by Elizabeth MILLER, at her dwelling in Potomac st, opposite John WEIS's Blacksmith's Shop.
Henry BECKLEY offers reward for horse missing from stable of Jacob KNODE, junr., near Funkstown.
Samuel PRATHER and James PRATHER admrs of James PRATHER, to sell at res of decd, 1 mile from Big Spring, personal estate of decd.
Michael POTTORF, 1 mile from Isaac BAECHTEL's Mill, offers reward for indented girl named Sarah PECK, about 15 yrs old.
Whereas the subscriber has been heretofore accused of harboring slaves, he hereby gives notice that he is determined from this date to take up and commit to jail all slaves on or near his premises, unless they have passess from their masters. Andrew LIGHTER
Thomas EDWARDS has taken the well known house lately occupied by Samuel PETTIT.
Wm. FITZHUGH will sell on a credit of 6 months, on bond with approved security, a number of slaves, as he contemplates the removal of his family to the state of New York.
List of letters at the Post Office. [Not included here.]

137. Apr 12 1815
Elected Commissioners for Hagers-town for the ensuing year: Henry KEALHOFER, Henry LEWIS, David HARRY, G. H. IRWIN, George EMMERT.
Commissioners of Tax for Wash Co have adjourned 'til Fri. Jacob MYERS, Clk.
House and lot for sale - Henry SHANE.
A. HATFIELD & Co. have commenced Boot and shoemaking business at the house lately occupied by John CRINER, Franklin st, opposite dwelling of Henry MIDDELKAUFF, Hatter.

THE MARYLAND HERALD AND HAGERSTOWN WEEKLY ADVERTISER

William O. SPRIGG, 5 miles from Hagers-town, offers reward for negroes
    CHARLES age 20, and Davy age 19.
As I intend to leave John HERSHEY's Fulling Mill on 1 May, I request persons
    to take away their cloth, &c. John DOWNIN, Junr.
Perry WAYMAN, saddler and harness maker, has removed to house lately
    occupied by Christian LANTZ, opposite Mr. IRWIN's tavern, Potomac st.
Mrs. WAYMAN has on hand an assortment of bonnets.
Sale at res of Stephen DAVIS, decd, on Chew's Farm, 1 mile from Mr. HAUSER's
    mill, personal estate of decd: 14 negroes, horses, cows, furniture, &c.
    Samuel MILLER, admr.
New book store, 214 Market st, near opposite Hanover, st, Baltimore. F. G.
    SCHAEFFER & Co.
J. M'CLEERY to open a new seminary in the house lately occupied by Mr.
    SNEIDER, Franklin st, Hagers-town.

138. Apr 26 1815
James LYNES and Tho. I. FUET, Hagers-town, offer reward for negro fellow
    named DAVID, black-smith.
Sale at dwelling of subscriber, Samuel HERR, in Franklin st, milch cow, sow,
    furniture, and joiner's tools, &c; also his house and lot.
Jacob LIGHTER and Lewis ZEIGLER exrs of Jacob LIGHTER.
Alexander MONTGOMERY, Sharpsburgh, is missing a note of hand given by
    Gabriel NOURSE and Elizabeth CHAPLAIN.
John BRUA exr of Gustavus BRUA, to sell at res of John FEIDT, 2 miles from
    John T. MASON's mill, personal estate of Gustavus Brua, decd: carriage
    nearly new, horses, clock, beds and bedsteads.
Samuel BEAR has commenced watch making business at the shop of David HARRY.
Valentine WACHTEL, 1 mile from Hoffer's mill, has taken up a stray mare.

139. May 3 1815
Married Thurs evening last by Rev RAHAUSER, William WILEN to Miss Sally
    BECKLEY, dau of Henry BECKLEY of Funks-town.
- On Thurs evening last, by Rev T. P. IRVING, Zebulon LOVEALL, to Mrs. Peggy
    KEEFER; and on Sun evening by same, John MARTENY to Miss Sophia SHUGART.
Frederick-town - Died yesterday afternoon, of the prevailing epidemic in his
    68th yr, Dr., Philip THOMAS.
D. SPRIGG, Hagers-town, to rent house where he now occupies.
Persons are forewarned against taking assignment on note dated Dec 19, 1814.
    Andrew PECK.
P. EDWARDS seeks employment as a tutor.
Daniel HARTSOCK, living on John RICE's Farm, 5 miles from Hagers-town,
    offers reward for missing mare.
Jerusalem Manufacturing Co. have erected a wooollen factory in Funkstown.
    Henry & J. I. OHR, D. A & G. W. BOERSTLER.
George KERSHNER admr of Catharine BELCH, late of Wash Co, to sell personal
    estate of decd.
Peter SMITH, Vendue Crier, Hagers-town.
Whereas my wife Susanna has left my bed and board without any just cause, I
    therefore forewarn persons from trusting her on my account. James WARREN

THE MARYLAND HERALD AND HAGERSTOWN WEEKLY ADVERTISER

140. May 10 1815
Married last evening by Rev RAHAUSER, Daniel HANE of Frederick-town, to Miss Maria WOLTZ, dau of late Dr. Peter WOLTZ, of this town.
Thomas BUCHANAN, Assoc Judge of the 5th Judicial Dist, vice Roger NELSON appointed Clerk of Frederick co court.
The powder mill belonging to Messrs, GRAYSON, STULL and WILLIAMS at Bladensburg, yesterday blew up with the loss of the lives of 4 workmen.
Frederick-town - Died last evening, after an illness of about a week, of the prevailing epidemic, John Hanson THOMAS, Esq. of this town.
Sale of Tavern Stand in Cumberland [described in detail]; apply to Henry M'KINLEY in Cumberland, or to S. MAGILL, Editor of the "Allegany Freeman."
The Potomac Co. will receive proposals directed to Joseph BREWER, Treasurer, for erecting locks and opening and completing the navigation of the Antietam Creek, from its mouth to the mill of Messrs. John and George HARRY.
John CRAWFORD, insolvent debtor, to be discharged from imprisonment in county gaol.
Jacob HESS and William TAYLOR, exrs of Peter HOOVER, to sell tract, 207 a., near Shepherds Town.
Joseph CROMWELL, admr of Philemon CROMWELL.

141. May 17 1815
Farmers and Mechanics Bank of Greencastle will be opened at the Banking House in Greencastle. Matthew LIND, Cashier.
William O. SPRIGG, 5 miles of Hagers-town, offers reward for negro man named ANTHONY, age 22 yrs.
Seasoned pine boards for sale - James NOWELL, Williams-Port.
Equity court case - Margaret BAUMWART vs. Richard M'DANIEL. To sell lots mentioned in mortgage from said Richard M'DANIEL to said Margaret Baumwrt.
Meeting of the managers of the Hagers-town Bible Society. F. ANDERSON.

142. May 24 1815
Committed to jail of Wash Co, small light coloured negro man who says he belongs to Mrs. Sarah LANE of Fairfax co, Va, about 22 yrs of age.
Mary RIDENOUR and Adam RIDENOUR admrs of Charles RIDENOUR.
Martin FUNK to carry on wool carding at his farm near the widow FUNK's Mill.
Hugh M'KEE, admr of Hugh M'KEE, to sell at res of decd, Franklin co, Pa, personal estate of decd.
Sale of tract in Berkeley co, Va, 413 a., near Falling Waters or John GREGG's Inn, adj river Potomack, 4 miles down from Williams-Port. Apply to Edward TABB, junr, or John PATTERSON, res thereon. George TABB.
A. KERSHNER, has his machine for manufacturing wool into rolls, near Ogle's Tavern, Cross Roads, in complete order.
Henry C. SCHNEBLY offers reward for red sorrel horse.

143. May 31 1815
Roxbury mills and farm for sale, whereon he now lives, on which is merchant and grist mill, 400 a, upper part of Elkridge. Isaac KNIGHT.
A. M. WAUGH candidate of sheriff.
Samuel MILLER admr of William DAVIS.
Journeyman weaver wanted. John ODERFER, living on John T. MASON's farm, 12 miles from Hagers-town.
Jacob BARR and Jacob ROHRER, Junr, admrs of John ROHRER.

THE MARYLAND HERALD AND HAGERSTOWN WEEKLY ADVERTISER

Samuel MILLER admr of Mary DAVIS.
Samuel MILLER admr of Stephen DAVIS.
Jacob STOVER has taken up a stray horse at his farm in Antrim twp, Franklin co, Pa, 1 mile from Col. Josiah PRICE's res.

144. Jun 14 1815
Shoe store. L. C. WILLIS & F. FECHTIG, have just received large assortment of ladies coloured kid, morocco and leather shoes.
John FREANER and Gera SOUTH have purchased the patent right for the iron bound Boots and Shoes, for the 3rd Election Dist of Wash Co.
Wm. O. SPRIGG offers reward for negro man named JACK, aged about 32 yrs, purchased of Peter M'KIERNAN, for several yrs owned by Leonard COKEN-DAFFER, of George-town (Col.). While in his employ he was accustomed to drive hack carries and is well acquainted in most of the large towns.
Jouneyman weaver wanted. William M'ELROY, Sheperedstown, Va.
Samuel HAWKEN, gunsmith, has commenced business in shop heretofore occupied by his father, Christian HAWKEN.
Jacob BOWER, 3 miles from Hagers-town, offers reward for missing colt.
L. PRICE, late of Hagers-town, has taken that large 3-story brick house in Bedford, lately built by Mr. SCHELL, in which he has opened a tavern.
Found 3 weeks since, cloth coat. Joseph LITTLE, Hagers-town.
Married at Baltimore on Thurs evening last by Rev Dr. KEMP, Thomas B. POTTENGER, Esq. of this co, to Miss Isabella HUDSON of Baltimore.
Frederick-town - Died on night of 7th inst, General Roger NELSON of this place, after a long illness and incredible suffering.
William BRAZIER has opened a Grocery Store on corner of Franklin and Jonathan sts, opposite the dwelling of Christian STEMPLE.
Meeting of the Mount Moriah Lodge, Hagers-town. Tho. COMPTON, Sec'ry.
Sale of negro man, 22 yrs old; can be seen at Matthias SHAFFNER's farm, near Hagers-town. M. MORGAN
Jacob MUCK and John WITMER admrs of Thomas MUCK, to sell at dwelling of decd, his personal estate which includes 60 gallon still with the hogsheads, iron apple mill, carpenter's tools, and other.
Daniel M'COY has taken up a stray mare. Certified by James D. MOORE.

145. Jul 5 1815
Statement by Daniel HUGHES, jun., on behalf of Samuel A. CHEW relative to Mr. O. W. W. STULL. Also involved: Isaac SWEARINGEN, Dr. Hammond
Huntingdon, Cambria & Indiana Turnpike Road - Meeting at house of John BLAIR at Blair's Gap of Allegheny Mountain, Huntingdon Co, Pa, to enter into contracts for making the first five miles of the road commencing at John Blair's. John Blair, Pres. David STEWART, Sec'ry.
Benjamin YOE to sell dwelling where he res, opposite the New Bank.
Committed to jail, as a runaway, stout made negro man, who says he is free; calls himself PETER, says he came from Danville, Va; 5 ft 6 inches high.
Letters remaining at Post Office (Not included here.)

146. Jul 12 1815
Appointments: Otto H. WILLIAMS, Lieut. Col. of the 1st Regt of Cavalry in the first Regt Cavalry Dist., vice Col. TILGHMAN, resigned.
More statements re Samuel A. CHEW, O.H.W. STULL, W. HAMMOND, Isaac S. SWEARINGEN, Daniel HUGHES, Jun.

THE MARYLAND HERALD AND HAGERSTOWN WEEKLY ADVERTISER

William ARMOR, taylor, has received large assortment of wearing apparel.
Sale of property whereon subscriber now lives, in Mercersburg, Pa, two story brick dwelling house, brewery, clear of quit rent. Isaac TAYLOR.
Michael EMMERT and George EMMERT, admrs of Leonard EMMERT, to sell personal estate of decd.
Persons indebted to Antietam Manufacturing co. are requested to call at the Domestic store to pay debts. Wm. DICKEY, Agent for the company.
New Grocery Store in town of Williams-Port, next door to Mr. SACKETT's tavern. M. & D. NEAD.
Committed to jail, small light coloured negro, about 22 yrs old, calls himself George TURNER; says he belongs to Mrs. Sarah LANE of Fairfax co, Va.
John BRADSHAW continues the Spinning wheel and Chair making business in Franklin st, 2nd door from George KREPS, Cabinet Maker.
Abraham HATFIELD has commenced the boot and shoemaking business.
The partnership of James LYNES and Tho: I. FUET, Hagers-town, is dissolved.
James Lynes will carry on the coach making business at the present stand.
Thomas SHUMAN will sell house in Potomack st, and other property.
David HARRY to sell wood work of new wagons.
Journeymen potters wanted. Daniel REICHARD, on Mercersburg road, 3 miles from Hagers-town.
Mantua making - Nancy FLORA, next door to Thomas COMPTON.
Jacob BINKLEY, senr., Hagers-town, has for sale a house now occupied by himself in Washington st, nearly opposite Samuel RIDENOUR's Tan-Yard.

147. Jul 19 1815
Banking house and lot for sale. William HEYSER, Jacob SCHNEBLY, Joseph M'ILHENNY.
Married Thurs last by Rev Thomas P. IRVING, John NUSE, to Miss Mary M'KISSACK, all of this co.
Died in Chambersburg, Wed 5th inst, Thomas KIRBY(?), Esq.
Thomas RAMSAY, Capt, 1st Rifle Regt, and Dr. Henry FIELD from Buffalo, N.Y. passed through this town on Wed, on their way to Washington.
Baltimore - Reward for negro MARY, slave for life, with 5 children, BOB (eldest, age 13), DICK, WILLIAM, DAVY and HANSON. Mary calls herself Mary DAVIS, is handsome dark mulatto. Her husband was apprehended for theft and committed to jail. She has brother, Benjamin GATES near Hagers-town.
Joseph BLACKISTON, living near Stover's Tavern, has negro girl for sale.
Ludwick ZIGLAR, near Baughman's Tavern, has taken up a stray colt.
Sale of 100-200 cleared land including Big Spring from source to its efflux into Potomac, with mill; 500 a.adj. Fayette BALL, Charles Burgess BALL, heirs of B. BALL, decd, exrs of George W. BALL, decd. Leesburg, Loudoun Co, Va.
Sale of Tavern Stand which he has occupied for a number of yrs, Indian Queen Inn, New Market, Frederick Co, Md. James WAGERS.
Philip SPRECHER, 2 miles from Williams-Port, offers reward for colt.
Daniel HUYETT, near Mount Etna Furnace, offers reward for negro DAVID, 18-19 yrs old.
Col. Wm. FITZHUGH has taken up a stray colt. Certified by Robert HUGHES, Justice of the Peace.
Found on road - fur hat, iron tea kettle and sickle and cane. John HYLAND, near Ogle's Cross roads.
Samuel FRANKENBERY, Boot and Shoemaker, continues business in Salisbury st.

THE MARYLAND HERALD AND HAGERSTOWN WEEKLY ADVERTISER

Burr mill stones - Benjamin G. SIDES, has established himself in town of Lisbon, on Turnpike road.

148. Jul 26 1815
Married yesterday by Rev RAHAUSER, James W. C. BAGFORD, to Miss Cassandra BARNETT, all of this co.
O.H.W. STULL condemns Samuel A. CHEW. "I furthermore dare Chew to prove by one solitary respectable certificate, that he himself has in any place he has ever resided, borne a tolerable character." John ASHBURY states Chew said that Mr. SWEARINGEN was too low bred for him. Samuel MILLER attests to Chew's calling Swearingen "you low bred son of a bitch." Wm. HAMMOND and Tho: B. HALL say that the language used by Mr. Stull was harsh and abusive, as it respected Mr. Chew, but not "wicked, outrageous and horrible." [This controversy apparently began when Isaac S. SWEARINGEN arrived at the bank to vote for the Directors of the Bank, in which a misunderstanding arose.] Edmund H. TURNER states he met with Swearingen after election of Directors of Concocheague Bank at Stover's tavern Cross roads.
Controversy between RAGAN and H. DILLMAN. Statement by Wm. HEYSER re a letter John RAGAN had of Upton BEALL, of Montgomery, which Mr. Quantrill said he would not publish until after the election. Thomas QUANTRILL states that he called on Col. Ragan and informed him that his father was circulating a report "very injurious to my election, and that I felt myself bound to publish the transaction from beginning to end." John RAGAN, jun. states that his father was under a wrong impression; also that the statement signed by Thomas Quantrill is partially incorrect.
By decree of Montgomery county court, subscriber will sell at Rockville, 300 a. of William WALLACE, decd, Montgomery co,, decd, 8 miles from George-Town, 3 miles from the Potomac. Apply to Charles WALLACE on the premises, to Robert Wallace at Rockville. Franklin ANDERSON, Hagers-town, Trustee.
Persons having demands against estate of Jacob HESS, Sen'r., decd, are requested to present their accounts to Andrew RINEHART. Henry SHAFER, Andrew RINEHART, Philip GROVE, John MUMMA, heirs of Jacob HESS, sen.
If Henry ATKINSON, son of Michael ATKINSON, late of Manor twp, Lancaster co, Pa, is still living, apply to subscriber, in Emmittsburgh, Frederick co, Md., he may hear of something of interest. Joseph HUGHES, Emmittsburgh.

149. Aug 9 1815
Sale of plantation, 170 a., 2 miles from Hagers-town, adj lands of Upton LAWRENCE, estate of heirs of John RIDENOUR. M. KERSHNER, J. ZELLER, D. SCHNEBLY, W. BOYD, commissioners.
Nathan CROMWELL and Anthony B. MARTIN have entered into partnership in the mercantile business, at their store in house next to Thomas EDWARDS' tavern in Potomac st.
Tavern stand in Funks-town for sale, now occupied by subscriber, Jacob KNOLL. It is weather boarded and painted, contains three rooms on the first floor and 4 on the second, with good kitchen adj and never failing well. On the premises are a large stable, spring house and garden.
Married Sun 6th inst by Rev T. P. IRVING, Isaiah FIELDS to Miss Esther STONEBREAKER, and on the same day John SAGER to Mrs. Mary BEARD.
O.H.W. STULL retracts his denouncement of Daniel HUGHES.
More comments by John RAGAN, sen. re Thomas QUANTRILL.

THE MARYLAND HERALD AND HAGERSTOWN WEEKLY ADVERTISER

New store in Funks-town, on the south west corner of Henry BECKLEY's lot. Dry Goods and groceries and liquors. A. DEGROFFT & W. WILEN.
House for sale in Franklin st, adj Abraham KING's Blacksmith's shop. Nicholas LANTZ, on the premises.
Henry BECKLEY cautions persons from purchasing property that Henry SHANE pretends to claim in Funks-town, which formerly belonged to Henry ZIMMERMAN, as he lately bought said property from the lawful heirs.
Grocery store, late the property of Messrs. NEAD and POSEY. Tho. I. FUET.
Lands for sale in Bethel twp, Bedford co, Pa; apply to Andrew MANN, Jun, in said twp, or to subscriber, David MANN, in Bedford.

150. Aug 16 1815
Died at his seat near George-town, 28th ult, of a fever, Philip Barton KEY, aged 58 yrs, whose talents as a lawyer and politician were unquestionable.
More from Thomas QUANTRILL and John RAGAN, sen.
Committed to jail as a runaway, negro man who calls himself TOM; says he was set free by Col. CARTER of Shenandoah co, Va.
Anthony STARLIPER, Junr, near Parkhead forge, has taken up a stray horse.
Henry B. FUNK, Hagers-town, opening a new store. Dry Goods, Queensware, groceries & liquors.
Journeyman saddler wanted. David WILSON, Hagers-town.
Journeymen tinners and coppersmith wanted in Brownsville, Pa. SHUMAN & HUMRICKHOUSE.

151. Aug 23 1815
More from John RAGAN, jun.
William DELAHUNT, Sprigg's mill, 5 miles from Hagers-town, offers reward for negro man who calls himself Emory SADLER, about 24 yrs of age.
John BRADSHAW, to remove to the Western country this fall, will at his dwelling in Franklin st, Hagers-town, sell all his wheelwright stuff and part of his tools, hogs, and furniture.
The Washington Hussars are ordered to meet the several Regiments in pursuance of Brigade Orders and parade at SACKETT's Tavern in Williams-Port, 12 Sept. John V. SWEARINGEN, Lieut. Com.
Whereas the subscriber has been informed that citizens of Hagers-town feel themselves aggrieved, for the great concourse of negroes that frequently infest the Public Square, especially on the Sabbath day, from the inattention of the magistrates and constables of the town; he will for a moderate compensation, devote part of his time, particularly on Sundays, suppressing this dangerous, odious and abominable practice. Peter SMITH
Purchasers at the sale of personal estate of Jacob BRUMBAUGH, decd, are informed that their notes will be due on Sep 1st.

152. Aug 30 1815
Statement from Thomas B. HALL on the Ragan-Quantrill controversy. Also statement from Thomas QUANTRILL, John RAGAN, Junr.
Sale at dwelling of subscriber in Franklin st, of 8-day clock, and other items. Henry BARKMAN.
Swan Tavern - George DOYLE, has taken that well known tavern stand, lately occupied by Mr. G. H. IRWIN, Potomac st.
New store. Alexander NEILL, & Co. have just received and are opening at their old stand, adj White Swan tavern, a large assortment of merchandize.

THE MARYLAND HERALD AND HAGERSTOWN WEEKLY ADVERTISER

153. Sep 6 1815
Married last evening by Rev RAHAUSER, Thomas I. MUSTIN of George-Town (Dist. of Columbia) to Miss Sophia W. HELM of this town.
Land for sale, 280 a., 3 miles of Hagers-town, part of the estate of Otho SPRIGG, decd, and where Samuel LONG lately lived. Samuel HUGHES, jr.
Coverlet, carpet and table linen weaving. William BIERSHING has commenced the business in Washington st, below George M. HARRY's store.
Flaxseed, clvoerseed and tallow wanted. William BRAZIER, Franklin st.
Fuller wanted. Jacob I. OHR, Funkstown.
Persons are forewarned against taking assignment on note of hand given by Godfrid STUTAMAN to John WINTER. Samuel SHATT.
Petition to lay out road from Hancock-town to Jacob LEANARD's mill and from thence up the river Potomack, to intersect the main road from Hancock-town to Old town at Barnhart's hill.

154. Sep 13 1815
Ordered that the 10th Regt, parade at Carey's Cross Roads. Jenifer T. SPRIGG, Adjt., 10th Regt.
By the power vested in me by my son John BRADSHAW, I will sell at his res, Franklin st, wheel wright stuff, furniture, and other. George BRADSHAW.
Gera SOUTH, Hagers-town, offers reward for apprentice to the Boot and Shoe making business named George COLE, about 19 yrs of age.

155. Sep 20 1815
Married last evening by Rev RAHAUSER, Samuel HAWKEN of this town to Miss Rosanna OSTER, dau of Conrad OSTER, of this co.
Hagers-town Races - George DOYLE, Samuel HAGER, managers.
Silk shawl found on my porch. Robert DOUGLASS.
Josiah PRICE to remove to the Western Country, will sell all the land he holds in Washington Co: tract on which he resides, between Mercersburg and Hagers-town, 7 miles from each, 500-700 a.; tract on which he formerly resided, 600-800 a.; another tract adj the last, 300 a.; another tract of 300 a. and another of 100 a.. Josiah PRICE.
William COLLIER, exr, to sell at late dwelling of Matthias HECKMAN, decd, upper end of Franklin st, two lots on which are a log dwelling house.
Plantation for sale, 1/2 mile from Boonsborough, 189 a.; enquire of Henry LOCHER, junr, living on the premises. George SHAFER, Henry LOCHER, Junr.
John RIDDLE and Joseph PARKS, Chambersburg, have opened a school under the style of "The Chambersburg Union School."
Sale of property of Nicholas SMITH, decd, 3 miles from Hagers-town. Benjamin SWINGLEY, exr.
Plaster land for sale, a farm in Fauquier Co, Va, 450 a. Thomas TURNER, near Haymarket Post Office.

156. Sep 27 1815
Married Sun evening last by Rev RAHAUSER, Nathaniel BATEMAN, to Miss Catharine PROTZMAN, all of this town.
Plantation for sale, 270 a., Antrim twp, Franklin co, Pa, adj lands of Joseph SNIVELY, Christian SHELLY, on which is a stone dwelling house, log house, barn, stone stable and a well. Jacob STEFFY.
Two story brick house in Potomac st for rent, late the property of John MILLER, decd. Jacob SCHNEBLY, Guardian.

THE MARYLAND HERALD AND HAGERSTOWN WEEKLY ADVERTISER

For rent - Tavern property oppisite the New Bank, now in the occupation of Major Robert BAILEY. Henry LEWIS.

157. Oct 4 1815
Martin KERSHNER, John BOWLES, Jacob SCHNEBLY and Edward G. WILLIAMS elected members of the Assembly. Daniel SCHNEBLY is elected Sheriff of Wash co.
Letter remaining at the Post Office [Not included here]
I have taken a lease of Mr. ABERNATHY's & 'Squire HUNTER's houses for term of 3 yrs. I hope to give general satisfaction by keeping cooks and waiters at each house, and entertaining customers at different prices. Robert BAILY.
New Goods - CROMWELL & MARTIN.
Anthony SNYDER and Jacob ASH, Parkhead forge, offer reward for two negro men, JACK, short, thick chunk of a fellow, about 20 yrs old, & LLOYD, stout, well made, about 25 yrs old.
Sale agreeable to last will of late Col. Wm. FITZHUGH, of right of Col. FITZHUGH to 12000 a. in Kentucky, of which 10,000 a. are on Cow Creek and Red River, Clark co. Patented about 1786 and 1808. William FITZHUGH, exr
Sale of cow and furniture - Jacob KNODE.
Alexander BAKER, 6 miles from Hagers-town, has taken up a stray heifer.
Anthony SNYDER, near Parkhead forge, has taken up a stray heifer. Certified by Jeremiah MASON, Justice of the Peace.

158. Oct 11 1815
Died Fri last, after long illness, Joseph STEEL, of this co, in his 29th yr.
Rebecca MALOTT and Theodore MALOTT, admrs of John MALOTT, to sell at res of decd, on Ringgold's Manor, 2 miles from Williams-Port, 2 negro men, 2 negro boys, negro woman, 3 female children, 8 horses, milch cows, steers, hogs, sheep, bee-hives, wagon, wheat fan, ploughs, and other.

159. Oct 18 1815
Married on Thurs last by Rev RAHAUSER, Jacob BRUA, to Miss Margaret ANKONY, all of this co.
- On the same day, by same, Daniel SMITH, of this place, to Miss Rosanna BRUNNER, of Funks-town.
David BARR has purchased the Tan-Yard and stock of Messrs. Charles and Matthias SHAFFNER, Washington st, Hagers-town.
ROHRER & MOTTER, have taken the Tan-yard, heretofore occupied by John HERSHEY, and lately by David BARR.
Persons having claims against Samuel YOUNG, decd (a man of colour), are requested to hand them to George I. HARRY. Judy YOUNG, Rachel YOUNG, Joseph YOUNG.
William S. MOORE, Baltimore, wishes to find articles he forwarded by a wagonner to his son at the Hagers-town Academy June last: a matrass, bedstead, sheets, pillows and cases, towels, &c., directed to I. L. MOORE, care of Col. Otho H. WILLIAMS, Hagers-town. The name of the wagonner is MYSEWINKLE, and at that time drove for Mr. SCHNEBLY, near Sharpsburg.
Merchant mill & saw mill for rent near Conococheague, 6 miles from Hagers-town. Michael HOFFER, 1 mile from the Mills.

THE MARYLAND HERALD AND HAGERSTOWN WEEKLY ADVERTISER

160. Oct 25 1815
Married Tues evening, 17th inst by Rev T. P. IRVING, Samuel BEAR, to Miss Catharine LANTZ, both of this town.
- On Sun evening last, by same, John BOWER, to Miss Mary CRUMBAUCH, both of this co.
John NESBITT admr of Elisabeth NESBITT.
Chancery sale of land, late of Thomas HELM, decd, called "Charlemont," 300 a., two tenements, one containing Stover's Tavern, the other adj. Call on Otho LAWRENCE, Trustee.
Christopher HILLAIRD, opposite Henry MIDDELKAUFF's has received assortment of Fall and Winter Goods, groceries and liquors.
David LITTLE, Hagers-town, offers reward for apprentice to tailoring business named John FEDRAY, about 17, 5 ft 5-6 inches.
Sale at res of John KNODE, 2 miles from Hagers-town, 1 mile from Funks-town, breeding mares, colts, milch cows, sheep, hogs, ploughs and other.
Jacob OLDAKER and Daniel SWITZER, exrs of Nicholas SWITZER, decd, to sell landed estate of decd, 760 a., one tract on main road from Winchester to Morefield and occupied as a Tavern Stand.
Sale of land on West Run, Frederick co, Va, 170 a., with merchant mill and saw mill. Apply to Robert M'CLEAVE on the premises, or Jacob OLDAKER in Hardy co, Va.

161. Nov 1 1815
Married Wed 25th inst, by Rev Robert KENNEDY, William H. MILLER, to Miss Agnes A. PARK, both of Green-Castle, Pa.
- On same day by Rev RAHAUSER, Peter SWORD, to Miss Mary MILLER, both of Wash Co, Md.
Edward FARRON, admr of John FARRON.
Cheap new store - Michael G. KESSINGER, has rented the house of Mrs. SHEARER in Williams-Port.
John EBERT, Hagers-town, offers reward for indented Apprentice to the comb-making business named Peter WAGGONER, about 19 yrs of age, 5 ft 7 inches, slim, fair complexion, down look, very hollow eyed with small scar above one of them. He was seen at his brother's (John WAGGONER) on Ray's Town Branch, near Huntingdon, Pa. It is expected that he and another brother, who lived at Jacob BELTZHOOVER's near Pittsburgh, will make their way towards the western country or Virginia.
John NEWSON, 1 mile from Mr. CHARLTON's tavern, 2 miles from Big Spring, offers reward for missing filly.
Sale of Tavern stand now occupied by subscriber, next door to the Post Office, Hagers-town. Christian FECHTIG.
Margaret COMPTON, William-Port, offers reward for stout negro girl named Lydia PILES, about 18 yrs old, rusty complexion, very rough skin, came originally from Prince William Co, Va.
Partnership of Matthias NEAD & Daniel NEAD is dissolved. Matthias Nead continues business in Grocery line at same stand, next door to Sackett's tavern.

162. Nov 8 1815
H. HOGMIRE, Hardtime Mills, having erected a fulling mill and engaged experienced workmen, to carry on the business of fulling, dying and dressing merino and country cloth.

THE MARYLAND HERALD AND HAGERSTOWN WEEKLY ADVERTISER

163. Nov 15 1815
Married Thurs evening last by Rev KURTZ, David SCHRYOCK, of Westmoreland co, Pa, to Miss Sarah Ann WILSON, of this town.
Frederick-town - On Fri 3d inst, Edward OWINGS was murdered by his own slaves, 6 in number.
Isaac BEAR, 1 mile from Ogle's Tavern, Cross roads, has taken up stray shoats.
John CARR, Senr., 2 miles from Williams-Port, has taken up a spotted shoat.
Daniel REICHARD, 3 miles from Hagers-town, has taken up a stray heifer.
Barton BEAN, living on the farm of John M. DAVISON, decd, 2 miles from Gordon's tavern, to sell work horses, colts, milch cows, cattle sheep, hogs, farm wagon, ploughs and other.
Hagers-town Academy - The Board of Trustees have appointed Aaron BEACH to superintend the English department.
Gerhart BUCHWALTER forewarns persons from taking away sand from his land.
George LEFEVER admr of John LEFEVER, to sell at dwelling of decd, 5 miles from Williams-Port, personal estate of decd: negro woman and her 2 children, horses, cows, cattle, sheep, hogs, farming utensils, wheat, rye and corn, hay, furniture; tract of 180 a., chiefly river bottom, lately occupied by John Lefever, decd.

164. Nov 22 1815
I gave formal power of atty to Thomas M'GEE, of Nelson co, Ky, on 21 Aug last, to transact business for me in Maryland, to collect money or other property, and sell lots in Hagers-town. This power is hereby revoked. Peter BRINER.
John RAMSBURGH, Fishing Creek, 9 miles from Frederick-town, 4 miles from Johnson's Furnace, Frederick co, offers reward for missing mare, saddle and blind bridle.
Schoolmaster wanted. Jacob FIREY, 2 miles from Gen. S. RINGGOLD's.

165. Nov 29 1815
Married Thurs last at Green-Castle, by Rev LIND, Christopher G. STANGE, of Phila, to Miss Mary WILKINSON of this place.
- On Sun evening last by Rev RAHAUSER, George WEIS, Cabinet Maker, to Miss Mary KREPS, all of this town.
Died Sat evening last, Mrs. Ann BRADSHAW, wife of George BRADSHAW of this town, in her 62nd yr.
Sale of land, 400 a., on main road from the Green Spring to Pa, 3 miles from Parkhead forge, with log dwelling house and barn, stone spring house. It will be shewn by George or Jacob DUNN, living thereon. Christian HAGER.
The Editor of the Political Examiner, wishes to dispose of his Printing Office and Establishment. Frederick-town.
Persons are forewarned against taking assignment on a note given to Alexander M'CLELLAND. Jacob RODRAUFF.
John HERR admr of Adam BOROFF, to sell at dwelling of decd, 1 mile of Williams-Port, personal property of decd.
Sale of bank stock by order of Orphan's Court - Jacob JONES, admr of George ANKONY.
Ann BERRY to sell at the farm where Peter RENCH formerly lived, 1 mile from Sprigg's mill: horses, cows, hogs, wagon, ploughs, farming utensils.
Letter carrier wanted at the Hagers-town Post Office. Wm. KREPS, P.M.

THE MARYLAND HERALD AND HAGERSTOWN WEEKLY ADVERTISER

166. Dec 6 1815
Married Wed 22d ult by Rev Tho. P. IRVING, Charles LITTLE, to Miss Elizabeth
   WATSON, both of this co.
- On Thurs last by same, Owen M'CARTY to Miss Ally RICE, both of Penn.
- On Sunday last at Frederick-town, by Rev David SCHAEFFER, Jacob MOTTER, of
   this place, to Miss Elizabeth DULL, of Frederick-town.
Trustee's sale, by decree of Washington co court, real estate of Leonard
   BEVENS, decd, lying on Licking Creek, 3 miles above Parkhead Forge, adj
   lands of Isaac BAECHTEL, called Leonard's Rest, 500 a. Enquire of Mr.
   Bevens residing thereon or Isaac Baechtel, adj. U. LAWRENCE, Trustee.
Sale of tract, 126 a., Bedford co, Pa, adj the Baptist Meeting Houses, 2
   miles from Hancock town. David SNYDER, living on the premises.
Robert COWEN, living on farm adj Joseph SPRIGG's, 5 miles from Williams-
   Port, removing shortly to the state of Ohio, to sell a few negroes.
Purchaser at the sale of Major C. CARROLL's Negroes, are notified that their
   notes are due Jan next. Elie BEATTY, Cash'r.
Committed to jail as runaway, bright mulatto man, who calls himself WILLIAM;
   about 22 yrs of age; says he belongs to Obed WAITE of Winchester, Va.
Committed to Jail as a runaway, negro man who calls himself DUNMORE, about
   23 yrs of age; says he belongs to Thomas BOWEN, near the White post, Fred-
   erick co, Va.
Eve NICHOLL to sell two story log house with kitchen adj, 2 doors from
   William BRAZIER.
Sale of 2-story log house in Franklin st, near opposite the dwelling of Rev
   RAHAUSER, kitchen adj. Jonas CRAMER, on the premises.
Two story house and lot in Antietam st, for rent, now occupied by Christian
   LANTZ. Apply to David HARRY or Theobald EICHELBERNER, Trustees.
Arthur BECK forewarns against taking assignment on note given to Alexander
   M'CLELLAND.

167. Dec 13 1815
Wm. HAMMOND, Hagers-town, offers reward for negro man who calls himself Noah
   YOUNG, about 35 yrs old, property of Col. Frisby TILGHMAN.
Martin KERSHNER, near Ogle's Tavern (Cross roads) has taken up a stray cow.
Sale of house and 2 lots in Funks-town, opposite dwelling of Dr. Christian
   BOERSTLER; also 2 milch cows, hogs, cart, hay, furniture. Patrick M'LAAR.
Conococheague Factory - John DOWNIN, junr. has again commenced the Fulling
   and Dying Business, at his former stand, 6 miles from Hagers-town.
Antietam Woollen Manufacturing Co. & Henry SWEITZER have entered into
   Co-Partnership, under the firm of Henry Sweitzer & Co. Henry SHAFER,
   Pres't, Henry Sweitzer.
William DILLAHUNT, 5 miles from Hagers-town, has taken up a stray cow.
Whereas my wife Barbara HAMMEL, has left my bed and board, without any just
   cause, persons are hereby cautioned against trusting her on my account.
   George HAMMEL.

168. Dec 20 1815
Sale of 2 wagon, and set of horses - William S. COMPTON.
Sale according to last will of Paul VERNER, decd, of all personal and real
   estate, including tract of land, at his late res near mouth of Opeckon,
   Potomack river, 2 miles from the Falling Watters, 200 a. with dwelling

THE MARYLAND HERALD AND HAGERSTOWN WEEKLY ADVERTISER

house, log barn, distillery; negro woman, furniture, and other - George SPERO, John GREGG, exrs.
Sale of 2-story stone house, on west side of Potomac st, at present in the occupancy of Nathan CROMWELL. Samuel HAMMETT.
Sale of tract of land, 360 a., adj place where Davis's Mill is on (now John GRAVES') 1/2 mile from Hancock-Town. Josias CARTER.
Journeyman cabinet maker wanted - George KREPS

169. Dec 27 1815
Married Sun last by Rev KURTZ, Frederick Benjamin Otto KINSELL of this town, to Miss Mary Magdalena YOUNG of this co.
John A. DONALDSON, Hagers-town, offers reward for negro man named Nace LENUM, 5 ft 10 inches, 24-25 yrs old, formerly property of Mr. SPALDING of city of Washington, sold by him to Mr. HARGETT of Frederick co. He worked at blacksmith trade at Navy yard, Washington.
Henry LANDIS, 4 miles from Hagers-town, offers reward for negro man named Harry THOMSON, but sometimes calls himself Harry GREEK, about 32 yrs old.
Peter SHENABERGER, offers reward for horse stolen from a wagon at Fechtig's tavern, Hagers-town.
Mary ALTER admr of Samuel ALTER, gives notice that the notes given by purchasers at the sale of Samuel Alter, are past due.
Ignatius DRURY, on Potomac river, 4 miles below Williams-Port, offers reward for mare missing from Barton BEAN's stable, 7 miles from Green-Castle, Pa.
John M'LANAHAN, Preceptor, living near Col. Josiah PRICE's, and contiguous to William HUNTER's, Franklin co, Pa, intending to remove to state of Tennessee, in March next, offers for sale his share of the farm belonging to the heirs of James M'LANAHAN, decd.
Michael G. KESSINGER, Williams-Port, offers reward for missing mare.
Jonathan HAGER to let house now occupied by Samuel HAGER as a Tavern, 2 doors from Messrs. John and Hugh KENNEDY's Store.

John M'LANAHAN, Preceptor, living near Col. Josiah PRICE's, and contiguous to William HUNTER's, Franklin co, Pa., intending to remove to state of Tennessee, in March next, offers for sale his share of the farm belonging to the heirs of James M'LANAHAN, DECD.
Michael G. KESSINGER, Williams-Port, offers reward for missing mare.
Jonathan HAGER to let house now occupied by Samuel HAGER as a Tavern, 2 doors from Messrs. John and Hugh KENNEDY's store.

HAGERS-TOWN GAZETTE

170. Jan 8 1811
Leonard SHAFFER, Williamsport, has taken that large and convenient warehouse near the mouth of Conococheague creek and is ready to receive flour, whisky, &c. on storage; and if requested, will have it delivered in George-Town.
Contracts solicited for bridge across the Conococheague creek at Williamsport - John CROSS, L. SHAFFER, John HOGG, managers.

HAGERS-TOWN GAZETTE

171. Jan 15 1811 - Charles M'CALLEY cautions persons against receiving a note drawn in favor of William JOBSON for $1220.

172. Jan 22 1811
Dissolution of partnership of Thomas SHUMAN and Charles MOORE; coopersmith business to be carried on by SHUMAN.
House for rent, presently occupied by Mr. FECHTIG as a shoemaker's shop-Peter ARTZ.
Peter HUMRICKHOUSE, Jr., Hagers Town, offers reward for indented girl Ann Thompson, about 14; had on dark brown coating frock and a lead coloured bonet.
Moses KNIGHT, a freeman of colour, living in the south Mountain, about 1 mile from Hays's saw mill, has taken up a stray mare.

173. Feb 5 1811 - Elected officers of the Hagers Town Academy: Otho H. WILLIAMS, Pres; William HEYSER, Treas,; Thomas B. HALL, Sec'ry; commissioners in managing the subscriptions: O. H. WILLIAMS, Fredk. DORSEY, Chris: HAGER

174. Feb 12 1811 - Died las eve, about 9 o'clock, after a short illness, Capt. Daniel STULL, an old and respectable inhabitant of this co.

175. Feb 19 1811 - Peter FAWBLE, Balt, offers reward for negro woman Lucy; supposedly has a husband in Hagers Town.

176. Feb. 26 1811
To sell in pursuance of the last will of Nicholas LOWE, Wash Co, decd, late dwelling house of decd, near the Big Spring, and negroes - George LOWE & James D. MOORE, exr.
Arthur JOHNSTON, HAGERS TOWN, seeks apprentice to the watch and clock making business
Alexander NEILL, Hagers Town, has removed his store to house lately occupied by Christian ARTZ, 3 doors from his former stand, nearly opposite Mr. SEITZ's tavern.
Dissolution of partnership of John HARRY and George HARRY of M., Hagers Town; business will be conducted in the future by George HARRY of M.
George SHOWMAN has taken up stray yearlings.

177. Mar 5 1811
Farm for sale, 600 a., 1/2 mile of Sharpsburg; John GOOD, Esq. on the place will shew the same; apply to Wm. McMECHEN, Balt City for terms.
Potters & Moulders wanted at Aetna Furnaces; apply to Wm. CONWAY at the Furnaces or the subscribers in Baltimore-town, William H. DORSEY and John E. DORSEY
Christian BORSTLER, Funks-Town, cautions persons from harboring his black man Ned (known as Kapp's Ned) who has habit of leaving home without permission. On Sundays he has liberty to visit his wife.

178. Mar 12 1811
Died at his place near Sharpsburgh, on 2d inst. William GOOD Senr. aged 72, after a short illness.

HAGERS-TOWN GAZETTE

The mill and 14 a. of land, late the property of Daniel STULL, decd, will be let for three years - Elie BEATTY, collector.
Wm. KREPS hs removed his store to new brick dwelling house in Washington st, nearly opposite Mr. BELTZHOOVER's tavern - dry goods, groceries and queensware; the post office is removed to the same house - Wm. KREPS, Post Master
Sale of tract in Wash Co, 3 miles of Hagers Town, 650 a. - WM. DOWNEY, Hagers Town
For sale - lands on the Ohio - Elie WILLIAMS, Hagers Town.

179. Mar 19 1811
George W. DAVIS, Franklin Co, Pa, cautions persons from taking notes given to James STERRETT (miller) of Wash Co.
Sale at res of Daniel STULL, decd of negroes, horses, grain, furniture, trace of 100 a. and other; farm will be shewn by Mr. J. I. STULL, living on the premises
William BROWN intending to remove his printing office after the first of April into one of the rooms lately erected by Mr. HAGER in Washington St, will let the house he at present occupies.
Land for sale, real estate of late Lewis BEALMER, for payment of his debts, part of estate in Montgomery Co - Harry W. DORSEY, Robt. P. MAGRUDER, Basil WATERS, Montgomery Co.

180. Mar 29 1811
Married Sun by Rev. RAHAUSER, Benjamin YOE of Hagers Town to Mrs. Mary HELM, of Williamsport.
Married same evening by Rev. SHAFER, William BRENTLINGER of Hagers Town, to Miss Charlotte FOUTZ, of Wash Co.

181. Apr 2 1811
Dissolution of partnership of Christian FECHTIG and Louis R. FECHTIG, of firm of C. FECHTIG and son.
George HAMMER has removed from his former stand into house lately occupied by Mr. FREANER, and next door to Seitz's tavern where he intends to carry on the tayloring business
William WILLIS, boot & shoe maker, has removed to house lately occupied by Adam LEPARD, in Potomac St., nearly opposite to Mr. MILLER's Appothecary shop.
James STERRETT, Wash Co, answers earlier advertisement signed by George W. DAVIS, Franklin Co, regarding sale of a stud horse.

182. Apr 9 1811
Died Tues. 2d inst., after a shore but painful illness, at his res near Hagers Town, Christian LANTZ.
Died Thurs 4 ins, Rev. John HERSHEY, in 71st year of his age; his affliction was long and tedious; left a number of relations and friends.
John GOOD, Sharpsburg, adm of William GOOD, decd, to sell personal property of decd.
Thos. C. BRENT and Ann DYCKE, Hancock Town adm of Valentine DYCKE.
Cash for negroes - enquire at Mr. C. HAWKENS, Hagers Town.

HAGERS-TOWN GAZETTE

Alexander STEPHENS, Mill Creek, Berkley Co, Va. offers reward for negro man named Bill, formerly property of Cephas BELL of Martinsburg, about 5 ft 8 inch, fond of liquor.

183. Apr 16 1811
Died Sun last, after a severe and lingering illness, in the 19th year of his age, Archibald VANLEAR, son of Matthew VANLEAR, Esq. of this co; he was near the completion of his education.
Letters of Collectorship have been obtained on the personal estate of Daniel STULL, decd - Elie BEATTY, Collector.
William B. WILLIAMS adm of Thomas WILLIAMS requests claims be produced.
David WILSON, saddle & harness maker, has removed to new building erected by Mr. HAGER in Washington St.
Charles G. BOERSTLER, Williams Port, intends quitting the mercantile business, offers for sale his stock in trade; also seeks an assistant miller.
Farm for sale on which he now resides on Potomac river, Wash Co, 8 miles above Hancocktown, 225 a. - David MISKIMIN, Hancock-town.
Samuel BAYLY, Hagers Town to petition for relief from debts.

184. Apr 23 1811 - Samuel BAYLY, Hagers Town, intends to open a school in back part of house which he at present occupies, confined to 20 pupils - $4.00 per quarter.

185. Apr 30 1811 - The firm of John I. STULL and John S. WILLIAMS has just opened as commission merchants at their warehouse and wharf at the end of High St in George-town, Columbia.

186. May 7 1811
Abraham MAYER, Hagers Town, has purchased well known inn formerly occupied by Mr. BRUMBAUGH and provided himself with a complete assortment of the best liquors, steady & sober ostler.
John STALLSMITH, boot and shoemaker, has commenced business, in shop formerly occupied by Mr. YOE, and at present occupied by William ARMOR, in Washington St, a few doors below Messrs John and George HARRY's Store.

187. May 14 1811
BEECHER & NEAD have formed a co-partnership - groceries and liquors.
Louis R. FECHTIG, ladie's shoe manufacturer, has commenced the business in Washington St, south of the Court House.

188. May 21 1811
Married Thurs evening inst by Rev. BOWER, Perry WAYMAN of Fred Co, to Miss Juliet HERBERT, of Hagers Town.
Work has commenced on the Williams-port Bridge; subscribers to pay immediately to Jacob T. TOWSON, Esq. Williams-port, 1/2 of their subscriptions.

189. May 28 1811
Married Tues evening last by Rev. RAHAUSER, George I. HARRY, merchant of this place, to Miss Amelia KNODE, dau of Jacob KNODE, of Funk's-town.
Gabriel NOURSE, Sharpsburg, offers reward for horse which eloped from stable of Christian FECHTIG.

HAGERS-TOWN GAZETTE

John WITMER and Peter NEWCOMER, exr, to sell at late res of Samuel NEWCOMER, decd, personal property of decd (listed).

190. Jun 4 1811
Furs & Peltries will be offered at auction at the stores of the Superintendent of Indian Trade.
William DENEAL, near Fairfax Court House, offers reward for negro woman named Hannah, about 22, chunky made, seen in Boonsborough about 2 weeks ago.

191. Jun 11 1811
WILLIS & CRAWFORD have entered into partnership in business of boot & shoe making, at their shop lately occupied by Adam LEPARD, in Potomac St.
Adam RIDANOUR, at the Broad Ford, Conococheague, offers reward for bound girl named Phebe HOLBERT, about 17, pock pitted, slender made; had on calico dress and barefoot.
Fleecy Dale Factory - Matthew BROWN, Fred Co, has completed his cloth factory (operation described).

192. Jun 25 1811 House and half lot for sale where he now res in Washington St, Hagers Town; has stable, smoke house and never-failing pump of good water at the door - George SHALL

193. Jul 2 1811
Benjamin LEWIS and William HITE exr of John HITE, to sell lands of decd in Rockingham Co, Va.
Andrew HERSHEY and John HERSHEY, exr of John HERSHEY.

194. Jul 16 1811
"Surviving partner" controversy, involving Matthew BROWN; John FRICK, Baltimore; David WINCHESTER; William NORRIS; Henry PAYSON; Joel MORGAN; Jacob NORRIS.

195. Jul 23 1811
Allegany Co - John BURBRIDGE, Old-town, certifies that John M. DAVIDSON has taken up a stray gelding.
Sale at house of Adam ROBB, tavern keeper, Rockville, the whole of the real estate of late William Prater WILLIAMS of said co, 800-1000 a. - Edward O. WILLIAMS, agent for the heirs.

196. Aug 6 1811
Dissolution of partnership of R. PINDELL, F. DORSEY and A. HANENKAMPF; Roderick DORSEY to collect for them; Dr. PINDELL having decline the practice of physic and contemplating to remove to Kentucky as soon as he can wind up his business; DORSEY and HANENKAMPF to be joined by Doctor William HAMMOND into partnership.
Charles G. BOERSTLER, at General Ringgold's Mill, seeks to hire distiller.
Isaac PANCAKE and John WRIGHT, living near Romney, Hampshire Co, Va, offer reward for two negro men, John & Lewis.
Daniel SCHNEBLY and Isaac S. WHITE, exr of Jacob RENCH, to sell personal property of decd: cattle, farming utensils.

HAGERS-TOWN GAZETTE

197. Aug 13 1811
10th Regiment to meet for exercises at Cary's Cross Roads - Charles G. BOERSTLER, Lt. Col.
Election for electors of the Senate of the State - Matthias SHAFFNER, Sheriff.

198. Aug 20 1811
Merino ram lambs for sale - O. H. WILLIAMS, U. LAWRENCE
Tract for sale adj property of Abraham HORSLER and Nicholas RIDANOUR - St. Leger NEAL or William CAPES.

199. Aug 27 1811
John ADAMS has opened tavern in Boonsborough at the sign of General Washington.
Catharine MILLER and George SMITH exr of David MILLER.
Sale of plantation now occupied by Abraham DITTO, on west side of Conococheague, 500 a. - M. & Wm. VANLEAR.
Matthew VANLEAR has taken up a stray cow.

200. Sep 3 1811 - Isaac McPHERSON, No. 54, Fayette St, Balt, has good assortment of bolting cloth.

201. Sep 10 1811
Thomas CRAMPTON certifies that Matthias RHODES has taken up a stray mare.
William REYNOLDS has taken up a stray steer.

202. Sep 17 1811 - Hezekiah EASTON of Wash Co has taken up a stray mare.

203. Sep 14 1811 - Thomas JONES, Senior, forwarns persons from taking assignment of notes given to Nicholas SWOPE.

204. Oct 8 1811
John BARR forewarns persons from taking assignment on note given to John DARBY.
John SHACKLETT living in Fauquier Co, Va, near Ashby's Gap, offers reward for negro man Nace, 30 yrs of age, 6 ft.

205. Oct 15 1811
Married Tues evening last by Rev. DUHAMEL, Moses TABBS, Esq. to Miss Jane CARROLL, dau of Charles CARROLL, Esq. of this town.
New stoves - John & Joseph M'ILHENNY.
Williams-Port Races - M.H. SACKETT, Jacob BROSIUS, Thos. EDWARDS, managers.

206. Oct 22 1811
Joseph CHAPLINE, near Sharpsbourgh, cautions persons from hunting with dogs or gun upon his inclosures.
J. STALLSMITH, boot & shoe maker, has removed his shop to house lately occupied by Messrs, WILLIS & CRAWOFORD.

207. Nov 5 1811 - Matthew BROWN, Fleecy Dale Factory, Fred Co, offers farm & mill for sale on Big Bennett's Creek, 3 miles by Buckey's town.

HAGERS-TOWN GAZETTE

208. Nov 19 1811
Rye Whisky for sale - I. S. WHITE or Danl. SCHNEBLY.
George KREPS, cabinet maker, has commenced business at the shop formerly occupied by his father Martin KREPS in Franklin St, Hagers Town.
William YATES, Justice of the Peace, certifies that Joseph HUNTER has taken up a stray horse.

209. Dec 3 1811
Salt-petre for sale - Frederick MILLER, Druggist and Apothecary.
Jos. CARLTON, Agent, George-Town, gives notice that a person will attend Mr. BELTZHOOVER's Tavern to receive prizes of the Potomac and Shennandoah Lottery.

210. Dec 10 1811 - Moulders & Potters wanted at the Aetna Furnaces, about 6 miles from Baltimore - Wm. H. DORSEY, John E. DORSEY.

211. Dec 24 1811 - Washington Tavern for sale, in Williams-Port, at present in the tenure of Thomas EDWARDS - Benjamin YOE, Hagers Town.

212. Dec 31 1811
Married Thurs evening last by Rev. KENNEDY, Joseph BRUMBAUGH, to Miss Elizabeth ANGLE, dau of Joseph ANGLE, Franklin Co, Pa.
Sale of tract of 8 a., adj Rohrer's addition to Hagers Town - William REYNOLDS.

213. Jan 7 1812 - Tavern to rent in Potomac St, at present in the tenure of John SEITZ; has 10 rooms, besides large ball room, kitchen, cellars, wash house, smoke house &c. Good stables and sheds, pump of water at the door - Christian LANTZ.

214. Jan 14 1812 - Married Tues evening last by Rev. SCHAUFFER, John ROBERTSON, merchant to Miss Mary HARRY, dau of late Jacob HARRY, all of this town.

215. Jan 21 1812 - Sale of 300 a. - David DUNHAM, Monogahala Co, Va; apply to subscriber or Jacob LYMAN or Moses KNIGHT, whose lands adj the plantation.

216. Jan 28 1812 - Plantation of 267 a. for sale on Potomac 1 mile below McPherson and Brian's iron works - John WADE, living on the premises.

217. Feb 4 1812 - Thomas M'CARDELL, Hagers Town, wants an overseer to superintend a small farm.

218. Feb 18 1812
Christian HERSHEY and John HERSHEY exr of Isaac HERSHEY, to sell personal property of decd at late res.
John WITMER and Peter NEWCOMER, exr of Samuel NEWCOMER, requests that claims be exhibited.

HAGERS-TOWN GAZETTE

219. Mar 3 1812
On Fri last a dinner was given to Col. John P. BOYD by the citizens of this
place in respect to his undaunted conduct at the battle of Tippacanoe.
Alexander M'DONALD, res Ashville, Buncome Co, NC, offers reward for 2 negro
men, who ran away while he was on his way home from Martinsburgh, Va; one
once belonged to Major CARR and the other to Mr. DAVIS, both of Wash Co.
Journeymen plasterers wanted - Michael WAGGENER, Greencastle.
William WILSON, Prospect-Hill, wishes to sell tract in eastern part of Hampshire Co, Va, known as Bloomery Mills and Sherrard's Store, 200 a.

220. Mar 10 1812 - Book-binding - Samuel B. DAVIS, Hagers Town

221. Mar 17 1812
Grocery store - Matthias NEAD, continues business at the old stand, formerly
Beecher & Nead.
Samuel HAGER, Hagers Town, wants apprentices to the saddle & harness
business

222. Mar 24 1812
Died at York, Pa, on Wed last, after a very short illness, George F.
HAUGMAN, formerly of this place.
Abraham FORCE continues to carry on the hatting business at his present
stand, 2 doors above Messrs. P. ARTZ and EMMERT's Store, in Potomac
street.
Horse, Young Florizell, will stand for mares at James MUIR's Tavern in
Williams Port and John FREANER's stabe in Hagers Town, near the jail -
Stephen ENOS

223. Mar 31 1812
Office of the Hagers Town Gazette to remove to house lately occupied by
Jonathan HAGER in Potomac st, a few doors from Mr. FERGUSON's store and
directly opposite German printing office.
Officers and non commissioned officers attached to 1st Regiment Cavalry
District to meet - Frisby TILGHMAN, Lieu't Col.
Partnership of George HARRY & Co. dissolved, to be carried on under the firm
of John & George HARRY.
Jacob GILBERT, living in Antrim township, Franklin Co, Pa, 7 miles from
Hagers Town, near Cunkleton's mill offers reward for missing mares.

224. Apr 7 1812
Died 16th ult after a short illness, Mrs. Sarah CRESAP, wife of Joseph
CRESAP, of Allegany Co, Md, in 54th yr of her age, mbr of Meth Episc
Church 30 yrs.
WILLIS, boot & shoe maker, continues at his old stand.
First installment of 1/4 becomes due on Antietam Loan, payable at the Hagers
Town Bank - J. THOMPSON, Superintendent P.C.
Jacob LITER, living near Baughman's tavern, on road leading to York, offers
reward for apprentice to blacksmith business names John HENTZELMAN, about
18, 4 ft 4-5 inch; had on black cloth coat and olive velvet pantaloons and
waistcoat.

225. Apr 24 1812 - Wanted immediately - 2-3 journeymen saddlers - Samuel
HAGER

HAGERS-TOWN GAZETTE

226. Apr 21 1812
Meeting of officers of 24th Regt. M. M. - John Ragan, Jr., Lt. Col. Comdt. 24th Regt.
John BRADSHAW, wheelwright and chair maker, has commenced business in Washington St.
John LANE, wool stapler, for Fleecy Dale Wool-Factory, offers highest market price for clean Merino or country wool; carding will be done, oiled with clear oil - Charles MOSS, manager; fulling, dyeing & dressing by Andrew QUIGLEY, clothier.
Meeting of cordwainers of Hagers Town, held at Mr. FECHTIG's tavern, adopting certain prices for their work (schedule given) - John FREANER, George BRENDLE, John HOFFMAN, Gera SOUTH, William WILLIAM, John STALLSMITH, Fred'k FECHTIG.

227. Apr 28 1812 - John WITMER, living on Beaver creek, about 6 miles from Hagers Town, has taken up a stray horse.

228. May 5 1812
The Washington Hussars and American Blues ordered to parade in squadron at Hagers Town - Otho H. WILLIAMS, Major, 1st Regimental Cavalry District.
Officers of the 1st and 2nd Battalion, 10th Regiment, M. M. to meet - John BLACKFORD, Daniel MALOTT, Majors.
Benjamin FREED, living in Montgomery township, Franklin Co, 3 miles of Greencastle, offers reward for missing mare; bring to him or Mr. HOCHLANDER's Tavern in Greencastle.
Sale agreeable to will of Jacob RENCH, Wash Co, decd, at Coffee-house in Hagers Town, part of real estate consisting of following: lot of 11 acres adj lands of Daniel RENCH, the heirs of John RENCH, Junr., decd, and Jacob YOUNG; lot adj lands of Jacob YOUNG, and heirs of John RENCH, Jun., decd; land conveyed by Peter RENCH to Jacob RENCH and a conveyance from Charles CARROLL, Esq. to Jacob RENCH and part conveyd by John BUCHANAN, Esq. as trustee for John RENCH's estate to Jacob RENCH - Daniel SCHNEBLY and Isaac S. WHITE, exr.

229. May 12 1812
10-12 youths of either sex to be taken by indenture to learn the superfine broad-cloth business; apply to Matthew BROWN, proprietor of Fleecy Dale Factory, or Charles MOSS, Manager, Fred. Co.
John WELLS, Druggist & Apothecary, has commenced business in the house lately occupied by John P. HERR, next door to BAYLY's tavern.
James BROWN & Co. are now receiving and opening at their store (corner of the Globe Tavern) in Shepherd-Town, an assortment of merchandize.
Andrew NEWCOMER, about 6 miles from Hagers Town, on road leading to Frederick, near FUNK's mill, has taken up a stray horse.

230. May 19 1812
Hat manufactory - KEEN, KAIGHN & Co., established on Washington st.
James M. CRESAP will give the use of a shop and tools free of rent to any sober industrious blacksmith who will carry on the business; it adjoins his mill near Old-town, Allegany Co.

HAGERS-TOWN GAZETTE

231. May 26 1812 - MAYER & IRWIN, have commenced business in house formerly occupied by Alexander NEILL, next door to Jacob SAILOR's tavern, where they intend keeping assortment of Queen's & Glass Ware, also groceries & liquors.

232. Jun 16 1812 - William WILLIS, Hagers Town, requests payment of debts.

233. Jun 23 1812 - Charles M'DOWELL, Bedford, offers reward for apprentice to the printing business, named John PATTON, 19, 5 ft 6-7 inch, stout made, surly look, a little marked with the small pox.

234. Jun 30 1812 - Sale of 7 negroes - Thomas QUANTRILL

235. Jul 7 1812
Died Fri 3d inst, after a short illness, in 95th year of her age, Mrs. Mary PINDELL.
Ezra SALIFER certifies that John SHUEY has taken up a stray mare.
Hezekiah BOTELAR cautions that a young man who calls himself Benedict ATHUM, supposed to be about 24 yrs of age, 5 ft 10-11 inch, fair smooth complexion, has lost a part of his fore finger on the left hand, left the house of the subscriber in Pleasant Valley, about 7 miles from Harpers Ferry, Wash Co and took a bay mare, property of subscriber and pair of saddle bags, property of Daniel ORTMAN.

236. Jul 14 1812
Joseph HUGHES, Emmittsburg, offers reward for gelding missing from stable.
Letter from Benjamin GALLOWAY, Hagers Town, against Thomas GRIEVES and the Maryland Herald.
Carpenter wanted to finish steeple on German Lutheran Church in this place - David HARRY, D. EICHELBERGER, Christ. EMBICH.

237. JUL 18 1812
John CRAWFORD had commenced the boot and shoemaking business at the stone house on corner of public square.
Benjamin WILLIAMS has rented Washington Hotel in Patrick st opposite Mrs. KIMBOLL's.

238. Aug 4 1812 - Fancy Goods at their store in Shepherds-town - James BROWN & CO.

239. Aug 11 1812
More from Benjamin GALLOWAY regarding the Democratic "caucus squad."
Volunteers attached to my company are ordered to repair to my quarters for purpose of being uniformed - Thomas QUANTRILL, Capt., Hagers Town.

240. Sep 1 1812
Taxes & Officers fees are due - M. SHAFFNER, Sheriff & Collector.
Zachariah SHUGERT, wheel-wright and chair maker, carries on business in Potomac St.
George SMITH certifies that John STOVER, living near Mr. EINGLER's store, has taken up a stray mare.

HAGERS-TOWN GAZETTE

241. Sep 8 1812
Christian HENSMINGER and Eve MARSHALL adm of James MARSHALL.
John NICHOLSON, living near Sharpsburgh, has taken up a stray mule.

242. Sep 15 1812
Candidates for Gen. Assembly; Robert HUGHES, Otho H. STULL, Thos. C. BRENT, John BLACKFORD.
Tavern stand for sale in town of St. Clairsville, Belmont Co, Ohio - Zebulon WARNER.

243. Sep 22 1812
Meeting of the "Friends of Peace" in Washington Co, at Sharpsburgh - Jacob MUMMA appointed chairman, Joseph CHAPLINE Sec'ry; Committee appointed: Dr. CLAGGET, John BRIEN, Jacob T. TOWSON, John BLACKFORD, John MILLER, Edward BOTELER, William GOOD, Samuel D. PRICE and John RHODE.
John LYNN of Allegany and John Hanson THOMAS of Fred, candidate for electors of the Pres and Vic Pres of U.S.
Negroes for sale - William LEE, Georgetown.

244. Sep 29 1812
Married in Baltimore, Tues evening last, by Rev. Geo. ROBERTS, George HUSSEY, Jr., formerly of this place to Miss Sarah PRESTON, of that city.
Another letter from Benjamin GALLOWAY.

245. Oct 6 1812
Samuel D. PRICE, Mang. S.L., Sharpsburg, cautions persons against hunting, cutting down or injuring the timber on the lands belong to Jeremiah CHAPLINE, decd.
Sale of land in Wash Co, in the neighborhood of John MASON, Esq. and JACQUES iron works, called the resurvey on Pipe Tomahawk, 654 a. - Thomas PETER, David PETER.

246. Oct 13 1812 - Chancery case: William EVANS and Sarah his wife, Samuel D. PRICE and Catharine his wife, Joseph CHAPLINE, Jas. N. CHAPLINE, Elizabeth CHAPLINE, Susanna CHAPLINE, Mary Ann CHAPLINE and Ruhemia CHAPLINE against Matthias KUHNS. Petition filed to record deed executed by Matthias KUHNS to Jeremiah CHAPLINE, father to the petitioners in 1802 for 6 lots in Sharpsburg; the petition states that Matthias KUHNS does not res in this state.

247. Oct 20 1812
Daniel RENCH and Henry WILLIAMS (res in Emmittsburg district for many years, candidates as electors of Pres and Vice Pres.
Married in Fred Co, Sun evening 1th inst by Rev. HELSENSTEIN, Nathaniel POSEY, of Hagers Town, to Miss Margaret KEMP, dau of late Rev. Kemp of Fred. Town.
Petition to open a public road from ferry on Potomac below mouth of Antietam, commonly known as McCHANS or TAYLOR's ferry, from thence to M'PHERSON and BRIEN's iron works, from thence to CRAMPTON's Gap, on south mountain, from thence to RINGER's tavern, & from thence toward EVERHART's mill, until it intersects the Baltimore, Frederick and Boonsborough turnpike road.

HAGERS-TOWN GAZETTE

248. Oct 27 1812
Letter to the public from John Hanson THOMAS.
Matthew VANLEAR has taken up a stray steer at his farm near Williamsport.
Funks-town Factory - Jacob & Michael CONRADT, having received their cards, are now putting up their machinery and will begin to card and spin wool some time next week.

249. Nov 3 1812 - Gideon BOYD offers reward for mare which strayed or was stolen from his waggon at Joseph HOLLAR's tavern, 1 1/2 miles west of town of Bedford; deliver to George MULLIN, at foot of Dry Ridge, Bedford Co.

250. Nov 10 1812
G. I. CONRADT, Funks-Town seeks to hire black woman to do house work and plain cooking.
Chancery case: John WADE against James CHAPLINE and John BUCHANAN. To obtain from John BUCHANAN as trustee for James CHAPLINE a conveyance for 125 a. of tract called Loss and Gain, in Wash Co.

251. Nov 17 1812 - Steuart GAITHER and Edward GAITHER, adm of Henry GAITHER, decd to sell at farm of decd, about 5 miles from Hagers Town and 2 from Col. HUGHES's Furnace, part of personal estate of decd.

252. Nov 24 1812 - A daring robbery was committed on John MAUCHERMAN, living near Sharpsburg on Fri last, while on his way from his residence to Hagers Town. Between CAREY's Cross roads and STOVER's tavern he was attacked by two villains, one white man with a scar across his nose and the other a mulatto blind in one of his eyes, taking $150 in bank notes.

253. Dec 1 1812
Dissolution of partnership of A. MAYER and G. H. IRWIN, Hagers Town; business to be continued by IRWIN.
Tract for sale near head spring of Bulliskin, Jefferson Co, Va. 370 a. - Samuel MENDENHALL.

254. Dec 8 1812
Sale of tract in mouth of Little Cove, 8 miles from Mercersburg, in neighbourhood of Michael POTTORFF and Captain John's, and about 3 miles from Isaac BAIGHTLE'S, 400 a.; also farm of 140 a. now occupied by Martin TICKERHOOF near Leonard BEVIN's on Licking Creek, about 1 mile from Mr. DUNN's forge - apply to Otho H. WILLIAM, Hagers Town or to Elie WILLIAMS.
Michael LOWMAN, Jun., has lost a white woolen cloth of 7 1/2 yards; leave at COFFROTH's store in Greencastle or Mr. M'ILHENNYS store in Hagers-Town.

255. Dec 22 1812
Daniel GEHR, living at the plantation of John BEARD, Wash Co, has taken up a stray bull calf.
Sale of tavern stand in Williams-Port, now in tenure of Mr. MUIR - Benjamin YOE.

256. Dec 29 1812
Died Mon morn, 28 inst in 70th year of her age, Mrs. Barbara BARR.
Negro man for sale - William CURTIS.

HAGERS-TOWN GAZETTE

257. Jan 5 1813
Married Sun evening last by Rev SCHAEFFER, William HEYSER, Jun., to Miss Sally ARTZ, dau of Peter ARTZ, merchant of this town.
For rent - plantation being part of Chew's farm, now in the possession of Col. Jonas HOGMIRE, property of Doct. Elisha HARRISON. Enquire of Samuel HUGHES, Jun., at his office in Hagers-town.
Negro man for sale, 22 yrs old - William CURTIS.
2500 lbs of good corn fed pork, each hog weighing not less than 130 lbs and not more than 160, delivered in the City of Washington. O.H.W. STULL.

258. Jan 12 1813
George KREPS has resumed cabinet-making at his old stand in west Franklin st.
The fulling mill at Jacob & Michael CONRADT's cloth factory in Funk's Town goes into operation this week.
George HAGER, House Joiner & Cabinet Maker, has commenced in the shop nearly opposite the German Printing Office in Potomac St.
Chancery sale of tract in Wash Co, 107 a., called Free-Stone, and part of tract called "the resurvey on lot Justice take place," late the property of Charles TALBOTT, Paul TALBOTT, Archibald TALBOTT, Elisha HYLAND and Anna his wife and John R. HYLAND and Charlotte his wife - situated on Conococheague creek, opposite to P. & M. Miller's mills, now in the tenure of Elisha HYLAND. Henry SWEITZER, Trustee.

259. Jan 19 1813 - Nathaniel POSEY has commenced the Hatting Business at the shop lately occupied by Abraham FORCE, Potomac st.

260. Jan 26 1813
Died on night of 24th inst., Miss Elizabeth YOUNG, aged about 29 yrs, only child of Doctor Samuel YOUNG of this p[lace, after a lingering and painful illness.
Sale of horses, cattle, hogs, 2 stills with apparatus, grain, and other, 3 1/2 miles from Hagers-town, at my res - Ch. HESLETINE.

261. Feb 2 1813
Samuel BAYLY will sell household, barr and kitchen furniture.
George SHEISS has taken up a stray colt.

262. Feb 9 1813
Jacob SHOLL carries on rope making in Hagers-town, opposite Gottlieb ZIMMERMAN's, pump-maker.
Janet LINGAN admr Gen. James M. LINGAN, to sell at Middlebrook Mills, res of late Gen. James M. Lingan, all his personal property: number of slaves, furniture, plantation utensils, copper stills, blacksmith's, cooper's and joiner's tools, horses, and other. Henry WARRING and Robert P. MAGRUDER of Montgomery co, will attend the sale and settle the business of the estate.
Sale of land on Mill creek, Berkeley co, Va, with merchant mill, distillery and dwelling house. William B. KING, Mill Creek.

263. Feb 16 1813
Members of Robertson's Military school to meet at the lot nearly oppposite the Stone Church.

HAGERS-TOWN GAZETTE

Sale at subscriber's res, near Hagers-town, horses, cows, cattle, sheep, hogs, furniture. Frederick ROHRER.
Sale of 4-wheel carriage with plated harness, plank, barr iron, milch cow, furniture. Leonard SHAFER.

264. Feb 23 1813 - Died Mon evening 22d inst, Jacob MILLER, old inhabitant of this town.

265. Mar 2 1813 - Sale at late res of Henry SCHRIVER, 1/2 mile from Burkhart's mill. Geo. HARBAUGH, John STRITE, admrs, of Henry SCHRIVER.

266. Mar 9 1813 - Married Sun evening last by Rev SCHAEFFER, Robert HAYES, to Miss Sally RICHARDSON, both of this town.

267. Mar 16 1813 - Sale in Antrim twp, Franklin co, Pa, of horses, cattle, steers, sheep, swine, waggon, wheat, rye, oats and buckwheat, apple brandy, rye whisky, Latin and Greek books, furniture. Lazarus BROWN, John SNIVELY, Andrew SNIVELY, exrs.

268. Mar 23 1813
Sale at late dwelling house of Isaac HERSHEY, decd, near Booth's mill, horses, horse gears, cows, sheep, hogs, waggon, cart, ploughs, harrows, windmill, cutting box, rye, corn, furniture. Barbara HERSHEY
Head miller wanted. John & Geo. HARRY.
15 Negroes for sale at Levy's tavern - Thomas S. LEE, Frederick co.
Oliver EVANS to the Millers - detailed account of the savings possible with his improvements in the manufacture of flour.

269. Mar 30 1813
Sale by decree of Orphans' Court of Anne Arundel co, number of negroes. Gustavus WARFIELD, Chas. A. WARFIELD, admrs.
Trustees of Allegany County School have engaged Rev Henry R. WILSON, late professor of languages in Dickinson College, Carlisle, to preside over the Classical and Scientific Department.

270. Apr 6 1813
Died in Alleghany co, Md, after 4 days illness, of a pleurisy, Col. John LYNN, one of the bravest of patriots and best of men. Fed. Rep.
2 negro men for sale at Mr. Strause's tavern, Hagers-town. Addison WHITE.
William WILLIS, Boot & Shoe Maker, had removed to house lately occupied by Samuel HAGER.
Jacob SAYLOR has removed to the tavern stand, lately occupied by Christian LANTZ, sign of the Indian King.
John HENNYBERGER, Cabinet-maker, has removed to house lately occupied by Abraham MAYER, formerly occupied by Leonard KUHN, Cabinet maker, next door and above the dwelling house of Otho H. WILLIAMS, Esq., Potomac st.

271. Apr 13 1813 - Frederick KINSELL, Barber and Hair-Dresser, has just arrived from Georgetown and opened a shop in the corner room adj William BEECHER's Store, lately in the occupation of George BEECHLER, Confectioner.

HAGERS-TOWN GAZETTE

272. Apr 20 1813
Daniel PIPER admr of Jacob PIPER.
Martinsburg Academy, under the direction of Thomas CALDWELL. Trustees: David HUNTER, Elisha BOYD, Obed WAITE, John S. HARRISON, Philip C. PENDLETON.
Geo. SMITH, Swearingen's ferry, has taken up a stray horse. Certified by Geo. SMITH, Justice of the Peace.

273. Apr 27 1813
Managers of the Hagers-town and Westminster turnpike road company will receive proposals for completing the said road. John SCOTT, Treasurer.
Proposals will be received for building bridge across Big Conococheague, at the Broad Fording. David MARTIN, Trustee.

274. May 4 1813
Died yesterday morning in her 74th yr, Mrs. Barbara ROHRER, relict of the late Christian ROHRER.
Charles CANDERWINE, Waynesburgh, Franklin co, Pa, offers reward for missing horse.

275. Jun 8 1813
Daniel GEHR has taken up a stray mare.
Benjamin HOSKENS, living between Sharpsburg and the Antietam Iron works, has taken up a stray horse.

ALLEGANY FREEMAN

276. Nov 27 1813 Vol. 1, no. 2 [Library of Congress].
Published weekly by S. MAGILL, near the Bank, Cumberland, Md.
Edmund BOYD has a large assortment of stills for sale; also tin ware, at his Copper and Tin Manufactory, Cumberland.

277. Dec 4 1813 [Md. Hist. Soc.]
J. STRIDER, Brother, & Co. have just opened a new store in Hancock Town: cloths, cassimers and flannels, velvets, teas, sugars, &c.
Thomas REID, Cumberland, offers reward for apprentice to the Distilling business named William SHOMAKE, Deaf and Dumb.
Michael KERSHNER, Cumberland, offers reward for John BROWN, by occupation shoemaker, blind of the right eye, scar under his chin; took from the subscriber one full set of shoemakers' tools and one new pair of men's shoes.
Edmund BOYD has for sale at his copper and tin manufactory in Cumberland, an assortment of stills.
Labourers wanted early in Spring. James COCHRAN having finished 5 miles of the U.S. Western Road and contracted for 18 miles more, to be finished by November next, solicits labourers.
John MURRELL, Junr., Cumberland, has just received from Phila, Seasonable goods.
Deserters: Deserted from Cumberland Recruiting Rendezvous, Allegany co, enlisted soldier named William RANDOLPH, born in Windham co, Connecticut, aged 19 yrs, 5 ft 9 1/2 inches, fair complexion, gray eyes, light hair, by

ALLEGANY FREEMAN

profession a farmer, can beat the drum - also enlisted soldier named James
DAVIS, born in Bedford, N.Y., aged 45 yrs, 5 ft 10 1/2 inches, dark complexion, dark eyes, black hair, by profession a shoemaker. He has lost
the little finger of his right hand. Wm. JONES,Lieut. 38th Regt, U.S.I.
Persons having notes in the Cumberland Bank which shall become due will take
notice that their notes must be drawn on paper duly stamped. M. WALLACE,
Cashier.
John WRIGHT & co., Watch-makers, silversmiths & jewellers, have commenced
business in town of Cumberland, Main st, nearly opposite Mr. CARICO's
tavern.
James BOYD to teach the theory and practice of sacred music.
James SCOTT offers for sale, house and lot in tenure of Henry M'KINLY, on
west side of Will's Creek; and other.
Frederick CHRISTMAN, Cumberland, to sell lot in Cumberland, fronting on
Bedford st, with log dwelling and commodious shop, presently occupied by
him as a waggon-maker's shop.

278. Dec 11 1813 [Md. Hist. Soc.]
Caution. On November the ninth day, My wife Agnes ran away:
From bed and board did flee, and say ... She would no longer with me stay.
But since she left me without cause, I'll give her time enough to pause,
That she may see her error When I live happy with a fairer!
Therefore I warn both great and small, Not to credit her at all:
And for her contract from this day Not one farthing will I pay.
Gabriel KIMMEL, Somerset Co, Pa.
Aza BEALL, Collector of the Revenue for the 9th Collection Dist., Md., gives
notice re Acts of Congress, laying Internal Duties, requiring retailers of
wines, liquors, foreign merchandise, to apply in writing for a license.

279. Dec 18 1813 [Md. Hist. Soc.]
Wm. AULL, contractor, on great U.S. Western Turnpike, wishes to employ early
next spring, hands to work on the road.
James KINKADE has house for sale and 2 lots, adj Mr. NEFF and near Dr.
MORROW's, presently occupied by Ninian COCHRAN.

280. Dec 25 1813 [Md. Hist. Soc.] - Charles M'KINNEY, contractor on the
Great Western Turnpike, seeks to employ hands.

281. Jan 1 1814 [Md. Hist. Soc.] - Letters remaining at Post Office,
Cumberland: Francis ADELSPEYER; James ANDERSON; Elizabeth ARMSTRONG;
Jonathan ARNOLD; ; Dennis BEALL Isaac BEALL; Thomas BEALL of Samuel; Gideon
BOYD; Benjamin BROWN; John BROWN; George BRUCE; Upton BRUCE; James P.
CARLTON; Richard CARLTON; Jacob CORN; Polly CRESAP; Thomas CRESAP; James
DAILEY; William R. DAWSON, Collector of the Taxes; William DUFFIELD; Hugh
DUNN; John ECHART; Zedock ELLIOTT; Rebecca FEE; John GILMUR; Daniel GRIMES;
Adam GROSS, Jun.; David HOFFMAN; William HOUSE; Peter HOWELL; John HOYE;
George JONES; John KIMBERLY; William LODGSDON; Ludwick LYBERGER; John LYNN;
George M'COLLOCH; John MATHEWS; Jacob MYERS; Magy NEYNULDS; John ORME; James
PARMORE; Charles PERRIL; John READ; John M. READ; William RIDGLEY; Jacob
RISHELL; George RIZER; Henry ROCK; John SCOTT; Walter SELBY; Thomas STEWART;
George THISTLE; Thomas THISTLE; Benjamin TROUTMAN; Benjamin VAUGHN; Mary

ALLEGANY FREEMAN

WALLS; Israel WELSEY, Wann County surveyor; Michael WEYER; George WINTERS; John ZIMBLY. Samuel SMITH, P.M.

282. Jan 8 1814 [Md. Hist. Soc.] - For sale - Shad and Herrings; also some fine hats. George HOBLITZELL.

283. Jan 29 1814 [Md. Hist. Soc.]
Whiskey for sale - John PATTERSON, at his store.
D. ESPY, Captain, 22d Regt, U.S. Inf., Bedford Rendezvous, offers reward for enlisted soldier named John OAR, native of Dauphin co, Pa, aged 22 yrs, 5 ft 8 inches, fair complexion, blue eyes, brown hair, by profession a farmer; had on a brown linsey coatee, pair of white and blue twilled woollen pantaloons and a round hat - also from this rendezvous, on 3rd Jan, enlisted soldier named Joel THOMPSON, native of Virginia, aged 20 yrs, 5 ft 8 inches, fair complexion, grey eyes, brown hair, by profession a black-smith.
Reward for Thomas DAVIS who broke jail, low in stature and dark complexion, last place of res was on Big Capon in neighborhood of Springfield, Hampshire co, Va. He was formerly a copartner in a team with one CRAMPTON. George M. HOUX, Deputy Sheriff.
Lewis DUNN, admr, to sell a dwelling house of Silas PRICE, decd, Frankfort, Hampshire co, personal property of decd.
Barton CARICO offers reward for stolen saddle, bridle and blanket. On each stirrup leather is a strip of silver with J. THOMPSON engraven on it.
Samuel LOWDERMILK, Cumberland, offers reward for villain who broke into the house of Mrs. BRIDENHART and stole from him a silver watch.
Saddle and Harness Making - Wm. J. A. POLLOCK, & Co., have commenced in Cumberland.

284. Feb 5 1814 [Md. Hist. Soc.] - Isaac WORKMAN, Allegany Co, to sell plantation on which he lives, 1 3/4 a. of the great Western Turnpike.

285. Feb 12 1814 [Md. Hist. Soc.]
Persons having claims against estate of William H. BURNS, decd, are requested to produce them to the subscribers, Thos. B. CRAWFORD and John MATHEWS, admrs, Western Port.
Daniel Wm. M'HENRY, admr of John LYNN.
Frederick RICE, of Andrew, admr of John CAMPBELL.
Upton BRUCE and Geo. BRUCE, admr of William BRUCE.

286. Feb 19 1814 [Md. Hist. Soc.] - House and lot for sale in Cumberland, now occupied by Barton CARICO as a tavern. David HOFFMAN, Sen.

287. Feb 26 1814 [Md. Hist. Soc.] - John RESONER, Old Town, offers reward for apprentice to the blacksmith business, named John WAGGONER, about 19, dark complexion, about 5 ft 8 inches.

288. Mar 5 1814 [Md. Hist. Soc.]
Walter B. SELBY, Shepherdstown, offers reward for negro man named BILL, 5 ft 9 inches.
Jacob VANMETER, Fort-Pleasant, Old Fields, Hardy co, Va, offers reward for mustee or mulatto man, named JACK, about 33 yrs old.

ALLEGANY FREEMAN

289. Mar 12 1814 [Md. Hist. Soc.]
Licensed Auctioneer - John MILBOURNE, Cumberland.
The Commissioners of the Tax will meet in Cumberland. L. HILLEARY, Clk.

290. Mar 26 1814 [Md. Hist. Soc.]
M. C. SPRIGG will sell at his dwelling house, 2 miles from Old Town, his personal property.
William HOUX, Chair-maker, carries on the business in the last house on the south side of Bedford st.
Benjamin BROWN will sell a farm 1 mile of town, 165 a.
Auctioneers: George M. HOUX, John GEPHART, Peter PRESTON.
M. C. SPRIGG and Joseph SPRIGG will sell plantation on which they now reside on North Branch of the Potomac, Hampshire Co, Va.

291. Apr 2 1814 [Md. Hist. Soc.]
Wm. M'MAHON, Cumberland, has on hand: writing paper, spun cotton, iron and castings, seneca oil, whiskey, tea, &c.
Chancery sale in case of CAMPBELL and RITCHIE against Gilbert STRONG and others: house and lot in Cumberland, presently in the tenure of James CARLTON, and nearly adj store of John MURRELL. Hanson BRISCOE, Trustee.
Letters remaining at the Post Office, Cumberland: John BARCUS; Peter BARNWARD; Thomas BEALL; Thomas BEALL, of Saml.; Jeremiah BERRY, 3rd; Chs. H. J. BRISCOE; Benjamine BROWN; Joseph CLARK; Thomas CLINTON; Daniel COLLINS; John CREAMOUR; James CREEGAN; Joseph CRESAP; Mrs. DANNY; Solomon DAVIS; Frederick DEAMS; Lewis DENT; Maret DERROYGH; Levin DUNTON; Thomas EMORY; Andrew EMRICK; Samuel EVANS; Ann FITLER; Jacob FULLER; Ely GASAWAY; William Seph GATES; John GELLER; George GETTER; Robert GORDON; James GRAYHAM; Jacob GUNN; George GUNNETT; Francis HAMMER; Daniel HARRIS; George HAUCK; William HOBLITS; John HOLDRIDGE; David HUFFMAN, sr.; Gosepli HUNTER; Joseph JEFFERISS; John JOHNSTON; Lewis KLIMMER; Levi LEWMAN; Elizabeth M'DANILS; Richard M'DANILS; Mrs. M'GARVEY; Allen M'KENNA; Andrew M'LEERY; William M'MAHAN; John M'NEAL; Elias MAJERS; James MALLEM; Jacob MARTZS; Samuel MATTINGLY; James MAXWELL; Phillip MERRELL; Stephen MILLHOLLAND; Hance MITCHELL; George MORE; Thomas PERKINSON; Roger PERRY; Jacob POOL; Henrey RAFTER; John REID; James ROBESON; John SCHUCK; John SCOTT; Adam SHEET; Polly SIMKINS; Jacob SPEALMAN; Christian STATTS; John STEPHENSON, care John M'Neal; David STOVER; William STREET; Thomas STUART; Josiah THOMPSON; James TIMMONDS; John VAUN; Josua WILSON. Sam'l SMITH, P.M.
Geo. P. HINKLE has taken up a stray gelding.
Jacob VANDIVER, Patterson's Creek, Hampshire Co, Va, offers reward for negro man THOMAS, 32 yrs of age.

292. Apr 9 1814 [Md. Hist. Soc.]
Dry Goods, Hardware, Groceries & Liquors. John MURRELL, Jr., Cumberland.
Zadok CLARK has removed his hat factory to the house 3 doors above Mr. NEFF's Pottery, and directly opposite to Mr. WIRE's dwelling.
John CRUSE will sell plantation on which he now lives, 400 a. on Evit's Creek.
James ORD, Lieut, 36th U.S. Infantry, offers reward for John WALTON, born in New Jersey, aged 24 yrs, 5 ft 11 inches, fair complexion, blue eyes, light hair, by profession a joiner. He had his wife along with him when he deserted.

ALLEGANY FREEMAN

293. Apr 16 1814 [Md. Hist. Soc.]
Saddles, bridles and other - W. T. A. POLLOCK, Cumberland.
Andrew BRUCE to sell 1095 a. in Allegany Co, below the lands of Oliver CROMWELL at the mouth of Town Creek, patented in 1774.
Charles HOUSER, on New Creek, Hampshire Co, Va, offers reward for indented apprentice to blacksmith trade, named William THOMAS, 5 ft 8 inches, sandy complexion, grey eyes.
Mary MURDOCH, exr of Patrick MURDOCK.

294. Apr 23 1814 [Md. Hist. Soc.] - Isaac MEANS, living near Paddytown, Hampshire co, Va, offers reward for negro man named GLOSTER, about 29 yrs old.

295. Apr 30 1814 [Md. Hist. Soc.]
Two tracts for sale on Evits Creek, 3 miles from Cumberland, 1/2 of 11 a. on Jennings's Run in Pennsylvania on which is a coal mine. Upton BRUCE or John PATERSON.
James MORRISON, Westernport, admr of Henry CLOUSE.

296. May 14 1814 [Md. Hist. Soc.] - Chancery sale to complete the execution of the power given by Joseph FORREST to Benjamin STODDART and Archibald CAMPBELL, at the house of Walter SLICER, Cumberland: right of Joseph Forrest to 18 a., part of tract called Walnut Bottom, adj Cumberland on which is a Grist Mill. Roger PERRY.

297. May 21 1814 [Md. Hist. Soc.] - Thomas STALLINGS has purchased patent right of "The Pleasant Spinner," for spinning wool or cotton. Call on James HOOK, wheelwright, Cumberland.

298. May 28 1814 [Md. Hist. Soc.]
Mr. PERRY has not right to make the sale as advertised of the lot and grist mill of Mrs. Mary MURDOCH. Josiah M. ESPY, atty for Mary Murdoch.
Chancery case: Peter WOLFE & Magdalena WOLFE his wife; Peter MILLER & Elizabeth MILLER his wife; John WESTFALL & Lovice WESTFALL his wife vs. John COBLENTZ, Jacob COBLENTZ, Philip COBLENTZ, Catharine HESSON, Baltzer HESSON, Ann Maria HESSON, and Jacob HESSON and Barbara COBLENTZ - to obtain decree for sale of real estate of Philip COBLENTZ, Frederick Co, decd. John Coblentz resides in the state of Ohio.

299. Jul 30 1814 [Md. Hist. Soc.]
NEAL, WILLS & COALE, 174 Market st, Balt, offer reward for Joseph DEAL, apprentice to the Book-binding busines, about 18 yrs old, 5 ft 7 inches, dark complexion, has scar on right side of his chin.
New-Orleans sugar - Jacob LANTZ, Mechanic St, Cumberland.

300. Aug 5 1814 [Md. Hist. Soc.]
Upton BRUCE and George BRUCE admrs of William BRUCE request settlement of accounts of estate of decd.
Samuel HOWELL, Charlestown, Jefferson Co, Va, offers reward for apprentice to the tanning business named Franklin W. GIBBS, about 19 yrs old, 5 ft 8-9 inches, slender made, fair complexion, down look. He has a sister living somewhere in Louisiana.

ALLEGANY FREEMAN

301. Aug 13 1814 [Md. Hist. Soc.]
By virtue of several writs of Fierie facias, one in favor of Joseph RIDDLE, surviving partner of RIDDLE & DALL against Charles Frederick BRODHAG; one in favor of Frederick LINDENBERGER & co., against same; one other in favor of M'DONALD & RIDGELY against the same; and one other in favor of Matthew VANLEAR against the same. To sell several lots westward of Fort Cumberland, 50 a. each - late the property of Charles Frederick Brodhag.
John RICE has taken up a stray mare.

302. Aug 20 1814 [Md. Hist. Soc.]
Aza BEALL has opened a store in Mechanic St, in this town, next door of Mr. J. MURRELL, Junr. - Dry Goods, Groceries, Glass-Ware, &c.
Samuel STALLINGS has taken up a stray bull.

303. Sep 17 1814 [Md. Hist. Soc.] - Committed to jail as a runaway, negro man who says his name is SAM and that he belongs to Reason PUMPHREY, near Wheeling, Va; about 25 yrs old, 5 ft 8 inches.

304. Oct 15 1814 [Md. Hist. Soc.]
William R. DAWSON candidate for sheriff.
John M'HENRY admr, d.b.n. of John LYNN.
Margaret HOOK admr of Elias HOOK.

305. Oct 22 1814 [Md. Hist. Soc.]
Jacob HOBLITZELL, Cumberland, has sold his entire stock of merchandize to his brother, William HOBLITZELL, who solicits former customers to call at the corner store near the Brick Mill and who sells lot on Mechanic st adj Barton CARRICO's Tavern, a house opposite the Brick Mill, lately occupied by him as a store; a house and lot in Blocher's addition to Cumberland, 60 shares of bank stock, black woman and 3 children, furniture.
James P. CARLTON, taylor, carries on the tayloring business near Mr. SLICER's Tavern.
James M. WHITE has just returned from a tour of duty at Baltimore and intends to carry on the saddling business in Cumberland.
Letters remaining at Post Office, Cumberland, Sep 1814: John ATHY; Andrew BARTRUFF; David BEALL; Thomas BEALL; Thomas BEALL, of Sam'l; Montgomery BELL; John BLACK; Charles BRADY, care of C. M'KINNY; William CATHERS; Anna CLARK; Hiram CLARKE; George CLEAVER; Lewis CLEMMER; Amariah COBURN; Daniel COLLINS; John Conner; Mary COOK; Thomas DANDER; Rezin DAVAGE; Lewis G. DAVIDSON; John DELOUGHERTY, care of M'KINNA; George DUCKWORTH; William DUDDY; Michael FEE; John FREDRICKS; Josiah FROST; Peter GEPHART; George GILLER, Junr.; William GRAHAM, care C. M'CINNEY; Moses GREENWADE; Miss Rebecca HARNESS; Charles HECK; Henry HETHERINGTON; Daniel HICKMAN; Daniel HILLFORTEE; Beal HOWARD; Jacob HUFFMAN; Ann JACKSON; Lieut. William JONES; Elizabeth KELLER; James KING; Eli LEWMAN; Elijah Lewman; Peter LOWDERMILK; Henry M'DERMIT, care of C. M'KINNEY; John M'MAHAN; John MACKLEFISH; Zachariah MANN; John MARKEY; Ignatia MIDDLETON; Daniel MILHOLLAND; Benedict MILLER; Hamilton MOORE; James MOTHERD; John MUMMA; Samuel MURPHY; Jacob NEFF; Rinald PINDLE; George PLUCHER; William POLLOCK; Mrs. Christy PRATT; William QEREE; George RAINHART; Frances REID; John REID & others, Esqrs.; Martain RIZER; John ROBINSON; Baltzel H. SHELLHORN; David SHORT; John SIGLAR; Sophia SIMKINS; Fredrick SIMONS; John SIMPKINS; John SMITH; Michael

ALLEGANY FREEMAN

C. SPRIGG; Elihue STIVERS; David TOY; Jacob TRULLINGER; Francis TWIG; Benjamine G. VAUGHN; Nathaniel WALLAS; James WARD; John WELCH; John WONN; William WYATT. Samuel SMITH, P.M.
Nicholas BRADLEY, to sell at the Little Crossings, where Henry O'DONALD now resides, horses, carts, gears and other.

306. Oct 29 1814 [Md. Hist. Soc.]
Tax under act of Congress, Aug 1813, due and payable at the following places, at the house of: Archibald ARNOLD on Jennings's Run, Matthew BALL on George's Creek, William PRICE in Western Port, John MATHEWS near the State Road, John RINEHART in the Green Glades, Alexander SMITH in Rine's Glades, Andrew HOUSE at the Ginsenging Ground, Joseph FRANCE on the Great Crossings, John WELCH on Little Crossings, George M. LAUBINGER, in Old Town, John ROBINSON, Samuel OSBURN on Fifteen Mile Creek, Thomas STALLINGS, on Murley's Branch. Aza BEALL, Collector for 19th Coll. Dist.
James P. CARLTON, taylor, carries on the tayloring business near Mr. SLICER's Tavern.

307. Nov 5 1814 [Md. Hist. Soc.]
Elizabeth SHOCKY and Jacob CLEMMER, admrs of Valentine SHOCKY request settlement of accounts.
Henry O'NEALE, Jr., Captain 38th Regt., U.S. Infantry, offers reward for William WARD, soldier in 38th Regt, who deserted from my Rendezvous, Cumberland. He was born in Ireland, 24 yrs of age, 5 ft 10 inches, fair complexion, blue eyes, dark hair, by profession a labourer. One of his fingers is crooked and a large piece is cut out of one of his ears. - Escaped from jail of Allegany co, Thomas ARMSTRONG, soldier in the 38th regt, U.S. Inf. He had previously deserted from said regt, had been apprehended as such and confined to jail. He was born in Harford co, Md., about 30 yrs of age, 5 ft 6 1/2 inches, fair complexion, dark eyes, dark hair, by profession a house carpenter. He absconded with a woman he calls his wife.

308. Nov 12 1814 [Md. Hist. Soc.]
Petition to establish ferry over the North Branch of the Potomac river on state road from Winchester, Va, passing through Romney and thence by Wm. ARMSTRONG's, being the mail route now established and used, and thence to cross the said North Branch of the Potomac River at or near Benjamin DAWSON's farm, in Allegany Co, Md.
Fulling, dyeing and finishing - Frederick SIMONDS can now execute orders in this business. The mill is 7 miles from Cumberland, on Evitt's Creek, Cumberland Valley, Bedford Co, Pa.

309. Dec 10 1814 [Md. Hist. Soc.]
During my absence, Samuel LOWDERMILK is authorised to collect and settle accounts. Wm. M'MAHON, Cumberland.
Fulling, dyeing and finishing - Jonathan HENDRIXSON now has in complete readiness to execute orders. Cloths may be left at store of Thomas THISTLE, Cumberland. The mill is 14 miles from Cumberland, on Evatt's Creek, Cumberland Valley, Bedford Co, Pa.

310. Dec 17 1814 [Md. Hist. Soc.]

ALLEGANY FREEMAN

Sale at James BLACK's Tavern, all personal estate of Philemon CROMWELL, decd, furniture, hogs, horse, saddle and bridle. Joseph CROMWELL, admr. Ignatius MIDDLETON, Cumberland district, 4 1/2 miles from Cumberland, has taken up 2 stray horses.

311. Dec 14 1814 [Md. Hist. Soc.] - Henry INGMAN has carding machine for sale, in operation 2 seasons in his mill near the Flowery Meed Store, on George's Creek.

312. Dec 31 1814 [Md. Hist. Soc.] - Michael WILT, on Savage River, Glade Hundred, has taken up stray cattle.

313. Jan 7 1815 [Md. Hist. Soc.] - Letters at Post Office, Cumberland: Elizabeth ARTHER; Rev Daniel BEAIN; Fanny BEVINS; James C. BLAIR; John BRANT; Charles F. BRODHAG; Richard I. BUGH; Barnabas BURNS; Joseph CARTER; Mrs. CARTER; James COCHRAN; Daniel COLLINS; John CONNER; Mary CONNER; Joseph CRESAP; Mary CRESAP; Joseph CROMWELL; James CUGING; John CUSTER; Lewis DAVIDSON; Joseph DAVIS; Solomon DAVIS; Fredrick DECUIS; John ELLIOTT; John FOLK; Jonathan FRAEE; Josiah FROST; Louisa GRAHAM; Ester GRIFFITH; Daniel HAINES; Daniel HARRIS; Ezra HAUSER; John HOBLITZELL; John HOLTZMAN; James HOOK; John HOUSE; John HOYE; John G. HUFFMAN; J. JACOBS; Hugh JAMES; James KING; Philip KNIGHT; Jacob KOONTZ; John LANCASTER; John LICKLIDER; Peter LICKLITER; Tabitha M'COY; John M'DONALD; Peter M'KINEY; Mary M'MAHAN; John M'MAHAN, care James CORCORARD; Peter MAGERS; Jonthan MARGAART; Thomas MONNET; Charles L. MOORE; Peggy NEWMAN; William OSBORN; Michael OSWALT; Thomas PARKINSON; Lathrop PARMLEE; Elizabeth PEIRCE; Roger PERRY; John PORTER; Thomas RUSSELL; Jacob SAP; Jacob SEESE; Walter SELBY; Baltzer H. SHEELHORN; Joseph SMITH; Jacob SNIDER; Robert STEWART; Henrey SUFLING, care Js. TOMLINSON; Samuel TEVIS; Josiah THOMPSON; James TIDBALL; James TIMMONDS; Samuel TOMLINSON; Nicholas WALTER, care John MILLER; Rachal WARD; Charles D. WARFIELD; John WELTZHIMER; Peggy WHITE; Samuel WHITE; George WINTERS; Mr. WITMER, above Macandonke; John WORKMAN; Eliza E. YOUNG; Mathias ZIMERLY - Samuel SMITH, P.M.

314. Jan 14 1815 [Md. Hist. Soc.] - Hanson BRISCOE, desirous of settling all his worldly affairs and extricate himself from his present difficulties, to sell his farm near Cumberland, 1100 a., at present under rent for $600 per annum, with saw mill and distillery. Also house, my present res in Cumberland and plantation adj the town, 100 a., and other small tracts.

315. Jan 28 1815 [Md. Hist. Soc.] - Peter GARY, Cumberland, offers reward for apprentice to the weaving business named John MARTIN, in his 20th yr, 5 ft 2 inches, well set, fair complexion.

316. Feb 4 1815 [Md. Hist. Soc.]
Silver wanted - John WRIGHT & Co, Mechanics St, Cumberland.
Hopkins's celebrated Razor Strop and Diamond paster sold at the following
    stores: George THISTLE, John MURRELL, Jr., Thomas THISTLE, Cumberland.
Chair Making - James HOOK continues the business.

ALLEGANY FREEMAN

317. Mar 4 1815 [Md. Hist. Soc.] - Jonathan COX to sell all his real property in Allegany Co: house in Cumberland and lot on which he resides in Cumberland, with tannery.

318. Mar 11 1815 [Md. Hist. Soc.]
The horse, Rattlesnake will stand for mares. Henry M'KINLEY.
Sale of furniture, waggon and gears. Barton CARICO.

319. Mar 18 1815 [Md. Hist. Soc.]
Died at Ellicott's Mill where he had recently removed to, Edward AISQUITH, Esq. in his 36th yr, leaving widow and 4 small children.
John MURRELL, Junior, has removed his store to the frame building adj the Bank.
Notice to heirs and creditors of John DEAKINS, late of Allegany co, decd. Letters of admin will be granted to John M'DONALD. Geo: BRUCE, Reg'tr.
For sale - tract of land, 34 3/4 a., adj lands of Frederick RICE of Andrew, Mathias ZIMMERLA, Jeremiah PLUMMER and heirs of John CAMELL; also tract of 11 3/4 a. with coal mine, adj lands of Ralph LOGSDON, senr., Jacob WIT and Martin BANE, on road from Cumberland to Somerset. Ninian COCHRAN.

320. Mar 25 1815 [Md. Hist. Soc.]
Peter SMOUSE cautions trespassers on his property.
Notice to heirs and creditors of Ovid M'CRACKIN, late of Allegany Co, decd, letters of Testamentary proposed for John F. LANCASTER, one of the legatees.

321. Apr 1 1815 [Library of Congress]
Died lately at an advanced age, Andrew BRUCE of Allegany Co, native of Scotland, emigrated to this country at an early period. He espoused the revolution when it came on, settled in this co when it was little more than a wilderness, pursuing agriculture; reared a large family.
The horse, North Star, will stand for mares at Cornelius BEVORE's Mill, and at stable of Henry WINENOU; his sire kept by Joshua JOHNSON and his grand sire kept by Daniel WHITMER. Robert ANDERSON.
John F. STAFFORD forewarns persons from purchasing a note of hand which he gave to Noah HIDER.
Sale of Elijah DANISON's right and interest to tracts, Resurvey on St. George and part of Joseph & William's Adventure, at suit of Daniel FETTER - Thomas POLLARD, Sheriff.
Sale of stud horse - Henry M'KINLEY.

322. Apr 8 1815 [Library of Congress]
John SIMMONS has purchased tavern stand, lately occupied by Mr. B. CARICO.
Tract for sale, 224 1/2 a. adj lands of James PRATHER, near Oldtown - Ninian COCHRAN, Barton CARICO, Cumberland.
Henry M'KINLEY offers reward for apprentice, James GRIMES, age about 16 yrs.
Letters remaining at Post Office, Cumberland: George ARTHUR; John BARCUS; George BLOCHER; Gideon BOYD; Mrs. BRANT; Hanson BRISCOE; Alexander BROWN; George BROWN; Aqa. H. BROWNE; Fielder BURCH; Barney BURNS; John BUSY; Joseph CLARK; Thomas CLINTON; John COLLINS; John CONAWAY; John CONNER; Hariot CRESAP; James CRESAP; James M. CRESAP; Mary CRESAP; Emanuel CUSTER, sen.; James DYSART; Elizabeth G. ENNALLS; Dennis FANNING; Peter GAREY; Patrick GORMLEY; Philip HANSEL; James HENDERSON; James HENDRICKSON; Jacob V.

ALLEGANY FREEMAN

HOFFMAN; John HOG; James HOOK; James HORNER; William HOUX; John IRONS; Lieut. William JONES; Carber JULIUS; Elizabeth KELLER; James KINKADE; Edward LATHAN; Phillimon T. LEACH; Samuel LINGAL; Samuel LORMOR; Peter M'CANN; Mary M'CULLOH; Lettice M'DANIEL; Richard M'DANIEL; Archabald M'DONELD; Martha M'HENREY; William MAGRUDER; Henrey MATTINGLY; Daniel MILLHOLLAND; Mary MORRIS; James NARGNEY, Recruiting Officer(?); Jacob NEFF; Wil. OSBURN; Thomas PARKERSON; Charles PATTERSON; Thomas I. PERRY; John PORTER; James PRATER; Thomas PRATT; John PRIEST; Walter RITE; George ROBINETT; Jacob SEAS; William SHAW; Adam SHEETS; John SIESS; Walter SLICER; James SMITH; Jacob SNIDER; Cathrine TAYLOR; Nathan TRACY; Benjamin TROUTMAN; Bengeman G. VAUGHN; Obed Francis WAITE; Josua WILLSON; Henrey WINEOUR; Walter WRIGHT (spelled RITE); Rashael WYATT; Charles C. YELGHMAN Samuel Smith, P.M.
About 200 barrels of flour for sale - James KINKEAD.

323. Apr 15 1815 [Library of Congress] - Alexander KING and William M'MAHON, Cumberland, to close an old partnership, will sell 3 tracts in Hampshire Co, Va.

324. Apr 22 1815 [Library of Congress] - James STODDARD, Cumberland, cautions against receiving forged notes drawn in favor of William FARMER, Walter SLICER, security and witnessed by Joseph GORDON.

325. Apr 29 1815 [Library of Congress] - Barton CARICO requests persons to settle their accounts with him. John GEPHART is keeping the books.

326. May 6 1815 [Library of Congress] - William CUNNINGHAM, senr., and John CUNNINGHAM, near Moorfield, Hardy Co, Va, offer reward for 2 negro boys, BERRY and BILL, both about 20 yrs old. Berry about 5 ft 8-9 inches, caught before in Pa, about 12 months ago on Will's Creek. Bill is about 5 ft 5-6 inches.

327. Jun 3 1815 [Library of Congress]
Sale of house near centre of town of Western Port, at mouth of George's Creek, north branch of the Potomac, calculated for a tavern or store. James MORRISON.
Wm. HOBLITZELL & Co. have just received an assortment of dry goods from Phila.
For sale - in Allegany Co, about 8 miles above Jesse TOMLINSON, the road to Dr. T. F. BROOK'S run through it; on waters of Little Youghagany and adj tract, The Dung Hill, owned by Gen. SWAN of Balt. Apply to George HOFFMAN near Cumberland or subscriber, John GEBHART, Fredericktown.
James PEAL forewarns persons from crediting his wife, Ruth PEAL, as she has left his bed and board.
Young man wanted to assist in a distillery. Thomas REID.
Jacob BLOCHER, Youghagany River, offers reward for missing mare; deliver to him or to George BLOCHER in Cumberland.

328. Jun 10 1815 [Library of Congress]
Died at his res in Allegany Co, 1 Jun, after an illness of a few days, of an asthma, Robert LAMAR, native of this state, in his 92d yr.

ALLEGANY FREEMAN

Daniel LANTZ, Old Town, will sell farm on Potomac adj land of Jos. TIDBALL, in Allegany Co, 130 a. Apply to subscriber or to Jacob LANTZ.
Jacob LANTZ, Old Town, to sell merchant mill and distillery.
Tavern stand for sale, with 490 a., about 15 miles from Cumberland, 4 miles from Simon HAYS's Mill. Philip WINGERT.
Thomas CRESAP has taken up a stray mare. Certified by Nicholas Durbin, J.P.

329. Jun 17 1815 [Library of Congress] - Letter to public from Joseph CROMWELL, Old Town. He states on Tues 14 May last, he and Nathan CROMWELL were at James BLACK's near Old Town when James M. CRESAP and Michael C. SPRIGG came there. The writer says he presumed Cresap came there to settle with them respecting the property he purchased of him by "my deceased brother, Philemon CROMWELL, as my brother, Nathan Cromwell, had come up from Washington for that purpose." An argument ensued. Cresap acted in a threatening manner (with cocked pistols). [Other persons mentioned: John SLICER, of Old town, Mr. LANTZ].

330. Jun 24 1815 [Library of Congress]
James M. CRESAP responds to earlier letter; referes to Phil. CROMWELL as an inmate in my family from 1st of April until sometime in June. When I gave him possession of my house, garden and stable..." "Phil CROMWELL died in July... In September I called on his brother Oliver with Mr. Lenox MARTIN and proposed to take back the property," provided the heirs of Phil. Cromwell would make a small compensation for trouble and expence; also wrote to another brother, Adjutant Nathan CROMWELL. [also included are letters from R. NEWMAN, statement from J. J. JACOB, note from John HANDY or BLACK JOHN, in Virginia, letter from Joseph CROMWELL accepting Cresap's challenge for satisfaction, statement from Phinehas REID regarding Joseph CROMWELL who called at his store in Old Town, statement by Elizabeth ROACH that Cresap chased after Joseph Cromwell (on horseback) and fired a pistol at Cromwell.
Proposals will be received for completing road from Cumberland to Brownsville, Pa. David SHRIVER, Jr, Superintendant, Western Road, Cumberland.
Henry O'NEALE, Montgomery Co, admr of Lawrence O'NEALE, of Montgomery Co.

331. Jul 1 1815 [Library of Congress]
Sale of 3 pair of mill stones and 1 merchant boulting cloth and 1 country cloth. James SCOTT.
New Store - Dry goods, Mechanic St, Cumberland, in the house lately occupied by John MURRELL, 1 door above Geo. THISTLE's. Ely SIGLER & Co.
Co-partnership of HUNTSBURY & STRIDER, dissolved - John STRIDER & Co., Hancock, Md.
George M. LAUBINGER admr of Nathan D. CLIFTON.
John SIMONS will receive boarders, horses received on livery at customary rates.
John RESONER offers reward for apprentice to the blacksmith business, John WAGGONER, about 20 yrs old, about 5 ft 8 inches, tolerably stout made, dark hair and eyes.

332. Jul 8 1815 [Library of Congress]
Joseph CROMWELL answers Mr. CRESAP.

ALLEGANY FREEMAN

Letters at Post Office, Cumberland: James ABBOT; Christian ALBRIGHT; Notley BARNARD; Barnabas BARNS; Tilghman BELT; Robert BENNETT; Jeremiah BERRY 3d; George BLOCHER; C. F. BRADHAG; Benjamine BRADY; Jesse BRASHEARS; Charles H. I. BRISCOE; John H. BROWAD; Alexander BROWN; Upton BRUCE; Pall BUSEY; Rev John G. BUTLER; George CALEMESE; Eve CALFLESH; Jacob CLARK; Benjamin CODDINGTON; Patrick COLEMAN; Rebecca COMPTON; Mrs. CONNER; Ezekiel COOK; George COOK; William B. COOKE; Jonathan COX; James M. CRESAP; William DAVIDSON; Moses DICKENS; Daniel DOUGHERTY, care of C. M'KINNEY; John DUFFY; Hugh DUNN; Benjamine DUVALL; Andrew EMRICK; Gabrial D. EVANS; Editor of Allegany Federalist & Gazette; Jacob FLATHER; Philip FLATHER; William GORDON; Mrs. William GREGG; John HARKESS; Adam HIDER; John HOUSE; William HOUX; John HOY; William IJAMS; Samuel JOHNSTON; Thomas JOHNSTON; John JOURDAN; Nicholas KOONSE; James LANCASTER; Susannah LEACHLIGHTER; Benjamine LEANARD; John LEAZEAR; Dudly LEE; Samuel LINGO; Archabald LOGSTON; William M'CLUNG; Archibald M'DANIEL; Henrey M'DONNEL; Henrey M'KINLEY; Charles M'KINNEY; Peter M'KINNY; William M'MAN; John M'MULLEN; William MACOY; William MAGRUDER; Benjamine MASTERS; John MATHEWS; John MATTHEWS; Thomas MATTHEWS; Philip MINOCK; Peter MURRY; Athanatius NEWTON; Mathew PATTON; Thomas PERRY; Mary PORT; Henry PORTER; Michael PORTER; John M. REID; Miss Catherine REID; James REYNOLDS; Martain RIZER, Jun.; Eliza ROBINET; George ROBINET; Benjamine ROBOSON; Thomas RUSSEL; John SIMKINS; George SMITH; Elizabeth STONE; William TAYLOR; Charles C. TILGHMAN; Bazil TOMLINSON; Singleton WELSH; John WELTZHIMER; Thomas WHEELER; William WHITE; William WILLSON; Amos WILSON; Philip WINGERT; Jacob WORKMAN. Samuel SMITH, P.M.

333. Aug 19 1815 [Library of Congress]
Thomas Beall of N. has taken up a stray mare. Certified by George P. Hinckle, Justice of the Peace.
Daniel UHL, wheelwright and chairmaker, about 9 miles from Cumberland, on road from Cumberland to Pittsburgh and 1/2 mile from Jacob UHL's new mill.
Jeremiah BERRY, 3d, Cumberland, to rent plantation 9 miles from Cumberland on Merly's Branch.
Jacob HOBLITZELL candidate for sheriff.
Samuel SMITH, Principal assessor 9th District of Md. opens tax lists for inspection by all persons in Cumberland.
Edmund BOYD and John HOFFMAN, coppersmiths & tin business, Mechanic St.
John KIMBERLY admr of Motalena KIMBERLY.

334. Sep 9 1815 [Library of Congress]
William FOX and John INSKEEP, exrs of Dr. John SNYDER of Romney, Hampshire Co, Va, to sell lot, house, furniture, farm, grist and saw-mill on Patterson's Creek. Property will be shewn by John SNYDER of Romney or John MARSHALL, on the premises; also 30 negroes, 150 bushels of wheat at Joseph CRESAP's mill and other items.
L. HILLEARY declines candidacy as sheriff.
Reward offered for John PORTER who broke jail, confined for forgery. He is about 5 ft 10-11 inches, sandy hair, whiskers, believed to have had accomplice named John HULING who is short, chunky man, about 5 ft 6-7 inches.
Co-partnership formed by Robert M'GUIRE and Frederick T. HARRISON, Clock & Watch making, in house lately occupied by John PATTERSON, 1 door above Jacob HOBLITZELL'S and opposite Post Office, Cumberland.

ALLEGANY FREEMAN

John BURBRIDGE, near Cumberland, offers reward for negro man, Peter, about 5 ft 10 inches, stout, 26 yrs old, yellow complexion, yellow eyes, scar on left hand occasioned by cut of sickle in reaping; plays on the violin; has many friends near Williamsport.
Mesheck FROST and Isaiah FROST have laid out small town on U. S. Turnpike, 10 miles from Cumberland; offer lots for sale.
Partnership of John WRIGHT & Ebenezer VOWELL (John WRIGHT & Co.), Cumberland, is dissolved. John Wright offers his jewelry on lowest terms.

335. Sep 16 1815 [Library of Congress]
John KIMBERLY Of M., candidte for Sheriff.
Ashes wanted at the Cumberland Glass Factory - Roger & Thomas PERRY & Co.
John SIMKINS candidate for General Assembly.

336. Sep 23 1815 [Library of Congress] - George HAINS cautions persons from trusting Hannah HAINS on his account.

337. Oct 21 1815 [Library of Congress]
Institution in Plain and Ornamental Needlework - and Spelling, reading, &c. - Miss BRADLEY, next door to Dr. VIER's.
Patent portable steam bath - apply to Rev John J. JACOBS, Hampshire Co.
Negro NED committed to jail of Allegany Co by John BOYLE, Somerset Twp. He is 5 ft 6-7 inches, says he belongs to John JOHNS who lives 16 miles from Balt.
Riding horse for sale; also real property in Cumberland. B. S. PIGMAN.
John MURRELL, Jr. has opened a store in the corner of the large brick building occupied as a tavern by late Barton CARICO and recently by Mr. SIMONS.
William M'MAHON admr of Rev John HAYES.
Letters remaining at Post Office, Cumberland: James ABBERT; Henrey ABRAMS; Thomas BEALE of Samuel; Alphus BEALL; James BLAIR; John BOOSE; John BRANDT; James BUGH; Miss Isabella CALMEES; Joel CATTELL; John CAYLOR; Collimore CHAPMAN; George CLARK; Joseph CLARK; Miss Harriot COLLINS; Mrs. Rebecca COMPTON; John CONWAY; Dr. William R. COZENS; Robert CRESAP; Joseph CRESAP and others, Esqrs.; Lewis DAVIDSON; Thomas DORSEY; Thomas DOWDEN; Jacob DURKET; JOHN ECKHART; Evan EVANS; John B. FELVER; John FRENCH; Stephen GLANVILL; John GREENLAND; George GUNNETT; James HADLAY; Patrick HARKINS; John HAUGHEY; Samuel E. HENDERSON; John HOBLITZELL; Samuel HOBLITZELL; Prescilla HOLDEN; Isaac HOLLINGSWORTH; Mrs. Ann HOLTZMAN; All--e HOUSE; Elijah HOWELL; John HOYE; Elisha HUFF; Morgan HUFF; Hugh IJAMS; Ignatius JARBOE; Moses JOHNSON; Adam KAMP; Charles KELLY; John A. KILGORE; John KIMBERLY; Jacob LANTZ; John V. LARIMORE; William LAWHEAD; Jesse LESSURE; Mrs. LINN, widdow; Adam LITTLE; Ralph LOGSDEN, sen.; Samuel LOUDERMILK; Peter M'CANN; Joseph M'GAHEN; William M'GRUDER; John M'KINNEY; Charles and Mary M'KINNY; Jane M'KINTOSH; John M'MAHON; William M'MAHON; Jereh MANET; John MARKEY; John MATHEWS; Miss Nancy MATTINGLY; Daniel MILL-HOLLAND; Mrs. MINER; Miss Elizabeth MINICK; James MORRISON; David OLIVER; William OQUIM; John PRICE; Conway RECTOR; Miss Catherine REED; Mrs. Mary REYNOLDS; John SAYLOR; Walter SELBY; John SHRYER; John SIMKINS; Walter SLICER; Jacob SNYDER; Jacob SPEELMAN; Michael SPRIGG; Christian STATTS; David STEMPLE; James SULLIVAN; Jeremiah SULLIVAN; Robert SWAN; Moses TABBS; Michael TIERNAN; Benjamine TOMLINSON; P.M. TOMLINSON; Peter TOOL; John TWIGG and

ALLEGANY FREEMAN

Nathan WILLSON; John VAW; Ebener. VOWELL; Samuel WALLS; Thomas WHITE; Henkrey WINEHOUR; Jacob WITT, senr.; John WORKMAN; William WRIGHT; Mrs. Rachel WYATT; William WYATT, sen. - Samuel SMITH, P.M.
530 a. for sale on great Western Turnpike Road, 6 miles east of the Big Crossings, 30 miles from Cumberland and 30 miles from Uniontown, Pa, by the heirs of John JONAS, Allegany Co, decd. - Lucy JONAS, Adolph JONAS, admrs.
Francis MADORE gives notice to persons indebted to him for meat, etc.

338. Oct 28 1815 [Library of Congress] - Dissolution of partnership of Robert M'GUIRE & Frederick T. HARRISON.

339. Nov 4 1815 [Library of Congress]
U. BRUCE, expecting to be absent from home for a few months during the winter, requests persons having business with him to call on Mr. M. C. SPRIGG.
Fashionable goods - BRUCE & SPRIGG, Cumberland.
Margaret COMPTON offers reward for stoute negro girl named Lydia PILES, about 18, rusty complexion, rough skin, generally wears hair in plaits, good house servant and seamstress; came originally from Prince William Co, Va.

340. Dec 23 1815 [Md. Hist. Soc.]
Samuel THOMAS will soon submit reply to Walter SLICER who entirely "misrepresented [Thomas] for the purpose of answering his own malicious views."
Journeyman blacksmith wanted - William RIELY, Old-Town, Md.
Federal Direct Tax is due and payable at the following places [rearranged in alphabetical order]: Mathew BALL on George's Creek; Joseph FRANCE on the Big Crossings; Meshec FROST; James KING, Fifteen-mile Creek; George M. LAUBINGER, Old-Town; John MATHEWS, near the state road; William PRICE, Western Port; George RINEHART, Green Glades; John ROBISON; Alexander SMITH, in Rine's Glades; Thomas STALLINGS, Murley's Branch; Jesse TOMLINSON, Esq on the Little Crossings.
Wm. M'MAHON and Samuel THOMAS have formed a co-Partnerhsip, under the firm of M'MAHON & THOMAS and are now opening for sale Seasonable Goods, selected in Phila and Balt.
Fulling, dyeing and finishing - Frederick SIMONS. Goods will be taken in at the Tavern in Cumberland where he resides.
Philip WINGERT and Peter TOOLE have formed a co-partnership in the fulling, dyeing and dressing of cloth at Philip and John WINGERT's on Jenning's Run, 3 miles from Cumberland.
Noah RIDGELY, sole proprietor of Lee's Family Medicines, continues carefully to prepare Lee's Highly approved family medicines. Available from Samuel MAGILL's Book and Stationary Store, Cumberland.
Sale of farm on banks of Potomac, 10 miles above Cumberland, 800 a., with saw-mill, orchard, 2-story dwelling house, kitchen, stables. Thomas CRESAP, living on the premises.
The Market-House in Cumberland, is now nearly completed.
John HAYS & Co. have opened store in the frame building owned and occupied by Charles F. BRODHAG, near the Post-office. Dry Goods, hardware, Queensware and Groceries.
John RODEHEAVER offers reward for steer which strayed from a drove of cattle of his, near Cumberland.

ALLEGANY FREEMAN

John SIMONS has removed his tavern stand to large building opposite his late stand, owned by Mr. M'KINLEY.

341. Dec 30 1815 [Md. Hist. Soc.]
George THISTLE requests indebted persons to settle accounts.
Moses KELLY requests those indebted to settle their accounts.
Michael LANE to commence a brewery in Cumberland and seeks farmers to supply him with quantities of malt.

CUMBERLAND GAZETTE

Published by William BROWN, Cumberland

342. Thursday, Jul 21, 1814. Vol. 1, No. 23 From Microprint at Lib. of Congress.
The Friends of Peace, in Allegany co, are to assemble and choose three delegates to represent them in General Committee. The Committee will meet at the house of Walter SLICER to recommend four suitable persons to represent this county in the next general Assembly.
Reply by Roger PERRY, Cumberland, to recent publication of Josiah M. ESPY, wherein "my character [was] most wantonly asaailed." [Apparently involves sale of property which Espy said Perry had no legal authority to make.] Reference is made to Mrs. MURDOCH and her family.
Robert M'GUIRE - Clock and Watch maker, Cumberland, has commenced business in the room lately occupied by Doctor READ as a shop.
Jonathan HENDRIXSON has commenced the fulling & dyeing business at Mr. HUSHER's mill, in Cumberland Valley, Bedford co, Pa, 14 miles from Cumberland. Cloth will be taken in at Jacob HOBLITZELL's store in Cumberland and returned every three weeks dressed.
Large quantity of Bacon, assorted hams, shoulders and middlings - Wm. M'MAHON, Cumberland.
Doctor READ has lately received a fresh supply in addition to his former stock of Drugs and Medicines.
Deer Skins wanted. Peter LOWDERMILK, Cumberland.
For sale - wagon and four horses. Roger PERRY, Cumberland.
John RESONER, Allegany co, insolvent debtor, to be discharged from the custody of the Sheriff. Hanson BRISCOE, Clk. of Allegany Co.
I am authorized by David COX to receive the several sums due him and to sell a tract of land called the Promised Land in Allegany co, 179 a., 1 1/2 miles from Cumberland. Thomas THISTLE.
Persons indebted to Joseph RODEFER are to make payments to Thomas THISTLE.
Dry Goods, Hardware and Groceries. William HOBLITZELL.
Reward offered for deserter, George HESS, private in the 36th Regiment, U.S. Infantry, deserted from Piscataway, Prince George's co, Md. on 14 May. He was born in Hagers-Town, 22 yrs of age, black hair, small black eyes, dark complexion and pock marked, very stout form, by profession a waggoner or blacksmith. Has been seen in vicinity of Martinsburgh, Va, where he has of late resided. Wm. JONES, Lt. 38th Regt. "Desertion is one of the least of his crimes."

INDEX

ABBERT James 337
ABBOT James 332
ABERNATHY Mr. 157
 William 98
ABRAMS Henrey 337
ADAM Catharine 95
ADAMS James 63
 John 7, 13, 17, 47, 88, 92, 96, 119, 199
 Otho 92
 Peter 26
 William 103
ADDISON Reverend 58
ADELSPEYER Francis 281
AISQUITH Edward 319
ALBRIGHT Christian 332
ALEXANDER William 8
ALLABAUGH John 28
ALLCOCK John 103
ALLEN James 88
 Martha K. 88
ALLINDER William 83
ALLISON John 32, 54
 William 103, 128
ALTER Frederick 87, 94, 118
 Mary 169
 Samuel 134, 169
AMIS --- 28
AMMERSON John 28
AMOS James 82
ANDERSON F. 141
 Franklin 129, 149
 Jabez 4
 James 281
 Richard 32
 Robert 321
ANGLE Elizabeth 212
 Jacob 47, 121
 Joseph 212
ANIBA William 135
ANKONY George 165
 Henry 49
 Margaret 159
ANTHONY 141
APRICE Edward 36
ARMOR William 11, 22, 27, 28, 89, 118, 125, 146, 186
ARMSTRONG Elizabeth 281
 Thomas 307
 William 308

ARNOLD Archibald 306
 Henry 4, 131, 132
 Jonathan 281
ARTHER Elizabeth 313
ARTHUR George 322
ARTZ Christian 8, 78, 134, 176
 P. 222
 Peter 15, 19, 72, 79, 172, 257
 Sally 257
 Widow 28
ARTZ & EMMERT Messrs. P. 48, 98
ASH Jacob 157
ASHBURY John 148
 Mary 134
ASHBY 204
ATHUM Benedict 235
ATHY John 305
ATKINSON Henry 148
 Michael 148
AULL William 279
AVEY Christian 28
AYERS James 28
AYRES James 112

BACHTEL Martin 57
BAECHTEL Isaac 136, 166
 Jacob 95
 Martin 7, 30, 115, 135
BAECHTELL Martin 40
BAGFORD James W. C. 148
BAIGHTLE Isaac 254
BAILEY Edward B. 128
 George 16
 Robert 104, 128, 156
BAILY Robert 157
BAKER Abraham 96
 Alexander 157
 Anne 15
 John 28
 Nicholas 34, 36, 57
 Richard 15
 Sarah 36, 57
BAKER & ZIGLAR 59
BALL B. 75, 147
 Charles Burges 75, 147

 Fayette 75, 147
 George W. 147
 George Washington 75
 Mathew 306, 340
BANE Martin 319
BANKS Clement 28
BARBER Resin 125
BARCUS John 291, 322
BARGELD Michael 28
BARINGER George 28
BARKDOLL Joseph 110
BARKHART Christopher 49
BARKMAN Henry 152
 Mary 28
BARNARD Notley 332
BARNES Mary 130
BARNET Jacob 1
BARNETT Cassandra 148
 Elizabeth 28, 34
 Henry 17
 Henry Jacob
 Jacob 10, 17, 27, 34, 79
 John 27, 35, 39
BARNHART 153
BARNS Barnabas 332
BARNWARD Peter 291
BARR Barbara 47, 256
 David 69, 100, 159
 Jacob 26, 99, 106, 111, 112, 118, 126, 143
 John 88, 204
BARRICK John 36
BARTLETT John 55, 132
BARTON Mr. 22, 107
 Stephen 41
BARTRUFF Andrew 305
BATEMAN Nathaniel 156
BATES William H. 64
BAUGHMAN 77, 147
 Andrew 114
 George 1
BAUMWART Margaret 141
BAXTER William W. 99
BAYLY 229
 George 23
 Mr. 40, 41, 47
 Samuel 21, 27, 28, 35, 133, 183, 184, 261
BEACH Aaron 163
BEAIN Daniel 313

INDEX

BEALE Samuel 337
  Thomas 337
BEALL Alphus 337
  Aza 278, 302, 306
  David 305
  Dennis 281
  Isaac 281
  John Lee 42
  N. 333
  Samuel 281, 291, 305
  Thomas 281, 291, 305, 333
  Upton 32, 148
BEALMER Lewis 179
BEAN Barton 163, 169
  George 46, 94, 117
BEAR Isaac 163
  Samuel 138, 160
BEARD Andrew 101
  John 3, 9, 25, 75, 101, 118, 255
  Mary 149
  Michael 3
  Nicholas 92
  Nicholas P. 101
BEARD & KESSINGER 7, 135
BEATTY Elie 6, 19, 48, 67, 80, 93, 94, 166, 178, 183
  Elizabeth 76
  James 36
  William 71, 76, 122
BEAVER John 124
BECK 130
BECK Arthur 166
BECKLEY Henry 121, 122, 136, 139, 149
BECKLEY Sally 139
BECKLY Henry 53
BEECHER Mr. 34
  William 26, 27, 53, 271
BEECHER & NEAD 187, 221
BEECHLER George 271
BEELOR Barbara 25
  Samuel 25
BEIGHLER George 53, 90
BEIGLER George 34
BELCH Catharine 139
  James 2, 38
  Susanna 38
  William 6

BELL Andrew 70
  Anthony 70
  Benjamin 36
  Cephas 182
  Frederick 70
  Jacob 70
  Montgomery 305
  Peter 26
BELLER Benjamin 119
BELT Richard G. 95
  Tilghman 332
BELZHOOVER 27
BELTZHOOVER 35
  George 24
  Jacob 161
  Mr. 2, 26, 178, 209
BEN 37, 100
BENCE Henry 86
  Mary 86
BENDER George 48, 96
BENNER Henry B.T. 3
  John B. T. 22, 23
BENNETT 207
  Robert 332
BERNET Hezekiah 125
BERRY 96, 326
  Ann 36, 165
  Jeremiah 291, 332, 333
  John 36
BESHORE John 103
BETTY 19
BEVENS Basil 47
  Henry 47
  Leonard 47, 60, 166
  Mr. 166
BEVINS Fanny 313
  Leonard 254
BEVORE Cornelius 321
BIERSHING William 153
BILL 92, 182, 288, 326
BILMYER Martin 60
BINKLEY Eve 91
  George 15, 26, 27, 29, 91, 97
  Jacob 4, 15, 40, 122, 146
  Philip 53
BIRELEY John 7
  Lewis 7, 132
  William 7
BIRLY William 132

BLACK James 310, 329
  John 305, 330
BLACKBURN John 125
BLACKFORD John 31, 43, 57, 88, 228, 242, 243
BLACKISTON Joseph 114, 118, 147
BLAIR Andrew 30
  James 337
  James C. 313
  John 145
BLAKEMORE William 28, 114
BLAKENEY Perren 23
  William 103
BLEAKNEY William 128
BLENTLINGER Jacob 24
BLOCHER 305
  George 322, 327, 332
  Jacob 327
BOB 115, 147
BODENHAMER William 88
BOERSTLER Charles G. 26, 183, 196, 197
  Christian 167
  Colonel C. G. 8
  D. A. 139
  Daniel 78
  G. W. 41, 129, 139
  George
  Jacob 41
BOND Edward 81
  Mrs. 106
BOONE Mordecai 23
BOORD Andrew 7
BOOSE John 337
BOOTH 28, 68, 268
  John 100
  Maria 100
  Maria C. 28
BOROFF Adam 165
BORSTLER Charles G. 28
  Christian 177
  Doctor C. 41
BORTLE John 125
BOSTATER Jacob 64
BOTELAR Hezekiah 235
BOTELER Edward 88, 243
  Thomas 128
BOUDON David 82
BOURNS John 117, 119
BOWARD Michael 40

100

INDEX

BOWART Margaret 48
BOWEN Thomas 166
BOWER Abraham 10
  George 72, 80, 94, 106, 135
  Jacob 134, 144
  John 5, 160
  Lucinda 94
  Moses 125
  Rev. 8, 10, 188
BOWLES Daniel 109
  James H. 11, 21
  John 7, 44, 88, 136, 157
  Samuel 91, 130
BOWMAN Margaret 28
BOWSART Mr. 114
BOWSER John 125
BOYD Edmund 276, 277, 333
  Elisha 272
  Gideon 249, 281, 322
  James 277
  John 60
  John P. 219
  Joseph 97, 132
  W. 149
  Walter 79, 134
BOYER Abraham 55
  Detrick 64
  Jacob K. 15
  Joseph 125
  Peter 130
BOYLE John 337
BRADHAG C.F. 332
BRADLEY Miss 337
  Nicholas 305
BRADSHAW Ann 165
  George 154, 165
  John 52, 146, 151, 154, 226
  Martha 28
BRADY Benjamine 332
  Charles 305
BRAGONIER Daniel 7, 30, 45, 66, 96
  George 7
  Henry 7
  Mr. 11
BRANDT John 337
BRANSTETTER Andrew 28

BRANT John 313
  Mrs. 322
BRANTNER George 28
BRASHEARS Jesse 332
BRAZIER William 19, 38, 71, 144, 153, 166
BREATHETT Edward 28
BRENDEL William 92
BRENDLE George 132, 226
BRENT Thomas 38, 43
  Thomas C. 182, 242
BRENTLINGER William 180
BREWER Joseph 48, 140
  Nicholas 49
BRIAN 216
BRIDENHART Mrs. 283
BRIDLEY Patrick 72
BRIEN 247
  John 243
  Mr 118
BRINER Peter 164
BRISCOE Charles H. I. 332
  Chs. H. J. 291
  Hanson 291, 314, 322, 342
BRISKER Joseph 133
BRODHAG Charles F. 313, 340
  Charles Frederick 301
BROGUNIER David 118
  Samuel 118
BRONAUGH John W. 75
BROOK Doctor T. F. 327
BROSIUS Jacob 11, 205
BROWAD John H. 332
BROWN Alexander 322, 332
  Benjamin(e) 281, 290, 291
  Elie 47
  George 34, 322
  James, & Company 229, 238
  John 94, 277, 281
  Lazarus 267
  Matthew 191, 194, 207, 229
  William 52, 179

BROWN & WATSON 115
BROWNE Aqa. H. 322
BROWNING John 60
BRUA Gustavus 92, 138
  Jacob 159
  John 138
BRUCE Andrew 293, 321
  George 281, 285, 300, 319
  U. 339
  Upton 281, 285, 295, 300, 332
  William 285, 300
BRUCE & SPRIGG 339
BRUMBAUGH Daniel 57, 100, 134
  David 48, 121
  George 2, 53, 98
  Jacob 120, 151
  Joseph 212
  Mr. 186
BRUNNER Jacob 98
  Rosanna 159
BRUSH Peter 28
BRYAN John 82
BUCHANAN John 7, 28, 30, 228, 250
  Judge 22, 56, 93
  Thomas 7, 134, 136, 140
BUCHWALTER Gerhart 163
BUCK John 125
BUCKEY 207
BUCKWALTER Gerhart 43
BUEHLER George 111
BUGH James 337
  Richard I. 313
BUMBERGER John 100
BURBRIDGE John 195
BURCH Fielder 322
BURCKHART 89
BURCKHART Christopher 88
BURCKHARTT Christopher 62, 96, 114, 117, 119
  Henry 119
BURGER John 28
BURKDALE Peter 28
BURKHART 265
BURNBRIDGE John 334
BURNS Barnabas 313
  Barney 322
  William H. 69, 285
BUSEY Pall 332

INDEX

BUSY John 322
BUTLER Jack 105
 Jacob 114, 135
 John G. 332
 Letty 51
 Polly 28
 Samuel 88
 William 51
BYERS Jacob 87

CAKE Henry 2, 99
 John 20, 123
CALDWELL Thomas 272
CALEFLESH Eve 332
CALEMESE George 332
CALMEES Isaa 337
CAMELL John 319
CAMPBELL 291
 Archibald 296
 John 285
 Thomas 62
CANDERWINE Charles 274
CAPES William 198
CAPRON Mrs. 26
CAREY 69, 154, 252
CARICO B. 322
 Barton 44, 283, 286, 318, 322, 325, 337
 Mr. 277
CARLTON James 291
 James P. 281, 305, 306
 Joseph 209
 Richard 281
CARR Elizabeth 50
 John 163
 Major 219
 Nicholas 50
CARRICO Barton 305
 Mr. 70
CARROLL Charles 1, 3, 7, 27, 30, 54, 133, 205, 228
 Jane 205
 Major 94
 Major C. 166
 Most Reverend Archbishop 88
 William 125
CARTER 37
 Colonel 150
 Jerry 103
 Joseph 313

 Josias 168
 Mrs. 313
CARY 197
 Robert T. 87
CATHERS William 305
CATTELL Joel 337
CAUFFMAN Samuel 28
CAYLOR John 337
CELLAR George 53, 114
 John 115
CELLER Isaac 35
CELLERS Joseph 127
CEZERON Mr. 71
CHAMBERS Robert 39
CHAPLAIN Elizabeth 138
CHAPLINE Catharine B. 8
 Elizabeth 131, 246
 James 250
 James N. 246
 Jeremiah 8, 245, 246
 Joseph 206, 243, 246
 Mary Ann 246
 Ruhemia 246
 Susanna 246
CHAPMAN Collimore 337
CHARLES 37, 100, 114, 137
CHARLTON 98
 Mary 92
 Mr. 161
CHENEY David 109
 Jeremiah 80, 109
 John 109
 Robert 22
CHESLEY Alexander 58, 77
 Elizabeth 77
 Sarah 58
CHESTON James 93
CHEW 38, 45, 134, 257
 O. H. W. 148
 Samuel 7
 Samuel A. 99, 145, 146
CHRISTIAN Daniel 23
CHRISTMAN Frederick 277
CLAGETT J. B. 135
 Mr. A. 62
 Zachariah 128
 Doctor 243

CLAPSADDLE Anna 65
CLARK Anna 305
 George 337
 Jacob 332
 John 64
 Joseph 291, 322, 337
 Mary 28
 Zadok 292
CLARKE Hiram 305
CLEAVER George 305
CLEMMER James 307
 Lewis 305
CLIFTON Nathan D. 331
CLINTON Thomas 291, 322
CLOPPER Francis C. 121
 Nicholas 47
CLOUSE Henry 295
COBLENTZ Barbara 298
 Jacob 298
 John 298
 Philip 298
COBURN Amariah 305
COCHRAN James 277, 313
 Ninian 279, 319, 322
COCKEY Joshua 44
CODDINGTON Benjamin 332
COFFROTH 254
 Conrod 10
COKENDAFFER Leonard 144
COLE George 154
COLEMAN Patrick 332
COLIFLOUR George 28
COLIFLOWER George 47, 101
 John 47
COLLIER William 155
COLLINS Daniel 291, 305, 313
 Harriot 337
 John 322
 Mathew 6
COMBS John 116, 133
COMPTEN William S. 6
COMPTON Margaret 161, 339
 Rebecca 332, 337
 Thomas 144, 146
 William S. 94, 168
CONAWAY John 322
CONGRADT G. M. 135
CONNELL James 28

102

INDEX

CONNER John 305, 313, 322
Mary 313
Mrs. 332
CONRAD John 99, 109
CONRADT G. I. 250
G. M. 115
J. 61
Jacob 32, 248, 258
M. 61
Michael 32, 248, 258
CONWAY John 337
William 177
COOK David 114
Ezekiel 332
George 332
Henry 98, 130
John 2, 3, 97, 103
Mary 305
Mr. 82
Mr. D. 114
COOKE William B. 332
COOKES Adam 65
Mary 65
CORCORARD James 313
CORL John 28
CORN Jacob 281
COSKERY Michael 103
COSS John 77
COW John 13, 66
COWEN Robert 6, 166
COX Charles 47
David 342
Jonathan 317, 332
COZENS William R. 337
CRAFT Henry 135
CRAMER Jonas 166
Peter 47
CRAMPTON 247, 283
Thomas 7, 53, 201
CRAWFORD John 27, 36, 46, 47, 140, 237
Thomas B. 69, 285
William 97
CREAGER Doctor 22
Peter 118
CREAMOUR John 291
CREEGAN James 291
CRESAP Hariot 322
James 322
James M. 230, 322, 329, 330, 332

Joseph 224, 291, 313, 334, 337
Mary 313, 322
Polly 281
Robert 337
Sarah 224
Thomas 281, 328, 340
CRINER John 137
CRISSINGER John 15, 92
CROMWELL John 36
John C. 47
Joseph 140, 310, 313, 329, 330, 332
Nathan 47, 79, 149, 168, 329, 330
Oliver 293, 330
Phil. 330
Philemon 39, 140, 310, 329
Stephen 39
CROMWELL & MARTIN 157
CROSS John 170
CRUMBAUGH John 48
Mary 160
Samuel 48
CRUSE John 292
CUGING James 313
CUNKLETON 223
CUNNINGHAM John 326
William 326
CURTIS William 125, 256, 257
CUSHWA David 39
John 5, 81, 91, 105, 111
CUSTER Emanuel 322
John 313
CUTAR George 124

DAILEY James 281
DANDER Thomas 305
DANISON Elijah 321
DANNY Mrs. 291
DARBY John 204
DAVAGE Rezin 305
DAVID 138, 147
DAVIDSON George E. 106
John M. 195
Lewis 313, 337
Lewis G. 305
William 332

DAVIS --- 168
Daniel 109
Eleanor 136
Ephraim 23, 88
George W. 179, 181
Henry 106
James 24, 56, 277
John 133
Joseph 313
Mary 45, 61, 143, 147
Mr. 219
Rezin 136
Samuel B. 26, 71, 220
Solomon 291, 313
Stephen 45, 61, 127, 137, 143
Thomas 283
William 8, 45, 61, 143
DAVISON John M. 163
DAVY 147
DAWSON Benjamin 308
William 125
William R. 281, 304
DEAKINS John 76, 319
DEAL Joseph 299
DEAMS Frederick 291
DECKART Mr. 92
DECKERT Catharine 92
DECUIS Fredrick 313
DEGROFF Abraham 28
DEGROFFT A. 149
DEHART Samuel 88
DEITZ John 3
DELAHUNT William 38, 151
DELOUGHERTY John 305
DENEAL William 190
DENT Lewis 291
DERROUGH Maret 291
DICK 36, 147
DICKENS Moses 332
DICKEY 54
W. 132
William 146
DICKSON James 99
DIDIE Solomon 118
DIEHL Catherine 87
Henry 87
DIETZ John 17, 92
DILLAHUNT William 167
DILLEHAY Thomas L. 28
DILLMAN H. 26, 85, 148
DILLMAN Henry 26

INDEX

DITTO Abraham 69, 199
DIXON William 27
DOAK Robert 37
DONALDSON James Lowry 119
  John A. 130, 169
DORSEY Doctor 47
  F. 196
  Frederick 3, 136, 173
  Harry W. 179
  John E. 177, 210
  Nicholas 115
  Roderick 196
  Thomas 337
  William H. 177, 210
DORSEY, NANENKAMPF, and HAMMOND 98
DOUGHERTY Daniel 332
DOUGLASS Robert 67, 155
DOWDEN Thomas 337
DOWNES Benjamin 125
DOWNEY Basil 125
  Robert 25, 72, 81, 99
  William 79, 81, 96, 99, 178
DOWNIN John 94, 99, 114, 125, 137, 167
DOWNS Charles 57
DOYLE George 125, 152, 155
DRURY Ignatius 169
DUBUISSON --- 21
DUCKWORTH George 305
DUDDY William 305
DUFFIELD William 281
DUFFY John 332
DUFFY Patrick 4
DUHAMEL Rev. 92, 205
DULL Elizabeth 166
DULY Barton 55
DUNHAM David 215
DUNMORE 166
DUNN George 11, 165
  Hugh 281, 332
  Jacob 7, 30, 165
  Lewis 283
  Mr. 254
DUNNX John 28
DUNTON Levin 291
DURBIN Nicholas 328
DURKET Jacob 337
DUVALL Benjamine 332

DYCKE Ann 182
  Valentine 182
DYSART James 322

EACKER George 28
EADS John 28
EARECKSON James 100
EASTON E. 74
  Elisha 88
  Hezekiah 202
EBERT John 26, 87, 161
ECARD John 111, 128
ECHART John 281
ECKERD George 37
ECKHART John 337
EDWARDS P. 139
  Thomas 11, 136, 149, 205, 211
EICHELBERGER D. 236
  Frederick 5
  Mrs. 52
  Theobald 36, 52, 166
  William 125
EICHELBERNER Theobald 115, 129
EINGLER Mr. 240
ELIJAH 39
ELLICKSON William 10
ELLIOTT John 313
  Zedock 281
EMBICH Christopher 26, 36, 236
  Philip 26, 37
EMMERT --- 222
  Benjamin 78
  George 79, 89, 94, 104, 135, 137, 146
  Leonard 146
  Michael 146
EMMERY George 31
EMORY Thomas 291
EMRICK Andrew 291, 332
ENNALLS Elizabeth G. 322
ENOS Stephen 222
ESPY Captain D. 283
  Josiah M. 298, 342
EVANS Evan 337
  Gabrial D. 332
  John 72
  Oliver 268
  Samuel 291

  Sarah 246
  William 39, 246
EVATT 309
EVERHART 247
Evit's (Evitt's) Creek 292, 295, 308

FACKLER Maria 28
FAIRFAX Ferdinand 114
FANNING Dennis 322
FARMER William 324
FARQUIER Captain 125
FARRON Edward 161
  John 161
FASTNAUGHT Barnabas 43
FAWBLE Peter 175
FEAGUE George 106
FECHTIG --- 169
  C. 61
  C., and son 181
  Christian 9, 17, 21, 24, 27, 48, 64, 95, 98, 161, 181, 189
  F. 144
  Fred'k 226
  L. 22
  Lewis R. 28
  Louis 97
  Louis R. 181, 187
  Margaret 27
  Mr. 172, 226
FEDRAY John 160
FEE Michael 305
  Rebecca 281
FEIDT John 138
FELBER John B. 337
FERGUSON Mr. 223
FERREE Cornelius 88
FETTER Daniel 321
FIEDT John 104
FIELD Henry 147
FIELDS Isaiah 149
FIERY --- 7, 36
  Henry 83
  John 69
FINLEY Michael A. 136
FIRESTONE Michael 62, 77, 116
FIREY Henry 94
  Jacob 94, 164
  Joseph 94
FISHACH Frederick 3

INDEX

FISHER John D. 28
FITE Peter 21
FITLER Ann 291
FITZHUGH Colonel 157
  William 28, 88, 114, 132, 136, 147, 157
FLATHER Jacob 332
  Philip 332
FLEMING Thomas 105, 134
FLENNER Philip 125
FLOOD William P. 88
FLORA Nancy 146
FLOREY Christopher 68
FOLK Casper 28
  John 313
FORCE Abraham 18, 49, 222, 259
FORD Joseph 114
  William 39
FOREMAN 86
  Conrad 32
FORMAN James 88
FORREST Joseph 296
FOUTZ Charlotte 180
FOX George 28
  William 334
FRAEE Jonathan 313
FRANCE Joseph 306, 340
FRANCIS Emanuel 34, 36
FRANKENBERY Samuel 147
FRANKINBURY & ROSS 98
FRANZ Emanuel 56, 131
  Eve 56
  Henry E. 56
FREANER John 78, 96, 125, 144, 222, 226
  Mr. 181
FREDRICKS John 305
FREED Benjamin 228
FRENCH George 81, 87, 100
  John 337
  Thomas 81
FRICK John 194
FRIEND Eleanor 118
  Jacob 118
  Robert T. 56, 118
FRITZ Nicholas 36, 57
FROST Isaiah 334
  Josiah 305, 313
  Meshec(k) 334, 340

FUET Thomas I. 104, 138, 146, 149
FULK Casper 123
  Joshua 28
FULLER Caleb 29
  Jacob 291
FULTON William 28
FUNK --- 229
  David 116
  Elizabeth 91
  Henry 100
  Henry B. 150
  Jacob 39
  John 100
  Martin 30, 57, 142
  Samuel 97
  Widow 30, 57, 142
FY William 3

GABBY John 119
  William 19, 72, 117, 119
GAITHER Edward 72, 74, 99, 134, 251
  Henry 46, 72, 251
  Steuart 72, 73, 251
GALLOWAY B. 1
  Benjamin 34, 236, 239, 244
  Mr. 36, 38
GARDNER Peter 125
GAREY Peter 322
GAREY & ZIGLAR 59
GARRETT James 133
  Thomas 3
GARY George 60
  Peter 315
GASAWAY Ely 291
GATES Benjamin 147
  William Seph 291
GAY Peter 125
GEBHART John 327
GEERHART Sophia 28
GEHR Daniel 28, 255, 275
GEISENDORF Mrs. 74
GEISER Michael 127
GELLER John 291
GELWICKS Charles 25
  John 25, 38, 60, 120
GENRES Mr. 27

GEORGE 57, 80, 306, 311, 327, 340
GEORGE John 101
GEPHART John 290, 325
  Peter 305
GERHART Christian 48
  Sophia 126
GERLACH Henry 83
GETTER George 291
GHEISTWEIT Reverend 48
GIBBONEY John 7, 40, 70
GIBBONS Moses 124
GIBBS Franklin W. 300
GIERHART Catharine 99
  Christian 99
GIESEY Valentine 121
GILBERT Jacob 223
  Wendel 1, 28, 36, 39
GILLER George 305
GILMUR John 281
GILPIN William 125
GIVIN James 38
GLANVILL Stephen 337
GLOSSBRENNER Peter 23, 70, 122
GLOSSBRINNER Adam 98
GLOSTER 294
GOLL Christian F. 127
GOOD Christian 47, 133
  John 12, 25, 177, 182
  William 12, 178, 182, 243
Gordon's Tavern 163
GORDON Joseph 324
  Robert 291
  Susanna 81, 99
  William 332
GORMLEY Patrick 322
GOWER Jacob 125
GRAFF Joseph 99, 107, 109
  Mr. 1
GRAHAM James 42
  Louisa 313
  William 305
GRAVES John 168
GRAY Anne 10
GRAYBILL Joseph 125
GRAYHAM James 291
GRAYSON, STULL, and WILLIAMS, Messrs 140
GREEK Harry 169

105

INDEX

GREENLAND John 337
GREENWADE Moses 305
GREGG John 142, 168
  William 332
GREGORY James 98
  William 98
GREINER William 20
GRIEVES Thomas 7, 28,
  81, 134, 236
GRIFFIN Thomas 125
GRIFFITH Daniel 12, 36
  Ester 313
GRIM Alexander 111
GRIMES Daniel 281
  James 322
  Robert 74
GRIMM Alexander 88
GROFF John 133
GROSH Frederick 88
GROSNICKEL Peter 8
GROSS Adam 281
GROUND George 95
  Philip 95
  Widow 57
GROVE Philip 3, 148
GRUBER Everhard 111
GUNN Jacob 29, 291
GUNNETT George 291, 337
GUY Bill 64
GUYTON Benjamin 7

HACKMAN Barbara 67, 75
  Henry 67, 75
HADLAY James 337
HAGER --- 99, 118
  Christian 3, 11, 37,
  43, 104, 165, 173
  George 100, 258
  Jonathan 1, 27, 130,
  169, 223
  Mr. 179, 183
  Samuel 52, 53, 155,
  169, 221, 225, 270
HAHN Henry 114, 122, 123
HAINS George 336
  Hannah 336
HALBERT William 87
HALL Richard 36
  Thomas B. 3, 26, 35,
  52, 55, 103, 136, 148,
  152, 173
HALLER Joshua 97

HAMILTON Samuel 115
HAMMEL Barbara 167
  George 167
HAMMER Francis 291
  George 181
HAMMET Samuel 33
HAMMETT David 130
  M'Kelvie 28
  Samuel 27, 110, 117,
  121, 168
  William 7, 17, 28
  William C. 17, 26
HAMMOND David 103
  Doctor 98, 118
  Peter 56
  W. 146
  William 26, 96, 148,
  167, 196
HAMMONS Thomas 3
HANDY John 330
HANE Daniel 140
HANENKAMPF A. 196
  Doctor A. 89
HANNAH 190
HANNENKAMPF Doctor A.
  99
HANSEL Philip 322
HANSON 147
HARBAUGH George 49,
  265
HAREGROVE Henry 125
HARGETT Mr. 169
HARKESS John 332
HARKINS Patrick 337
HARLAN Caleb 97
HARMAN John 123
HARNESS Rebecca 305
HARPER Lewis 115
HARRIS Daniel 291, 313
  Thomas 131
HARRISON Benjamin 64
  Doctor E. 1
  Elisha 1, 257
  Frederick T. 334,
  338
  John S. 272
  Harry's Town 48
HARRY 36
HARRY David 3, 36, 37,
  83, 87, 92, 132,
  137, 138, 146, 166,
  236

  George 1, 24, 58, 75,
  140, 176, 186
  George & Company 223
  George, I. 62, 77,
  103, 159, 189, George
  M. 153
  Jacob 214
  John 1, 3, 18, 22, 24,
  62, 75, 88, 89, 118,
  134, 135, 140, 176,
  186
  John & George 36, 43,
  50, 80, 223, 268
  Mary 214
  William 83, 92, 132
HARTMAN Isaac 107
HARTSOCK Daniel 139
HARTZOCK William 29
HARTZOG John 12
HATFIELD A. 137
  Abraham 146
HAUCK George 291
HAUGHEY John 337
HAUGMAN George F. 222
HAUN Mr. 1
HAUSER Ezra 313
  Isaac 67, 88
  Michael 87
  Mr. 137
HAUVERMALE Ludwick 114
HAWKEN Christian 51, 144
  Jacob 94
  Samuel 144, 155
HAWKENS C. 182
HAWPE Henry 37
HAYDON Robert 81
HAYES Jeremiah 36, 134
HAYS --- 172
  John 337
  John, & Company 340
  Robert 47, 266
  Simon 328
HAZARD 16
HEBB George 99
HECK Cahrles 305
HECKMAN Matthias 155
HEDRICK George 36
HEFFLEBOWER Daniel 37
HEFLEICH Peter 1
HEFLEICH & NEAD 77
HEFLEIGH Peter 48

INDEX

HELM Mary 180
  Sophia W. 153
  Thomas 160
HELSENSTEIN Reverend 247
HENDERSON Archibald 121
  Griffith 121
  James 322
  Samuel E. 337
HENDRICKSON James 322
HENDRIXSON Jonathan 309, 342
HENNEBERGER John 91, 104
HENNING Thomas 7
HENNYBERGER John 28, 51, 270
HENSMINGER Christian 241
HENTZELMAN John 224
HERBAUGH Jacob 28
  Ludwick 28
HERBERT Elisha 125
  Juliet 188
HERR John 165
  John P. 31, 101, 229
  Samuel 24, 138
HERSHBERGER Jacob 118
HERSHEY Andrew 193
  Barbara 268
  Christian 218
  Isaac 218, 268
  Jacob 66, 87
  John 7, 40, 41, 70, 88, 88, 94, 95, 97, 99, 114, 137, 159, 182, 193, 218
  Mary 28
HESLETINE Ch. 260
  Charles 133, 136
HESS George 36, 342
  Jacob 140, 148, 149
  Mr. 52
HESSON Ann Maria 298
  Baltzer 298
  Catharine 298
  Jacob 298
HETHERINGTON Henry 305
HEYSER Mr. 46
  William 3, 6, 12, 17, 51, 147, 148, 173, 257
HEZ 116
HICKMAN Jacob 305
  Joshua 106

HIDER Adam 332
  Noah 321
HIESTAND Henry 28
HILDEBRAND Conrod 47
HILL William W. 28
HILLAIRD Christopher 160
HILLEARY L. 289, 334
HILLFORTEE Daniel 305
HINCKLE George P. 333
HINE Jacob 125
HINES Daniel 313
HINKLE George P. 291
HINSON Mrs. 28
Hinton Charles 114
HITE John 193
  William 193
HOBLITS William 291
HOBLITZELL George 282
  Jacob 305, 333, 334, 342
  John 313, 337
  Samuel 337
  William 135, 305, 342
  William & Company 327
HOCHLANDER Mr. 228
HOCKMAN Henry 7
HODGES Thomas 7
Hoffer's Mill 138
HOFFER John 116
  Michael 7, 23, 40, 70, 94, 99, 159
HOFFMAN David 281, 286
  George 327
  Henry 108
  Jacob 44
  Jacob V. 322
  John 226, 333
HOG John 322
HOGG John 136, 170
HOGMIRE Conrad 130
H. 162
  Jonas 60, 88, 128, 257
HOLBERT Phebe 191
HOLDEN Priscilla 337
HOLDRIDGE John 291
HOLKER John 96
HOLL John 3, 7
  Mr. 46

HOLLAND Solomon 32
HOLLAR Joseph 249
HOLLINGSWORTH Isaac 337
HOLTZMAN Ann 337
  John 313
HOOK Elias 304
  James 297, 313, 316, 322
  Margaret 304
HOOVER Peter 140
HOPE David 125
HOPKINS 316
HORINE Adam 28
  John 28
HORNER James 322
HORSLER Abraham 198
HOSKENS Benjamin 275
HOSLER Jacob 135
HOTTMAN Isaac 32, 54
HOUCK Henry 22
HOUSE Alle-- 337
  Andrew 306
  John 313, 332
  William 281
HOUSER Charles 293
  Christian 114
  Isaac 114
HOUX George M. 283, 290
  William 290, 322, 332
HOWARD Beal 305
  Benjamin 122
  Lawrence 88
HOWELL Elijah 337
  Peter 281
  Samuel 300
HOWSER Isaac 56
HOY John 332
HOYE John 281, 313, 337
  Mariam 15
  Paul 15, 86
HUBER --- 41
HUDSON Isabella 144
HUFF Elisha 337
  Morgan 337
HUFFMAN David 291
  Jacob 305
  John G. 313
HUGHES Daniel 82
  Barnabas 28
  Colonel 7, 7, 9, 26, 101, 251
  Colonel D. 120

INDEX

Daniel 3, 26, 28, 110, 118, 145, 146, 149
  Joseph 72, 148 Joseph 236
  Robert 7, 43, 88, 98, 134, 147, 242
  Samuel 3, 153, 257
HUGHES & FITZHUGH 122
HUGHS Daniel 19
HULING John 334
HUMRICKHOUSE Albert 47
  John 49
  Peter 73, 94, 99, 172
HUNSBERRY Henry 114
HUNT Job 99
HUNTER David 272
  Gosepli 291
  John 32
  Joseph 34, 37, 208
  Mr. 8
  Squire 157
  William 169
HUNTINGDON Hammond 145
HUNTSBERRY George 118
HUNTSBURY & STRIDER 331
HURDLE Leonard 81, 87
HUSHER David 342
HUSSEY George 244
HUTCHESON Ruben 118
HUYETT Daniel 57, 80, 147
HYLAND Anna 258
  Charlotte 258
  Elisha 258
  John 147
  John R. 258

IJAMS Hugh 337
  William 332
INGMAN Henry 311
INGRAM Joseph 88
INNSKEEP John 334
IRONS John 322
IRVINE William 38
IRVING Patsey 92
  Rev. 77, 92, 96
  Rev. T. P. 139, 149, 160
  Thomas P. 147, 166
IRWIN G. H. 36, 97, 137, 152, 253
  George Hays 28

Gideon H. 96
  Mr. 137
ISENBERGER Gabriel 125

JACK 77, 144, 157, 288
JACKSON Ann 305
  Billy 74
  William 53
JACOB J. J. 330
JACOBS Corbin 36
  J. 313
  John J. 337
JACQUES --- 245
  Denton 15
  Lancelot 88
JAMES 53, 91, 124
JAMES Hugh 313
JARBOE Ignatius 337
JEFFERISS Joseph 291
JEFFERSON John 19
Jenning's Run 295, 306, 340
JEREMIAH 8
JERRY 106
JIM 52
JOBSON William 171
JOE 8
JOHN 7, 196
JOHN, BLACK 330
JOHN, Captain 254
JOHNS Aquilla 99
  John 337
  L. H. 55
JOHNSON Denton 46
  Joshua 321
  Moses 337
  Roger 39
JOHNSTON Arthur 34, 92, 176
  John 66
  John 67, 291
  Mr. 74
  Samuel 332
  Thomas 332
JONAS Adolph 337
  John 337
  Lucy 337
JONES George 281
  Jacob 165
  John 83, 134
  Joshua 125
  Thomas 95, 203

William 277, 305, 322, 342
JOSEPH & WILLIAM 321
JOURDAN John 332
JULIUS Carber 322
  John 119
JUSTIS Peter 5

KAELHOFER Jacob 124
  John 3
KAIGHN William 93
KAMP Adam 337
KAPP Michael 8, 51, 60, 97
KAPP's NED 177
KAUSLER Mr. 1
KAUSLER & GRAFF 7, 72
KAUSLER & GROFF 91
KAY James 78, 107
  Mr. 98
KEALHOFER Henry 81, 131, 137
  Jacob 131
  John 81
KEALHOVER Henry & John 91
KEAN Joseph 108
KEEFER Peggy 139
KEEN, KAIGHN & Company 33, 93, 230
KEENE Thomas 93
KEEPERS Isaac 28
KEIBER George 28
KELLAR Caspar 75
  George 92
  John 84
  Joseph C. 128
  Philip 132
KELLER Elizabeth 305, 322
  John 115
  Thomas 127, 132
KELLY Charles 337
  John V. 7
  Moses 341
KEMP David 28
  Margaret 247
  Rev. 247
  Rev. Doctor 144
KENNEDY Hugh 1, 27, 169
  John 1, 3, 27, 111, 619

INDEX

John & Hugh 52, 84
Rev. 39, 212
Robert 161
Thomas 28, 71
Kershner's Fording 66
KERSHNER A. 142
Andrew 30
George 46, 69, 99, 112, 131, 139
Jacob 7, 39, 69, 70, 94, 133, 135
Jacob P. 96, 123
John 131
M. 26, 149
Martin 28, 30, 72, 101, 123, 157, 167
Michael 277
Philip 26, 41, 70
KESSINGER George 28, 109
Jacob 78, 88, 92, 98, 101, 109, 130
Michael G. 161, 169
KEY Philip Barton 150
KIESACKER Simon 58
KILGORE John A. 337
KIMBERLY John 281, 333, 335, 337
M. 335
Motalena 333
KIMBOLL Mrs. 237
KIMMEL Agnes 278
Gabriel 278
KING Abraham 109, 149
Alexander 323
Jacob 81
James 305, 313, 340
John 36
John O. 81
Mr. 68
William B. 262
KINKADE James 279, 322
KINSELL Frederick 53, 271
Frederick Benjamin Otto 169
KIRBY Thomas 147
KIRKPATRICK 50
KISSINGER John 85
KITCHEN Uriah 46
KITTY 7
KLIMMER Lewis 291
KLINK George 134

KLOTZ Jacob 103
KNABLE Mr. 38
KNIGHT Isaac 143
Moses 172, 215
Philip 313
KNODE Amelia 189
Jacob 19, 86, 98, 136, 157, 189
John 118, 160
KNOLL Jacob 149
KOONSE Nicholas 332
KOONTZ Jacob 313
KOYLER Peter 28
KRAMER John 10
Jonathan 78
KREPS George 7, 20, 36, 50, 109, 146, 168, 208, 258
Martin 7, 109, 208
Mary 165
Michael 55
Mr. 79
Susanna 56
William 1, 11, 27, 28, 36, 53, 69, 81, 87, 91, 132, 165, 178
KRICK Peter 75
KUHN Adam 125
Leonard 17, 25, 44, 51, 94, 270
KUHNS Matthias 246, 246
KURTZ Reverend 163, 169

LAMAR Robert 328
LAMBERT Jacob 67, 75, 114, 123, 126
LANCASTER James 332
John 313
John F. 320
LANDIS Henry 169
LANE Elliot T. 122
James S. 81
John 226
Michael 341
Sarah 142, 146
LANGENECKER Christian 99
LANGLEY John 17

LANTZ C. 27
Catharine 160
Christian 23, 29, 48, 51, 60, 84, 93, 137, 166, 182, 213, 270
Daniel 328
Jacob 299, 328, 337
Mr. 329
Nicholas 109, 149
LARIMORE John V. 337
LATHAN Edward 322
LAUBINGER George M. 306, 331, 340
LAUMAN William 97
LAWHEAD William 337
LAWRENCE Mr. 80
Otho 127, 160
U. 40, 60, 75, 91, 130, 166, 198
Upton 3, 109, 136, 149
LEACH Phillimon T. 322
LEACHLIGHTER Susannah 332
LEANARD Benjamine 332
Jacob 153
Jeremiah 125
LEAR Jacob 104
LEASURE Elijah 28, 96
LEAZEAR John 332
LECKRON Jacob 109, 112
Simon 109, 112
Simon and Jacob 109
LEE 340
Dudly 332
Michael 6
Thomas S. 268
William 41, 243
LEFEVER George 163
John 163
LEIBEY Ann B. 107
LEIGHT Mr. 66
LENHART Elizabeth 48
William 48
LENUM Nace 169
LEONARD 166
LEPARD Adam 181, 191
LEROY 118
LESSURE Jesse 337
Levy's Tavern 268
LEVY Mr. 22
LEWIS 196

109

INDEX

LEWIS Benjamin 193
  Henry 1, 8, 19, 24,
    44, 47, 49, 84, 89,
    95, 98, 106, 115, 135,
    136, 137, 156
  Mr. 94
  William 21
LEWMAN Eli 305
  Elijah 305
  Levi 291
LICKLIDER John 313
LICKLITER Peter 313
LIGGET Jeremiah 28
LIGHTER Andrew 114, 136
  Cathaine 114
  Jacob 138
  John 114
LILLY Sarah 28
LIND Matthew 103, 128, 141
  Reverend 165
LINDENBERGER Frederick, & Company 301
LINGAL Samuel 322
LINGAN General 121
  James M. 262
  Janet 262
LINGO Samuel 332
LINN Mrs. 337
LINTON Joshua 74
LITER Jacob 224
LITTLE Adam 337
  Charles 166
  David 15, 160
  Joseph 144
LITTON James 39
  Mrs. 41
LLOYD 157
LOCHER Henry 3, 131, 155
LOCHRAY James 40
LODGSDON William 281
LOGSDEN Ralph 337
LOGSDON Ralph 319
LOGSTON Archabald 332
LONDON 92
LONG Conrod 1
  John 100, 109, 134
  Peter 109
  Samuel 119, 153
LORMOR Samuel 322
LOTTEBERGER George 99
LOTTERBERGER Mary 36

LOUDERMILK Samuel 337
LOVE Richard H. 66
LOVEALL Zebulon 139
LOVER Zebulon 125
LOWDERMILK Peter 305, 342
  Samuel 283, 309
LOWE George 36, 176
  Nicholas 176
LOWMAN Michael 254
LOWRY William 119
LOWRYE Henry 8, 55
LUCKETT Lawson 98
LUCY 175
LYBERGER Ludwick 281
LYMAN Jacob 215
LYNCH Samuel 95, 108, 134
LYNES James 104, 138, 146
LYNN John 243, 270, 281, 285, 304

M'CALLEY Charles 171
M'CANN Peter 322, 337
M'CARDELL Thomas 15, 19, 36, 114, 217
  William 80
M'CARTY Owen 166
M'CAULEY Hugh 67
M'CHESNEY Adam 37
M'CINNEY C. 305
M'CLAIN Barbara 100
  James 37, 73, 88, 100
  John 37, 49
M'CLANAHAN Alexander 28
M'CLEAVE Robert 160
M'CLEERY J. 137
  John 21
  Mr. 98
M'CLELLAND Alexander 165, 166
  William 61
M'CLUNG William 332
M'COLLOCH George 281
M'CONLEY Elizabeth 125
  William 125
M'CONNEL Samuel 28
M'CORMICK Samuel 60

M'COY Archibald 1
  Daniel 68, 144
  James 1, 60
  John 55
  Tabitha 313
M'CRACKIN Ovid 320
M'CREA James 6
M'CULLOCY Samuel 91
M'CULLOH Mary 322
  Robert 118
M'CULLUGH James 136
M'CUMSEY Thomas 121
M'CUNE Archibald 103
M'CURTIN Daniel 103
M'DANIEL Archibald 332
  Lettice 322
  Richard 141, 322
M'DANILS Elizabeth 291
  Richard 291
M'DERMIT Henry 305
M'DONALD Alexander 219
  John 313, 319
M'DONALD & Ridgely 301
M'DONELD Archabald 322
M'DONNEL Henrey 332
M'DOWELL Charles 233
M'ELFISH Thomas 130
M'ELROY William 65, 144
M'EWEN Samuel 128
M'GAHEN Joseph 337
M'GARVEY Mrs. 291
M'GEE Charles 42
  Thomas 164
M'GINNIS R. 92
M'GOLSBERG Harriot 28
M'GRUDER William 337
M'GUIRE Robert 334, 338, 342
M'HENERY Martha 322
  Sidy 28
M'HENRY Daniel William 285
  John 304
M'ILHENNY Ann 44
  John 4, 24, 61, 98
  John & Joseph 48, 97, 129, 205
  Joseph 4, 24, 36, 37, 61, 147
  Mr. 254
M'KANNA Michael 2

INDEX

M'KEE Hugh 142
  John 60, 121
  Robert 60, 119
M'KEEN Francis P. 28
M'KENNA Allen 291
M'KENNEY Charles 28, 70
M'KIERNAN Peter 144
M'KINEY Peter 313
M'KINLEY Henry 140, 318, 321, 322, 332
  Mr. 340
M'KINLY Henry 277
M'KINNA --- 305
M'KINNEY C. 305, 332
  Charles 280, 332
  John 337
M'KINNY C. 305
  Charles 337
  Mary 337
  Peter 332
M'KINSTRY William T. 122
M'KINTOSH Jane 337
M'KISSACK Mary 147
M'LAAR Patrick 167
M'LANAHAN James 169
  John 103, 128, 169
M'LAUGHLIN Henry 1, 10, 34, 54
  John 28
M'LEERY Andrew 291
M'MAHAN John 305, 313
  Mary 313
  William 291
M'MAHON John 337
  William 291, 309, 323, 337, 340, 342
M'MAHON & THOMAS 340
M'MAN William 332
M'MULLEN John 332
M'NAMEE Job 28
  Moses 30, 100, 133
M'NEAL John 291
M'PHERRIN Mr. 96
  Rev. 129
  William 124
  William M. 129
M'PHERSON --- 247
M'PIKE Charles 39
MACKLEFISH John 305
MACOY William 332
MADEIRA Charlotte 65
MADORE Francis 337

MAGERS Peter 313
MAGILL S. 140, 276
  Samuel 340
MAGRAW Patrick 114
MAGRUDER Robert P. 179, 262
  William 322, 332
MAINS Philip 30, 60
MAJERS Elias 291
MALLEM James 291
MALONE Benjamin 112
  Elias 48
MALOT Michael 36
MALOTT Daniel 31, 38, 69, 98, 109, 228
  John 158
  Michael 48
  Peter 98
  Rebecca 158
  Theodore 158
MANET Jereh 337
MANN Andrew 149
  David 149
  Zachariah 305
MANTZ Christiana 69
  Francis 69
MARGAART Jonathan 313
MARIA 3
MARKER George 55
MARKEY John 305, 337
MARSHALL Eve 241
  James 241
  John 334
MARSTELLER George 63
MARTENY John 139
MARTIN Anthony B. 70, 126, 149
  David 8, 53, 273
  George 37
  Honore 32
  John 315
  Lenox 330
  Nicholas 111
  Samuel 41, 47, 106
  Thomas 41
MARTINEY George 119
  John 88
MARTINI George 38
MARTZS Jacob 291
MARY 147

MASON J. T. 91
  Jeremiah 88, 157
  John 245
  John T. 3, 15, 21, 27, 28, 72, 75, 81, 105, 135, 138, 143
  William T. T. 84
MASTERS Benjamine 332
MATHEWS John 13, 69, 281, 306, 332, 337, 340
MATHIAS John 66
MATTHEWS John 285, 332
  Thomas 332
MATTINGLY Henrey 322
  Nancy 337
  Samuel 291
MAUCHERMAN John 252
MAUGHMAN John 28
MAXWELL James 291
MAY Daniel 28
MAYER A. 253
  Abraham 26, 127, 133, 186, 270
  Michael F. 1, 103, 107
MAYER & IRWIN 231
McCARTY Edgar 75
McCHANS 247
McMECHAN William 177
McPHERSON --- 216
  Isaac 200
MEADES Benjamin 134
MEANS Isaac 294
MEISHEIMER Rev. 31
MENDENHALL Samuel 253
MENTZER Conrod 70
MERIWEATHER Nicholas 84
Merly's Branch 333
MERRELL Phillip 291
MERRICK Joseph I. 26
MEYER Abraham 75
MIDDELKAUFF Henry 137
MIDDLEKAUFF Henry 51, 160
  Jacob 131
  Peter 82, 86
MIDDLEKAUFF & JULIUS 114
MIDDLETON Ignatia 305
  Ignatius 310
MILBOURNE John 289
MILHOLLAND Daniel 305
MILL-HOLLAND Daniel 337

INDEX

MILLER Ann 96
  Benedict 305
  Catharine 53, 99, 199
  Christian 91, 96
  Daniel 27, 47, 69, 103, 128
  David 199
  Elizabeth 91, 136, 298
  F. 29, 49
  Frederick 4, 4, 6, 55, 209
  George 30, 38, 42, 47, 48, 53, 56, 64, 88, 101
  Henry 30, 48, 56, 64, 100
  Jacob 1, 7, 29, 86, 110, 122, 264
  John 24, 26, 56, 84, 100, 156, 243, 313
  Mary 161
  Matthias 1, 53, 77, 79
  Michael 127
  Mr. 79, 181
  P. & M. 122, 258
  Peter 1, 4, 20, 53, 76, 77, 79, 114, 122, 298
  Peter & Matthias 91, 117, 121
  Reverend 36
  Robert 99
  Samuel 124, 137, 143, 148
  Susanna 28
  William H. 161
MILLERE Daniel 48
MILLERS & Beatty 53
MILLERS & Julius 53
MILLHOLLAND Daniel 322
  Stephen 291
MILLS Theodore 28
MILTON Philip 92
MINCHER Edward 125
MINER Mrs. 337
MINICK Elizabeth 337
MINOCK Philip 332
MISKIMIN David 183
MITCHELL Hance 291
MOATS Jacob 47
MOELLER Reverend 92
MOFFETT William 133

MOFFITT William 71
MONAHAN Frances 47, 92
MONG Barbara 133
  Jacob 128, 133
  Jacob B. 133
  Peter 19, 135
MONNET Thomas 313
MONTGOMERY Alexander 79, 138
MOORE Charles 172
  Charles L. 313
  Hamilton 305
  I. L. 159
  James D. 88, 144, 176
  William 38
  William S. 159
MORDEL George 23
MORE George 291
MORGAN Joel 194
  M. 144
MORRIS Mary 322
MORRISON James 295, 327, 337
MORROW Doctor 279
  William 103
MOSS Charles 226, 229
MOTHERD James 305
MOTTER Jacob 22, 166
MOUDY Casper 37
MOWEN Jacob 124
MUCK Jacob 144
  Thomas 144
Muir's Tavern 48, 98
MUIR James 36, 44, 95, 222
  Mr. 33, 255
MULHALL Thomas 24
MULLIN George 249
MUMMA Jacob 111, 114, 118, 243
  John 148, 305
MURDOCH Mary 293, 298
  Mrs. 342
MURDOCK Patrick 293
Murley's Branch 306, 340
MURPHEY Moses 28
MURPHY Christopher 11
  Samuel 305
MURRAY Matthew 49

MURRELL John 277, 291, 292, 316, 319, 331, 337
  Mr. J. 302
MURRY Peter 332
MUSTIN Thomas I. 153
MYER Martin 131
MYERS Jacob 98, 137, 281
  James 39
  Jonas 28
MYSEWINKLE 159

NACE 101, 204
NARBNEY James 322
NEAD Daniel 161
  M. & D. 146
  Matthias 26, 37, 92, 161, 221
NEAD and POSEY, Messrs 149
NEAL Saint Leger 198
NEAL, WILLS & COALE 299
NED 177, 337
NEEDY George 115
NEFF Jacob 305, 322
  Mr. 279, 292
NEIBB Mr. 135
NEIL Alexander 130
NEILL Alexander 1, 2, 3, 32, 33, 36, 47, 71, 85, 94, 136, 152, 176, 231
  Robert 32
NELSON Roger 140, 144
NESBITT Elisabeth 160
  John 160
NEWCOMER Andrew 229
  Christian 100
  David 26, 88
  Emanuel 94, 120
  Henry 92, 131
  Peter 47, 100, 189, 218
  Sameul 189, 218
Newkirk's Mill 104
NEWMAN Peggy 313
  R. 330
NEWSON Jane 98, 134
  John 12, 27, 28, 69, 70, 82, 86, 97, 98, 161
  Joseph P. 98
NEWTON Athanatius 332
NEYNULDS Magy 281

INDEX

NICHOLL Eve 166
NICHOLS George 13, 23, 88
NICHOLSON John 241
NICODEMUS Conrad 22
  Conrod 23
NISBETT Jacob 73
NOLAND Dade P. 113
  Samuel 11
NORRIS Jacob 194
  Stephen 65
  William 194
NOURSE Gabriel 131, 138, 189
NOWELL James 34, 141
NUMBER A. 26
NUNAMOCAN Samuel 119
NUSE John 147

O'BOYLE James 106
O'DONALD Henry 305
O'NEALE Henry 307, 330
  Lawrence 330
OAR John 283
OASTER Mr. 21
ODEN Benjamin 118
ODERFER John 143
OGLE Mr. 49, 69, 71, 99
  Thomas 132
OHR Henry 139
  J. I. 139
  Jacob I. 13, 153
OLDAKER Jacob 160
OLIVER David 337
  John 41, 118
OQUIM William 337
ORD James 292
ORME John 281
ORMSTON Ralph 28
ORNDORFF Susanna 47
ORTMAN Daniel 235
OSBORN William 313
OSBURN Samuel 306
  Wil. 322
OSTER Conrad 88, 155
  Rosanna 155
  Samuel 88
OSWALD Benjamin 26
  Eve 26
  John 24, 26
OSWALT Michael 313

OTT A. 48
  Adam 10, 28, 36, 51, 88, 97
  Colonel A. 88
  Justice A. 111
OTTO Henry 93, 123
  Isabella 93, 97, 123, 131
  Matthias 93, 123
OWINGS Edward 163

PALMER Perry A. 28
PANCAKE Isaac 196
PARK Agnes A. 161
PARKERSON Thomas 322
PARKINSON Thomas 313
PARKS Joseph 155
PARMLEE Lathrop 313
PARMORE James 281
PATERSON John 295
Patterson's Creek 291, 334
PATTERSON Charles 322
  John 142, 283, 334
  William 125
PATTON John 233
  Methew 332
PAYSON Henry 194
PAYTON Chambers 68
PEAL James 327
  Ruth 327
PECK Andrew 139
  Hiel 114
  Sarah 136
PEIRCE Elizabeth 313
PENDLETON Philip C. 272
PERKINSON Thomas 291
PERRIL Charles 281
PERRIN Rachael 28
PERRY Mr. 298
  Roger 291, 296, 313, 335, 342
  Thomas 332, 335
  Thomas I. 322
PETER 145, 334
PETER David 55, 245
  George 55
  Sarah 55
  Thomas 245
PETRY Philip 99
Pettit'S Tavern 59

PETTIT S. 52, 71
  Samuel 52, 97, 127, 136
PHIL 114
PHILLIPS Solomon 8
  Uriel 8
PIGMAN B. S. 337
PILES Lydia 161
PINDELL Doctor 27, 196
  Mary 235
  R. 1, 47, 196
  Richard 3
PINDLE Rinald 305
PINE Jacob 28
PIPER Daniel 272
  Jacob 272
PITRY Jacob 24, 26, 47
  John 26
  Ludwick 23
PLACINGER Mr 12
PLUCHER George 305
PLUMMER Jeremiah 319
POFFENBERGER 8
POLLARD Thomas 321
POLLOCK W. T. A. 293
  William 305
POLLOCK, William J. A., & Company 283
POMPHREY Silas 6
POOL Jacob 291
POPST Henry 114
PORT Mary 332
PORTER Henry 332
  John 313, 322, 334
  Michael 332
POSEY Nathaniel 49, 96, 98, 101, 247, 259
POST Thomas 34
POTTENGER James 110
  John B. 35
  Mary 7
  T. B. 26
  Thomas B. 7, 38, 144
POTTER Benjamin 125
  Josias 54
POTTORF Michael 136
POTTORFF Michael 254
POWLAS Catharine 84
  Jacob 87
  Margaret 80
PRATER James 322

INDEX

PRATHER James 36, 88, 134, 136, 322
Samuel 136
PRATT Mrs. Christy 305
Thomas 322
PRESTON James 52
Peter 290
Sarah 244
Price's Tavern 86, 96
PRICE Catharine 246
John 125, 337
Josiah 18, 22, 39, 47, 69, 143, 155, 169
L. 47, 53, 56, 71, 91, 115, 144
Levi 52, 84, 112, 128
Mr. 55, 71, 81
Sally 39
Samuel D. 8, 243, 245, 246
Silas 283
William 306, 340
PRIEST John 322
PROTZMAN Catharine 156
John 13
PUMPHREY Reason 303
PUTTER Andrew 29
PYLES Lydia 339

QEREE William 305
QUANTRILL Mr. 148
Thomas 5, 10, 36, 37, 39, 59, 71, 115, 148, 149, 150, 152, 234, 239
QUIGLEY Andrew 226

RAFTER Henrey 291
RAGAN Colonel 148
John 3, 33, 38, 56, 69, 84, 92, 93, 108, 148, 149, 150, 151, 152, 226
R. 11, 33
Richard 53, 98
RAGEN John 3
RAHAUSER Rev. 8, 36, 48, 53, 65, 86, 87, 100, 134, 135, 139, 140, 148, 153, 155, 156, 159, 161, 165, 166, 180, 189

RAHP Elizabeth 66
John 66
RAINHART George 305
RALPH George 57
RAMSEY Thomas 147
RAMSBURGH John 164
RANDOLPH William 277
RANKIN Archibald 103, 128
Ray's Town Branch 161
RAY Richard 125
REA A. P. 119
READ Dr. 342
John 281
John M. 281
REBECK Jacob 134
RECTOR Conway 337
REED Catherine 337
REICHARD Daniel 91, 146, 163
Jacob 31
REID Catherine 332
Frances 305
John 291, 305
John M. 332
Phinehas 330
Thomas 277, 327
REIDENOUR Matthias 28
REISHER David 78
Rench's Mill 99
RENCH Ann Maria 87
Daniel 6, 28, 30, 41, 87, 228, 247
Elie 103, 104
Elizabeth 41
Jacob 6, 30, 36, 196, 228
John 30, 35, 87, 228
Mrs. 111
Peter 30, 35, 72, 121, 165, 228
REPP John 125
RESONER John 287, 331, 342
REVENACHT Reverend 100
REYNOLD Peter 34
REYNOLDS James 332
John 33, 99
Mary 337
William 201, 212
RHODE John 243
RHODES Matthias 201

RICE Ally 166
Andrew 285, 319
Charles 136
Frederick 285, 319
John 139, 301
Richardson's Ferry 93
RICHARDSON Sally 47, 266
RICKETTS Gerrard 101
RIDANOUR Nicholas 198
RIDDLE John 155
Joseph 301
RIDDLE & DALL 301
RIDENOUR Adam 134, 142, 191
Charles 142, 134
Eve 84
Jacob 26, 41
John 149
Martin 65
Mary 36, 134, 135, 142
Nicholas 1
Samuel 5, 40, 146
RIDGELY Noah 340
RIDGLEY General 103
William 281
RIED James 105
RIELY William 340
Rine's Glades 306, 340
RINEHART Andrew 148
George 340
Henry 99, 134
John 306
Ringer's Tavern 247
RINGGOLD Brigadier General S. 38
General 8, 9, 26, 88, 116, 133, 196
General S. 164
Samuel 3, 28, 44, 48, 116
Tench 24
RINULL George 125
RISHELL Jacob 281
RITCHIE --- 291
RITE Walter 322
RIZER George 32, 281
Martain 305, 332
ROACH Elizabeth 330
James 88
Mahlon 88
ROBARDET James 79, 118
ROBB Adam 195
ROBERTS George 244

INDEX

Robertson's Military School 263
ROBERTSON John 214
William 52
ROBESON James 291
ROBEY Owen 38, 80
Susanna 29, 38
William 29, 38, 80
ROBINET Eliza 332
George 332
ROBINETT Asa 80
George 322
Jeremiah 80
ROBINSON James 118
John 305, 306
ROBISON John 340
ROBOSON Benjamine 332
ROCK Henry 281
RODEFER Joseph 342
RODEHEAVER John 340
RODRAUFF Jacob 165
ROHRER Barbara 96, 274
Christian 55, 96, 118, 274
Daniel 96
Frances 96
Frederick 28, 37, 46, 100, 263
Jacob 96, 100, 118, 119, 143
John 19, 100, 118, 143
Maria 96
Samuel 15, 55, 96
ROHRER & BARR 100
ROHRER & MOTTER 159
ROOT Jacob 81, 109
ROSS Samuel 23, 50
ROUCH Jacob 92
Philip 83
William 83
ROW Anthony O. 114
ROWLAND Christian 91, 119
Jacob 11, 31
RUDISILLI Michael 7
RUSSEL Thomas 332
RUSSELL Mrs. 19
Thomas 313
RUTTER Edmund 111

Sackett's Tavern 151, 161
SACKETT M. H. 11, 44, 205
Milton H. 61
Mr. 2, 146
SADLER Emory 151
SAGER John 149
SAILOR Jacob 231
Mr. 34, 46
Peter 13, 47
SALIFER Ezra 235
Sam 7, 10, 99, 303
SANDERS George 18
SAP Jacob 313
SARGENT George 125
James 125
SAYLOR Jacob 48, 52, 93, 270
John 337
Mr. 76
SCHAEFFER David 166
David F. 69, 129
F. G. 137
Rev. 27, 47, 65, 71, 80, 83, 84, 95, 257, 266
Rev. S. 129
Solomon 128
SCHAFFER John 135
Rev. 56, 104
SCHAUFFER Rev. 214
SCHELL Enos 94
Mr. 144
SCHILLING Mr. 105, 134
SCHIOLER Christopher 99
SCHLEIGH John 91
SCHNEBLY Cassandra 76
D. 149
Daniel 10, 15, 30, 36, 65, 73, 77, 87, 88, 98, 120, 127, 157, 196, 208, 228
David 7, 26, 26, 37, 39, 48, 54, 58, 69, 79, 116, 120
Doctor 28, 53, 127
Doctor J. 52
Henry 36
Henry C. 35, 142
J. 1, 2, 54, 56, 99

Jacob 3, 27, 35, 41, 76, 88, 94, 100, 103, 135, 136, 147, 156, 157
John 75, 79, 87, 123, 131, 135
Mr. 159
Sally 94
SCHRADER Henry 32, 34
SCHRECH John 49
SCHRIVER Henry 265
SCHRYOCK David 163
SCHUCK John 291
SCHYCAW William 55
SCIPIO 122
SCOTT George 87
James 277, 331
John 96, 273, 281, 291
SEAMON Charles 125
SEAS Jacob 322
SEESE Jacob 313
SEGUR Jacob 81
SEIBERT Henry 5, 91
Jacob 5, 7
Peter 82
Seitz's Tavern 73, 181
SEITZ John 10, 28, 29, 44, 63, 88, 98, 131, 213
Mr. 8, 94, 176
SELBY Walter 281, 313, 337
Walter B. 92, 288
SEMPLE Christian 75
SERGEANT Archibald 129
SEVIER John 28
SHACKLETT John 204
SHADRACH 6
SHAEFFER Reverend 123
SHAFER Catharine 87
George 22, 23, 131, 155
Henry 24, 32, 47, 104, 149, 167
John 36, 87, 122
Leonard 3, 38, 82, 95, 263
Mr. 7
Reverend 180
SHAFFER L. 170
Leonard 170
Mr. 136

INDEX

SHAFFNER Charles 98, 159
  M. 240
  Margaret 28
  Matthias 3, 7, 23, 66, 95, 136, 144, 159, 197
SHALL George 129, 132, 192
SHANAFELD Andrew 100
SHANE George 95
  Henry 23, 68, 92, 120, 137, 149
SHANK George 98
SHARER John 47
SHARKEY George 33
SHATT Samuel 153
SHAUMAN David 83
  John 86
SHAW George 64
  William 36, 322
SHEARER Mrs. 161
  Thomas 36
SHECHTER Wendel 23
SHEELHORN Baltzer H. 313
SHEET Adam 291
SHEETS Adam 322
  Frances 83
  Margaret 28
SHEFFY Philip 28
SHEISS George 261
SHELLER Christian 28
SHELLHORN Baltzel H. 305
SHELLY Christian 156
SHENABERGER Peter 169
SHENEFELT Henry 47
SHERFER John 26
SHERIDAN William 40
SHOCKY Elizabeth 307
  Valentine 307
SHOLL Jacob 33, 47, 262
SHOMAKE William 277
SHONG Abraham 125
SHOOP Henry 28
SHORT David 305
SHORTER Dick 95
SHOWMAN George 176
  John B. 53
SHRIVER David 330
  Henry 49
SHRYER John 337
SHRYOCK George 99, 125
  Henry 102
SHUEY John 235

SHUGART Sophia 139
  Zachariah 51, 240
SHULL Jacob 114, 115
SHULL, Jacob & BUTLER 99
SHUMAN Elizabeth 71
  Thomas 2, 18, 28, 67, 71, 88, 133, 146, 172
SHUMAN & HUMRICKHOUSE 150
SIDES Benjamin G. 147
SIESS John 322
SIGLAR John 305
SIGLER Ely, & Company 331
SILVER Francis 86
SIMKINS John 305, 332, 335, 337
  Polly 291
  Sophia 305
  William 38, 80, 99
SIMMONS John 322
SIMONDS Frederick 308
SIMONS Frederick 340, 305
  John 331, 340
  Mr. 337
SIMPSON John 28
SIVLEY John 105
SLEIGH John 47, 54, 81
SLICER John 329
  Mr. 305, 306
  Walter 296, 322, 324, 337, 340, 342
SLIFER Ezra 1, 22, 82
SMALL William 54
SMALLWOOD Samuel 125
SMITH Alexander 306, 340
  Barbara 53
  Christian 23, 26, 47
  Conrod 32, 54
  Daniel 159
  Ephraim 125
  Fleet 74
  George 8, 42, 52, 57, 60, 72, 88, 95, 132, 199, 240, 272, 332
  Jacob 2
  James 322

  John 23, 28, 305
  Jonathan 125
  Joseph 2, 92, 103, 313
  Mary Ann 122
  Michael 2
  Nicholas 53, 92, 114, 155
  Peter 68, 91, 139, 151
  Samuel 281, 291, 305, 313, 322, 332, 333, 337
  Thomas 28
  Widow 28
  Youst 125
SMOOT George C. 33, 47, 60, 81, 109, 118
SMOUSE Peter 320
SNAVELY Casper 95
  Jacob 116
  John 20, 121
  Samuel 20
SNEIDER Mr. 137
SNICKER 96
SNIDER Henry 8
  Jacob 28, 322
  Peter 97
SNIDERY Jacob 313
SNIVELY Andrew 267
  John 105, 267
  Joseph 103, 128, 156
SNOWDEN James 53
SNYDER Abraham 100
  Anthony 94, 157
  David 166
  Elizabeth 48
  Henry 38
  Jacob 337
  John 76, 334
  Mr. 95
SONTMON Jacob 125
SOUTH Gera 64, 144, 154, 226
SPALDING Mr. 169
SPEALMAN David 29
  Jacob 291
SPEECE Daniel 99, 134
SPEELMAN Jacob 337
SPEILMAN Jacob 80
SPEIS Daniel 30
SPEISS Daniel 47
SPERO George 168
SPICER Richard 125

INDEX

SPIELMAN Jacob 28
SPITLER Matthias 30
SPONSG Matthias 57
SPRECHER Philip 147
SPRENGLE Michael 124
SPRIGG D. 139
  Daniel 77
  General 1
  Jenifer T. 154
  Joseph 9, 47, 67, 118, 166, 290
  M. C. 290, 339
  Michael 337
  Michael C. 305, 329
  Osborn 21
  Otho 7, 153
  William 17, 109
  William O. 7, 44, 53, 137, 141, 144
SPRINGER Ann 78
  John 4
  Joseph 78
  Matthias 78
SPROUL William 28
STAFFORD John F. 321
STAKE Jacob 125
  John 125
STALLINGS Samuel 302
  Thomas 297, 306, 340
STALLSMITH J. 29, 49, 97, 206
  John 36, 92, 186, 226
STANGE Christopher G. 165
STANTON John 36
STARLING Abraham 131
  William 93
STARLIPER Anthony 150
STARTZMAN David 18, 25
  Henry 18, 25
  Martin 18, 25
STATTEN Jacob 9
STATTS Christian 291, 337
STAUFFER Daniel 105
STAUSE Henry 19
STEEL Joseph 158
STEELE Mr. 47
  Robert 37
STEFFY Catharine 48
  Jacob 156
STEINER Henry M. 28

STEMPLE Christian 52, 144
  David 337
STEPHENS Alexander 182
STEPHENSON J. 86
  John 291
STERRET James 118
STERRETT James 12, 61, 179, 181
STERRIT James M. 96
STERRITT James M. 134
STEUART Charles 8
STEVENSON James 86
STEWART David 145
  Robert 313
  Thomas 281
STINE Elizabeth 69
  Henry 69
  Matthias 121
  Mr. 35, 37
  Mrs. 88, 135
  Sergeant 108
STINEMETZ George 39
STIVERS Elihue 305
STODDARD James 324
STODDART Benjamin 296
STOLTZ David 39
  Henry 104
STONE Elizabeth 332
  John 16
STONEBRAKER George 114
STONEBREAKER Esther 149
  G. & M. 5
  George 79
  Gerard 1, 34, 61, 84, 122
  John 8
  Michael 79
  Mr. 98
STONER Abraham 32
Stover's Tavern 109, 128, 252
STOVER Christian 91, 119
  Daniel 39
  David 291
  Jacob 22, 143
  John 52, 96, 134, 240
  Mr. 47
Strause's Tavern 91
STRAUSE H. 71

Henry 21, 84, 97, 103
  Mr. 56, 99, 270
STREET William 291
STRIDER J., Brother, & Company 277, 331
STRITE John 49, 265
STRONG Gilbert 291
STUART Thomas 291
Stull's Addition to Hager's-town 40
STULL Captain D. 19
  Daniel 15, 19, 80, 174, 178, 179, 183
  J. I. 179
  John I. 3, 11, 185
  O. H. W. 24, 64, 91, 95, 106, 130, 146, 149, 257
  O. W. W. 145
  Otho H. 242
  Otho H. W. 10, 11, 43
  Sarah B. 28
STUTAMAN Godfrid 153
SUFLING Henrey 313
SULLIVAN James 337
  Jeremiah 337
SUMMERS Jacob 23
SWAN General 327
  Robert 337
SWAYNE Samuel 97, 125
Swearingen's Ferry 12, 272
SWEARINGEN Isaac 88, 145
  Isaac S. 146, 148
  John V. 151
  Mr. 148
SWEITZER Henry 12, 36, 69, 81, 118, 121, 124, 167, 258
SWINGLE Benjamin 53
  George 28
  Leonard 32
Swingley's Mill 79
SWINGLEY Benjamin 155
SWITZER Daniel 160
  Nicholas 160
SWOPE Catharine 12
  Catharine 36
  John 28
  Mr. 107
  Nicholas 203
  Peter 12, 36
SWORD Peter 161

INDEX

TABB Edward 142
  George 142
  Moses 26
TABBS Captain 39
  Moses 3, 26, 46, 118, 205, 337
TALBOTT Archibald 258
  Charles 258
  Paul 258
TALLY Josiah 125
TANEY Roger B. 43
TANLEY Betsey 11, 31
Taylor's Ferry 247
TAYLOR Cathrine 322
  Isaac 75, 146
  William 60, 140, 332
TEISHER John 53
TEVIS Samuel 313
THISTLE George 281, 316, 331, 341
  Thomas 281, 309, 316, 342
THOMAS 291
THOMAS David 125
  John 28
  John Hanson 140, 243, 248
  Philip 139
  Samuel 340
  William 293
THOMPSON Ann 172
  J. 224, 283
  Joel 283
  Josiah 291, 313
  Matthew 121
THOMSON Harry 169
  J. 28
  Josiah 21
THROCKMORTON J. E. 8
TICKERHOOF Martin 254
TIDBALL James 313
  Joseph 328
TIERNAM Luke 1
TIERNAN Luke 90
  Michael 337
  Miss M. A. 90
TILGHMAN Charles C. 332
  Colonel 52, 146
  Doctor F. 114
  F. 17, 28, 135
  Frisby 3, 7, 44, 72, 96, 118, 136, 167, 223
  Mary 96

TILMAN Sam 111
TIMMONDS James 291
TIMMONS James 313
TIMS Alexander 10
TOM 37, 60, 150
TOMLINSON Bazil 332
  Benjamine 337
  James 313
  Jesse 327, 340
  Joseph 135
  P.M. 337
  Samuel 313
TOOL Peter 337
TOOLE Peter 340
TOWNE Rev. 25
  Rev. E. 47
TOWSON Jacob T. 33, 61, 136, 188, 243
TOY David 305
TRACY Nathan 322
TRAVERSE John 135
TRAWINGER Jacob 28
TRESSLER Jacob 107, 135
TRITCH Catharine 48
TROUTMAN Benjamin 281, 322
TROVINGER John 55
TROXELL Jacob 81
  Philip 39
TRULLINGER Jacob 305
TUCKER Hansim 125
TUFTS Samuel 125
TURNER Edmund H. 88, 133, 148
  George 146
  Henry S. 79
  James 7
  Samuel 46
  Thomas 46, 155
TURNER & HESLETINE 98, 133
TUTWEILER Jacob 131
TUTWILER David 130
TUTWILLER Barbara 99
  Jonathan 99
TWIG Francis 305
TWIGG John 337
TYSON Benjamin 36

UHL Daniel 333
  Jacob 333
UNGER Frederick 134

VAL Samuel 93
VAN LEAR Doctor 96
  Matthew 88, 136
  William 56, 88, 120
VANDIVER Jacob 291
VANLEAR Archibald 183
  M. & William 199
  Matthew 183, 199, 248, 301
VANMETER Jacob 288
VANTZ Jacob 12
VAUGHN Bengeman G. 322
  Benjamin 281
  Benjamine G. 305
VAUN John 291
VAW John 337
VERNER Paul 168
VIERS Doctor 337
VOWELL Ebenezer 334, 337

WACHTEL Valentine 138
WADE John 216, 250
  Mr. 98
WAGERS James 147
WAGGENER Michael 219
WAGGONER John 22, 161, 287, 331
  Peter 161
WAGONER John 88
WAITE Obed 166, 272
  Obed Francis 322
WALLACE Charles 149
  M. 277
  Robert 149
  William 149
WALLACH Conrad 2
WALLAS Nathaniel 305
WALLING James 92
WALLS Mary 281
  Samuel 337
WALTER Nicholas 313
WALTON John 292
WARD James 305
  Rachal 313
  William 307
WARFIELD Charles D. 313
  Chas. A. 269
  Gustavus 269
WARNER Zebulon 242
WARREN Susanna 139
  James 139
WARRING Henry 262

118

INDEX

WARTZ Catharine 31
  Christian 31
WATERS Basil 179
WATKINS Horatio 131
WATSON Abraham 39
  Elizabeth 166
WATTS Thomas 24
WAUGH A. M. 9, 27, 103, 143
  Eleanor 100
  Mistress 96
  Mrs. 137
  Perry 22, 51, 96, 137, 188
WEAST Leonard 28
WEBB George 15
  William 28, 109
WEEKER Barbara 119
  Melchor 119
WEEKS Henry 125
WEIS George 165
  John 72, 136
  Samuel 53, 114
WEISEL Daniel 47
WEITZEL John 85
  Mr. 99
WELCH John 305, 306
  Maxwell 38
WELLS Elizabeth 90, 132
  John 31, 70, 229
  Rezin 30
WELSEY Israel 281
WELSH Singleton 332
  William 26
WELTY Daniel 97
WELTZHIMER John 313, 332
WENDALL Nancy 47
WEST David 106
  John 36, 134
WESTENBERGER David 97, 116
WESTFAL John 298
  Lovice 298
WEYER Michael 281
WHEELER Thomas 332
WHETSTONE Abraham 125
WHITE Addison 270
  I. S. 208
  Isaac S. 15, 30, 36, 196, 228, 305
  Peggy 313
  Samuel 313

Thomas 337
William 332
WHITESIDE Samuel H. 4
WHITHNEY Anne 27
WHITMER Daniel 321
WHITMORE Anna 65
WHITTING Carlyle F. 16
WILEN W. 149
  William 139
WILHELM John 125
WILKINSON Mary 165
WILL 277, 326
WILLIAM 19, 81, 147, 166
WILLIAM Otho H. 254
  William 226
WILLIAMS Anne Barbara 94
  Benjamin 237
  Captain E. G. 48, 104
  Captain O. H. 7, 17, 30
  E. G. 33, 131
  Edward G. 34, 111, 112, 157
  Edward O. 91, 195
  Elie 6, 94, 178, 254
  Elisha 55
  Esther 96
  Henry 247
  James 68
  John S. 185
  Major O. H. 50, 52, 85, 112
  O. H. 47, 54, 135, 136, 173, 198
  Otho H. 3, 5, 10, 51, 111, 159, 173, 228, 270
  Otho Holland 26
  Otto H. 146
  Richard 96
  Thomas 1, 28, 183
  William B. 1, 13, 44, 79, 136, 183
  William Prater 195
WILLIAMS & RAGAN 15, 130
WILLIAMSON David 90
  George 126

WILLIS --- 224
  L. C. 144
  William 27, 53, 91, 125, 181, 232, 270
WILLIS & CRAWFORD 9, 191, 206
WILLIS and FRANKENBERY 79
WILLSON Josua 322
  Nathan 337
  William 332
WILSON Amos 332
  David 150, 183
  Henry R. 269
  John 106
  Josua 291
  Samuel 81
  Sarah Ann 163
  William 28, 219
WILT Michael 312
WINCHESTER David 194
WINDHOUR Henrey 337
WINEMILLER John 97
WINENOU Henry 321
WINEOUR Henrey 322
WINGART Philip 1
  Philip 2
WINGERT John 340
  Philip 328, 332, 340
WINTER Benjamin 89, 101, 114
  John 98, 153
WINTERS George 281, 313
WIRE Mr. 292
WIT Jacob 319
WITHNEY Arthur 27, 32
WITMER Benjamin 107
  Christian 88
  Henry 107
  John 39, 88, 144, 189, 218, 227
  Mr. 313
WITT Jacob 337
WOLF Joseph 30, 47, 119, 129
WOLFARTH Mary 83
WOLFE Magdalena 298
  Peter 298
WOLFERSBERGER John 99
WOLFERSPERGER John 28

INDEX

WOLGAMOT Hannah 36
  John 28, 34, 109
  Mary 93, 109
WOLTZ Catharine 109, 116
  Doctor 99
  George 82
  Maria 140
  Peter 140
  Samuel 103, 109, 116
WOMELDORFF Catharine 99
  John 99
WONN John 305
WOODEN Randolph 39
WORKMAN Isaac 284
  Jacob 332
  John 313, 337
WORLAND Charles 13
WORLEY John 57, 94
WORSTER Frederick 134
WRIGHT John 196, 334
  John & Company 277, 316, 334
  Walter 322
  William 337
WYATT Rachel 322, 337
  William 305, 337

YAKLE Jacob 88
YANDES John 29
  Simon 40
YATES Amos 86
  William 46, 54, 88, 208
YEATS William 99
YEITER Abraham 28
YELGHMAN Charles C. 322
YOCUM Charles 57
YOE Benjamin 9, 18, 30, 128, 145, 180, 211, 255
  Mr. 186
YOUNG Eliza E. 313
  Elizabeth 260
  Jacob 30, 62, 66, 87, 228
  John 6, 10
  Joseph 159
  Judy 159
  Ludwick 91, 93
  Mary Magdalena 169
  Noah 167
  Rachel 159
  Samuel 159, 260

YOUNG & VAN LEAR 96
YUTSLER William 125

ZACK 8
Zeigler's store 45
ZEIGLER Lewis 138
  Mr. 36
  William 38, 56, 114
ZELLER J. 149
  Jacob 10, 28, 79, 136
ZETTER Jacob 3
ZIGLAR Frederick 19
  George 19
  William 59
ZIGLAS Ludwick 147
ZIMBLY John 281
ZIMERLY Mathias 313
ZIMMERLA Mathias 319
ZIMMERMAN Got(t)leib 135, Gottleib 33, 47, 99, 262
  Henry 149
ZUCK Jacob 55, 104

Other books by F. Edward Wright:

Abstracts of Bucks County, Pennsylvania Wills, 1685-1785
Abstracts of Cumberland County, Pennsylvania Wills, 1750-1785
Abstracts of Cumberland County, Pennsylvania Wills, 1785-1825
Abstracts of Philadelphia County Wills, 1726-1747
Abstracts of Philadelphia County Wills, 1748-1763
Abstracts of Philadelphia County Wills, 1763-1784
Abstracts of Philadelphia County Wills, 1777-1790
Abstracts of Philadelphia County Wills, 1790-1802
Abstracts of Philadelphia County Wills, 1802-1809
Abstracts of Philadelphia County Wills, 1810-1815
Abstracts of Philadelphia County Wills, 1815-1819
Abstracts of Philadelphia County Wills, 1820-1825
Abstracts of Philadelphia County, Pennsylvania Wills, 1682-1726
Abstracts of South Central Pennsylvania Newspapers, Volume 1, 1785-1790
Abstracts of South Central Pennsylvania Newspapers, Volume 3, 1796-1800
Abstracts of the Newspapers of Georgetown and the Federal City, 1789-99
Abstracts of York County, Pennsylvania Wills, 1749-1819
Bucks County, Pennsylvania Church Records of the 17th and 18th Centuries
Volume 2: Quaker Records: Falls and Middletown Monthly Meetings
Anna Miller Watring and F. Edward Wright
Caroline County, Maryland Marriages, Births and Deaths, 1850-1880
Citizens of the Eastern Shore of Maryland, 1659-1750
Cumberland County, Pennsylvania Church Records of the 18th Century
Delaware Newspaper Abstracts, Volume 1: 1786-1795
Early Charles County, Maryland Settlers, 1658-1745
Marlene Strawser Bates and F. Edward Wright
Early Church Records of Alexandria City and Fairfax County, Virginia
F. Edward Wright and Wesley E. Pippenger
Early Church Records of New Castle County, Delaware, Volume 1, 1701-1800
Frederick County Militia in the War of 1812
Sallie A. Mallick and F. Edward Wright
Inhabitants of Baltimore County, 1692-1763
Land Records of Sussex County, Delaware, 1769-1782
Land Records of Sussex County, Delaware, 1782-1789
Elaine Hastings Mason and F. Edward Wright
Marriage Licenses of Washington, District of Columbia, 1811-1830
Marriages and Deaths from the Newspapers of Allegany and Washington Counties, Maryland, 1820-1830
Marriages and Deaths from The York Recorder, 1821-1830
Marriages and Deaths in the Newspapers of Frederick and Montgomery Counties, Maryland, 1820-1830

Marriages and Deaths in the Newspapers of Lancaster County, Pennsylvania, 1821-1830
Marriages and Deaths in the Newspapers of Lancaster County, Pennsylvania, 1831-1840
Marriages and Deaths of Cumberland County, [Pennsylvania], 1821-1830
Maryland Calendar of Wills Volume 9: 1744-1749
Maryland Calendar of Wills Volume 10: 1748-1753
Maryland Calendar of Wills Volume 11: 1753-1760
Maryland Calendar of Wills Volume 12: 1759-1764
Maryland Calendar of Wills Volume 13: 1764-1767
Maryland Calendar of Wills Volume 14: 1767-1772
Maryland Calendar of Wills Volume 15: 1772-1774
Maryland Calendar of Wills Volume 16: 1774-1777
Maryland Eastern Shore Newspaper Abstracts, Volume 1: 1790-1805
Maryland Eastern Shore Newspaper Abstracts, Volume 2: 1806-1812
Maryland Eastern Shore Newspaper Abstracts, Volume 3: 1813-1818
Maryland Eastern Shore Newspaper Abstracts, Volume 4: 1819-1824
Maryland Eastern Shore Newspaper Abstracts, Volume 5: Northern Counties, 1825-1829
F. Edward Wright and Irma Harper
Maryland Eastern Shore Newspaper Abstracts, Volume 6: Southern Counties, 1825-1829
Maryland Eastern Shore Newspaper Abstracts, Volume 7: Northern Counties, 1830-1834
Irma Harper and F. Edward Wright
Maryland Eastern Shore Newspaper Abstracts, Volume 8: Southern Counties, 1830-1834
Maryland Militia in the Revolutionary War
S. Eugene Clements and F. Edward Wright
Newspaper Abstracts of Allegany and Washington Counties, Maryland, 1811-1815
Newspaper Abstracts of Cecil and Harford Counties, Maryland, 1822-1830
Newspaper Abstracts of Frederick County, Maryland, 1816-1819
Newspaper Abstracts of Frederick County, Maryland, 1811-1815
Sketches of Maryland Eastern Shoremen
Tax List of Chester County, Pennsylvania 1768
Tax List of York County, Pennsylvania 1779
Washington County Church Records of the 18th Century, 1768-1800
Western Maryland Newspaper Abstracts, Volume 1: 1786-1798
Western Maryland Newspaper Abstracts, Volume 2: 1799-1805
Western Maryland Newspaper Abstracts, Volume 3: 1806-1810
Wills of Chester County, Pennsylvania, 1766-1778

www.ingramcontent.com/pod-product-compliance
Lightning Source LLC
Chambersburg PA
CBHW070505100426
42743CB00010B/1771